THE RENAISSANCE LUTE CHORD BIBLE

(Standard 'G' Tuning)

by

Tobe A. Richards

A Fretted Friends Publication for Cabot Books

Published by:
Cabot Books
Copyright © 2015 & 2016 by Cabot Books
All rights reserved.

First Edition September 2013
Second Edition February 2016

ISBN-13: 978-1-906207-45-8

No part of this publication may be reproduced in any form
or by any means without the prior consent of the publisher.

Cabot Books
3 Kenton Mews
Henleaze
Bristol
BS9 4LT
United Kingdom

Visit our online site at www.frettedfriendsmusic.com
e-mail: cabotbooks@blueyonder.co.uk

TABLE OF CONTENTS

Introduction..4

Fingering..5

Chord Theory Questions & Answers......................................6-7

Alternative Chord Names and Lute Tuning on a Guitar........8-9

Understanding Chord Boxes...10

Renaissance Lute Fingerboard & Tuning Layout.....................11

Chords Covered in this Book...12-13

Slash Chords..13

Using a Capo or *Capo D'astra*..13

C Chords..14-18

C♯/D♭ Chords..19-23

D Chords...24-28

D♯/E♭ Chords..29-33

E Chords..34-38

F Chords..39-43

F♯/G♭ Chords..44-48

G Chords...49-53

G♯/A♭ Chords..54-58

A Chords...59-63

A♯/B♭ Chords..64-68

B Chords...69-73

Major Slash Chords..74-77

A Selection of Moveable Chord Shapes.............................78-81

The Lute Family Factfile and Tunings Guide......................82-84

Notes...85-87

Chord Window Blanks..88-110

INTRODUCTION

The Renaissance Lute Chord Bible provides the musician with 1,728 chords in all keys, featuring 68 different chord types, with 3 variations of each standard chord. 144 major slash chords (encompassing additional *diapasons* or bass strings) are also included, together with 48 moveable chord shape diagrams (providing access to a further 576 barré and standard moveable chords) making this the most comprehensive reference guide for the Renaissance lute currently available. For many years now, guitarists have been able to pick up a songbook and instantly play the songs in front of them, either with the help of one of the many published guides, or through the chord boxes supplied with most popular music. With the help of this *Chord Bible*, beginners and experienced lutenists alike will be able to take advantage of the many songbooks and musical compendiums by any artist you would care to name. With 68 different chordal variations in all keys, virtually any song should be playable!

Having a good chordal knowledge should arguably be the bedrock in any fretted or keyboard musicians armoury. Whether you're playing rock, pop, folk, jazz, classical, blues, country or other types of music, it's impossible to supply a suitable accompaniment to any vocal or solo instrumental music without providing a chordal or harmonic backing. The subtle nuance of an added ninth chord over a major chord is something that can't be captured simply by playing a melody line. In theory it is possible to approximate the harmonic intervals of any music using a limited palette of chords - probably around ten to twelve. But wherever possible it's best to use correct harmonies if they're available to you.

Having six to ten courses of strings, the Renaissance lute is a highly versatile musical instrument, making a wide variety of harmonic variations possible. But sometimes compromises have to be made, particularly when a chordal configuration isn't physically possible. By making acceptable compromises and omitting the least important parts of that chord, even the most complex musical structures are then viable. For instance, in the case of an eleventh, the third is generally omitted without the character of the chord being adversely affected. Equally, the root or key note isn't always necessary to achieve an effective approximation of the full chord. The third is rarely missing from the majority of chords (other than elevenths) as it determines whether the key is major or minor - although this isn't a hard and fast rule, particularly in folk music where the root and fifth form the basis of most traditional music. These two intervals are generally the starting point for a number of open tunings of instruments as diverse as the guitar, the bouzouki and the mountain dulcimer. The same interval is also used in a lot of heavy rock where a fifth chord is described as a *power chord*. Even though a power chord is technically neither major nor minor, it's more often used as an alternative for a major chord in most popular music.

One question which often pops up is *how many chords do I need to learn?* The smart answer is *'how long is a piece of string?'*, which is true, but it doesn't actually answer the question if you don't know where to start. My advice would be to begin with simple chord clusters like the popular G, C, D and Em progression and gradually work in new ones as you advance. If you intend playing within a pop or rock format, it's probably sensible to learn the E, A, B sequence which is the staple of most guitarists and bassists. As a generalisation, jazz probably requires the greatest chordal knowledge of any form of music, so the learning curve will be longer if you're planning to pick up any songbook and instantly produce a recognisable version of your favourite jazz number. The only truth as far as harmonic knowledge goes is you can never learn *too* much!

In this series of chord theory books, I've included a comprehensive selection of configurations of chords in all keys. As I mentioned previously, this will enable you to pick up virtually any chord-based music book (topline melody and chord symbols) and look up the chord shape that's needed. Obviously, you'll come across the occasional song which doesn't conform to the normal harmonic intervals which you find in this, or any other chord theory publication, but with a little experimentation and experience, you'll be able to make a reasonable stab at it. For instance, most players would be more than a little bemused if they suddenly came across an instruction to play a *Gbmaj7add6/D*. Fortunately, this is fairly unusual, but from the knowledge you'll have learned, you'll be able to use a similar chord or work it out note by note. Put simply, if every theoretically possible chord shape were to be included in this or any other book, the result would resemble something akin to several volumes of the *Yellow Pages*!

FINGERING

Always a tricky subject and one which seems to generate a lot of discussion and differing opinions as to which method is correct. Personally, I take the view that it's a largely fruitless exercise, as the number of variables involved make a definitive answer unlikely. So what I've decided to do in this book is to choose fingering positions which feel comfortable to me. Some chord shapes will dictate the fingering used, but others will be down to personal preference. If you can practise your two and three finger chords using different fingers, it will make your playing a lot more fluid when you change to another chord shape. But if you develop habits which limit you to one playing position, it isn't the end of the world either, if you can make the transitions seamless.

The only rules, if you could loosely call them that, are:-

a) Don't abandon using your pinky or little finger if you're just beginning to play, as you'll eventually need it for some of the four finger chords which frequently crop up.

b) Try to avoid fretting with the thumb unless you're learning an instrument like the mountain dulcimer which requires a longer stretch. I know a number of players employ it on slimmer necked instruments, but I personally feel it leads to bad habits.

c) Keep your left hand fingernails short or fretting becomes a major problem. Obviously do the reverse if you're a lefty.

d) If you're a beginner and you're naturally left handed, don't get persuaded into buying a right handed instrument - it won't work! The learning curve will be steeper and you'll never get the fluidity you'd achieve with your natural hand. Most acoustic instruments can be adapted for a left hander apart from cutaway guitars and f-style mandolins etc., by reversing the nut and strings. For the non-reversible instruments, always go for a left handed model.

e) Learn to barré with other fingers apart from your index finger. This will prove invaluable with more complex chords and increase finger strength as well.

f) Don't be afraid to use fingerings further up the neck in combination with open strings as these will give you interesting new voicings and are generally quite popular in folk music. A number of these are provided in this book.

g) The strings of a lute should generally be plucked rather than strummed. There are a number of reasons for this. Firstly, this is what gives the instrument its unique sound. Secondly, lutes are notoriously temporamental when it comes to staying in tune and as a result, vigorous strumming tends to hasten the detuning process. Thirdly, a lute sounds so much better plucked than strummed!

h) The right hand technique on a lute differs from the guitar in that the player's hand should be parallel to the strings and not in a vertical position, with the little finger anchored to the soundboard. The thumb should also sit inside the index finger, rather than above it as is common with guitar technique.

CHORD THEORY & FAQs

Q What is a chord?
A It's a collection of three or more notes played simultaneously. The exceptions in this book are the fourths and fifths (power chords) which aren't in the strictest sense, true chords. For convenience sake, they are classed as such.

Q What is a triad?
A A chord containing three notes. For example, G Major, Bm, D+ or Asus4.

Q What are intervals?
A Intervals are the musical distance between notes in a musical scale. For instance in the scale of C Major, C is the 1st note, D is the 2nd note, E the 3rd and so on. So if you're playing the chord of C Major, your intervals will be 1–3–5 or C as the *first* note, E as the *third* note and G as the *perfect fifth*.

Q What is a chromatic scale and which intervals does it contain?
A: A chromatic scale encompasses all twelve notes in a musical scale, including the sharps and flats. It's also the basis for the naming of every chord in existence. See the staff diagram below to see the intervals:

Q What is a seventh chord?
A: In its most basic form, an additional note beyond the triad. Sevenths can be either major or flattened. For instance, returning to our old friend, the key of C, a *Cmaj7* has an added *B* on top of the *C–E–G* triad. The resultant chord has a mellow quality often found in jazz. Now if you take the B and flatten it by dropping the fourth note in your chord down to a B flat, you get a C7.

Q: Then why isn't it called a C minor seventh?
A: Technically this *is* a minor seventh note, but this would create a lot of confusion when naming chords, as you already have a minor interval option in your triad (in the key of C major, E flat), so it's always referred to as a 7th to differentiate between it and a major seventh.

Q: What is an extension?
A: A chord which goes beyond the scope of triads and sevenths. Basically, extensions are additional notes placed above the triad or seventh in a musical stave, fingerboard or keyboard. It's important to understand these are, for theoretical purposes, always placed above the seventh. Or in layman's terms, higher up the scale. The confusion comes when you start to realise a 9th is identical to a 2nd - in the scale of C – a D note.

Q: So why is the ninth note the same as the second note?
A: This takes a little grasping, but if you remember that if your note goes higher than the seventh it's a 9th, but if it's lower, it'll be a 2nd. An example of this would be Csus2, which contains the root

note of C, a 2nd or suspended D note and a G, the perfect 5th. You'll see this even more clearly if you look at the piano keyboard diagram below. Count from the C up to the following D beyond the 7th (B note). From the C to the second D is exactly nine whole notes.

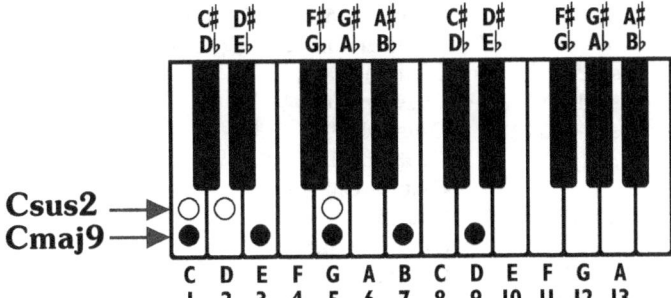

Q: *Do any other extensions share a common note?*
A: Yes, other examples include the *11th*, which is also a *4th* and the *13th* which shares a note with the *6th*.

Q: *What are inversions?*
A: In the root version of a chord, the notes run in their correct order from lowest to highest. In the case of G major, it would be G–B–D. With an inversion of the same chord the notes would run in a different order. For example, the first inversion of G major would be B–D–G and the second, D–G–B. In general, triads sound more or less the same when they're inverted, but that's certainly not the case with sevenths and extensions which can sound quite different and occasionally discordant when the notes are jumbled up in certain configurations. Inversions can also produce different chords using the same basic notes. A good example of this would be *C6 (C-E-G-A)* which produces an *Am7 (A-C-E-G)* when it's inverted (both contain the notes of C–E–G–A, but in a different order). The major variations are in the tonal properties of the chords, making them sound quite different from one another.

Q: *Do elevenths and thirteenths have any particular properties?*
A: Yes. In most cases the 3rd is omitted from eleventh chords and the 11th from the majority of thirteenths as they're deemed unnecessary and arguably, create unwanted dissonance.

Q: *Some chords are called by different names in different music books. What should I do?*
A: The alternative chord name reference chart at the back of the book should help sort out the confusion.

Q: *What is a suspended chord?*
A: It's simpler to think of suspended chords as a stepping stone to a major or resolving chord. In effect the third has been left in a state of suspension by either raising it to a fourth (sus4) or lowering it to a second (sus2). Sevenths also provide versions of the suspended chord in the form of C7sus4 or C7sus2 (using the key of C as an example).

Q: *What is a diminished chord?*
A: A diminished chord has a dissonent quality to it where the third and fifth notes in a triad are flattened by a semi-tone. Again, using C as an example, C major (C-E-G) is altered to Cdim (C-E♭-G♭). A second version of a dimished chord is also used in many forms of music, the diminished seventh. This retains the elements of a standard diminished chord, adding a double flat in the seventh (C-E♭-G♭-B♭♭). A B♭♭ in this case is, to all intents and purposes, really an *A* note.

Q: *What is an augmented chord?*
A: An augmented chord basically performs the opposite task to a diminished one. Instead of lowering the fifth by a semitone, it raises it by the same interval. A C+ (augmented) chord contains the triad of C-E-G♯. The major root and third are retained and the fifth is sharpened.

ALTERNATIVE CHORD NAMES

C	**CM** or **Cmaj**	Cm13	**C-13** or **Cmin13**
Cm	**Cmin** or **C-**	Cmaj13	**CM13, Cmaj7(add13),**
C-5	**C-5** or **C(♭5)**		**C△13** or **CM7(add13)**
C°	**Cdim**		
C4	**Csus4(no 5th)** or **Csus(no 5th)**	M	major
C5	**C Power Chord** or **C(no 3rd)**	m	minor
Csus2	**C(sus2)** or **C2**	-	minor
Csus4	**Csus** or **C(sus4)**	dim	diminished
Csus4add9	**Csus(add9)**	°	diminished
C+	**Caug, C+5** or **C(♯5)**	ø	half diminished
C6	**CM6** or **CMaj6**	sus	suspended
Cadd9	**Cadd2**	aug	augmented
Cm6	**C-6** or **Cmin6**	+	augmented
Cmadd9	**Cmadd2** or **C-(add9)**	add	added
C6add9	**C6/9, C$^6_9$** or **CMaj6(add9)**	dom	dominant
Cm6add9	**Cm6/9** or **Cm$^6_9$**	△	delta / major seventh
C°7	**Cdim7**	Q(3)	quartal / double fourth
C7	**Cdom**	♯	sharp
C7sus2	**C7(sus2)**	×	double sharp
C7sus4	**C7sus, C7(sus4)** or **Csus11**	♭	flat
C7-5	**C7♭5**	♭♭	double flat
C7+5	**C7+** or **C7♯5**		
C7-9	**C7♭9** or **C7(add♭9)**	Do	Spanish for C
C7+9	**C7♯9** or **C7(add♯9)**	Dó	Portuguese for C
C7-5-9	**C7♭5♭9**	Re	Spanish for D
C7+5-9	**C7♯5♭9**	Ré	Portuguese for D
C7+5+9	**C7♯5♯9**	Mi	Spanish & Portuguese for E
C7add11	**C7/11** or **C$^7_{11}$**	Fa	Spanish & Portuguese for F
C7+11	**C7♯11**	So	Spanish for G
Cm7	**C-7, Cmi7** or **Cmin7**	Sol	Portuguese for G
Cm7-5	**Cm7♭5, C-7-5** or **C°**	La	Spanish for A
Cm7-5-9	**Cm7♭5♭9**	Lá	Portuguese for A
Cm7-9	**Cm7♭9**	Si	Spanish & Portuguese for B
Cm7add11	**Cm**	H	German for B
Cm(maj7)	**Cm♯7, CM7-5, CmM7** or **C-△**		
Cmaj7	**CM7** or **C△(Delta)**		
Cmaj7-5	**CM7-5, C△♭5** or **Cmaj7♭5**		
Cmaj7+5	**CM7+5, C△5+** or **Cmaj7♯11**	**English Tonic Sol-fa**	
Cmaj7+11	**CM7+11, C△+♯11** or **Cmaj7♯11**	Do	**C**
C9	**C7(add9)**	Re	**D**
C9sus4	**C9sus** or **C9(sus4)**	Me	**E**
C9-5	**C9♭5**	Fa	**F**
C9+5	**C9♯5**	Sol	**G**
C9+11	**C9♯11**	La	**A**
Cm9	**C-9** or **Cmin9**	Ti	**B**
Cm9-5	**Cm9♭5**		
Cm(maj9)	**Cm9(maj7), CmM9** or **Cm(addM9)**		
Cmaj9	**CM9, Cmaj7(add9), C△9** or **CM7(add9)**		
Cmaj9-5	**CM9-5, Cmaj9♭5, C△9♭5** or **CM9♭5**	The majority of music books will use the chords featured in the first column (on the far left and top right), but should you come across alternatives, consult this guide for other naming conventions.	
Cmaj9+5	**CM9+5, Cmaj9♯5, C△9♯5**		
Cmaj9add6	**CM9add6** or **C△9add6**		
Cmaj9+11	**CM9+11, Cmaj9♯11, C△9♯11** or **CM9♯11**		
C11	**C7(add11)**		
C11-9	**C11♭9**	The list above includes most of the symbols and abbreviations that you're likely to encounter in the majority of music books.	
Cm11	**C-11** or **Cmin11**		
Cmaj11	**CM11, Cmaj7(add11), C△11, CM7(add11)**		
C13	**C7/6(no 9th)** or **C7(add13)**		
C13sus4	**C13sus** or **C13(sus4)**		
C13-5-9	**C13♭5♭9**		
C13-9	**C13♭9**		
C13+9	**C13♯9**		
C13+11	**C13♯11** or **C13aug11**		

LUTE TUNING ON A GUITAR

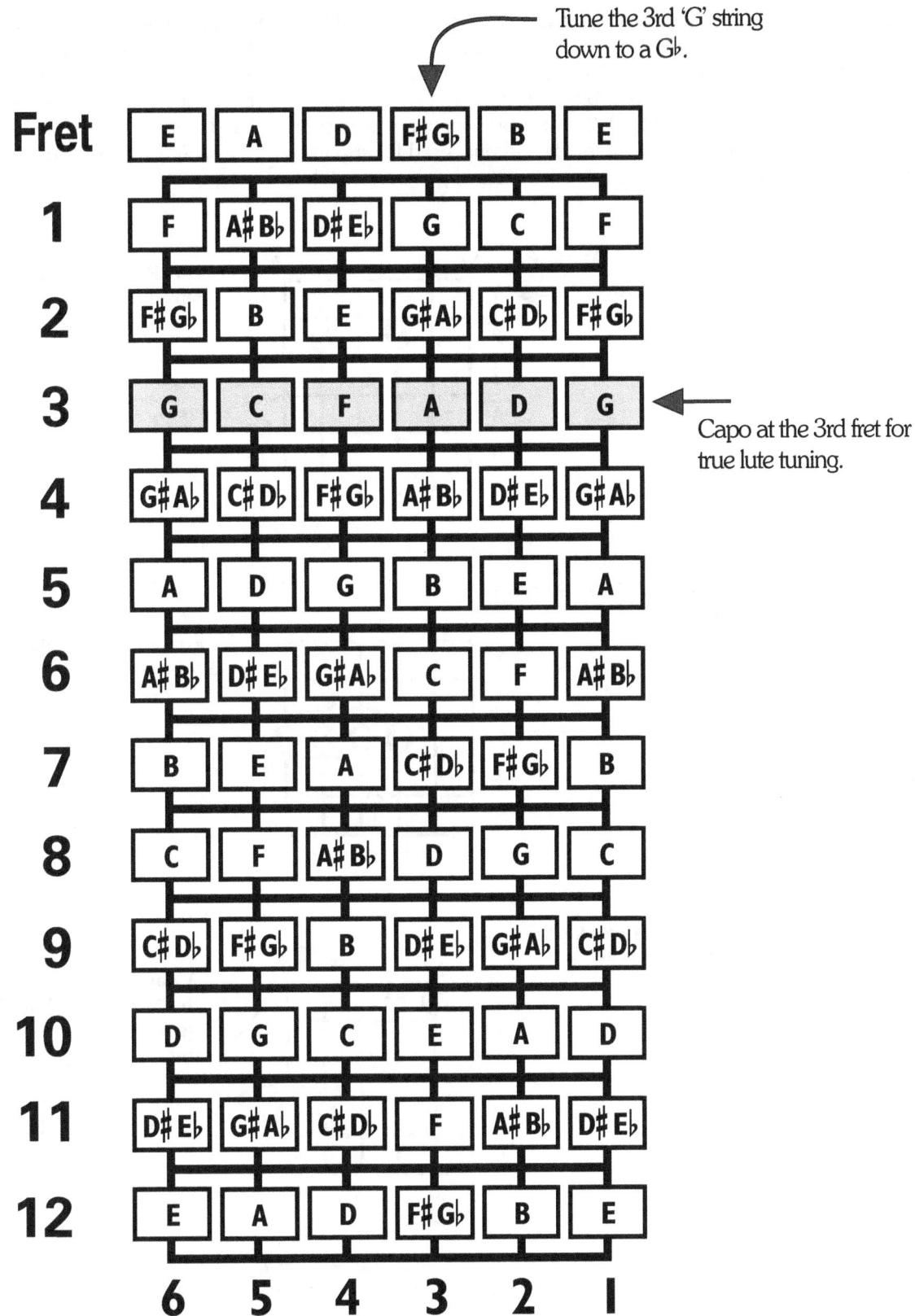

If you don't have access to a lute at the moment or just fancy playing music in lute tuning on the guitar, the above diagram shows you how to tune your instrument in tranposed lute tuning (E-A-D-G♭-B-E) or *'true'* lute tuning (G-C-F-A-D-G) by capoing on the third fret. I would heavily advise against trying to tune your guitar in *'true'* lute tuning without capoing or the strings will almost certainly break due to the extra tension on the longer scale instrument.

UNDERSTANDING THE CHORD BOXES

The three diagrams below show the chord conventions illustrated in this guide. Most experienced fretted instrument players should be familiar with them. The suggested fingering positions are only meant as a general guide and will depend, in many instances, on hand size, finger length and flexibility, so feel free to experiment. The location of the black circles is unalterable, though, if you want to produce the correct voicing. The chord windows in this guide feature the first six courses of strings (1st to 6th course viewed from right to left), with the lower pairings on courses 7 and 8 acting as bass strings. These are frettable, but the stretch is generally uncomfortable and only used for specific occasions. A few slash chord positions utilising these things are included in the book, where other fingerings aren't possible.

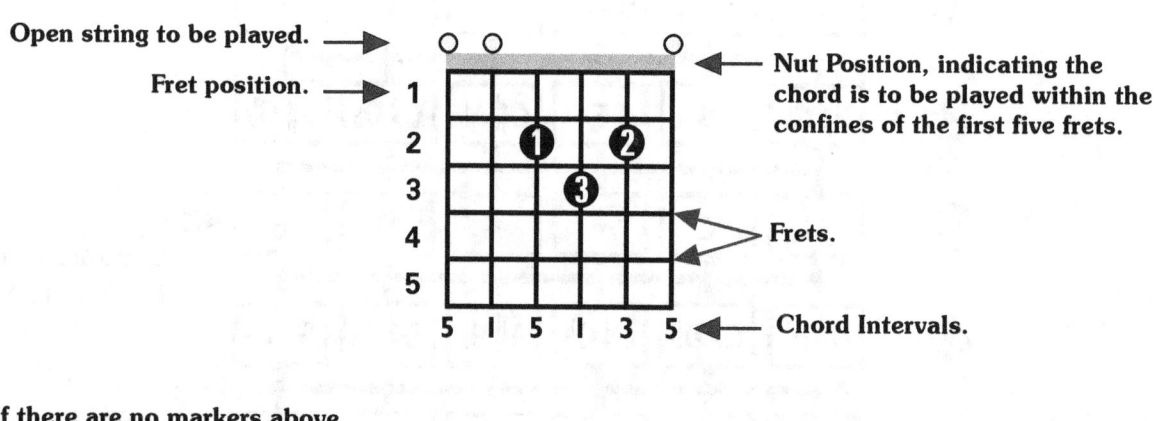

Whether a fretted instrument has single strings or pairs of strings, the chord boxes in this book, other chord dictionaries and songbooks treat it as a four stringed instrument. This convention is common to all double or triple course instruments such as the mandolin or tiple, making the diagrams a lot less confusing and free from unnecessary clutter.

RENAISSANCE LUTE FINGERBOARD & TUNING LAYOUT

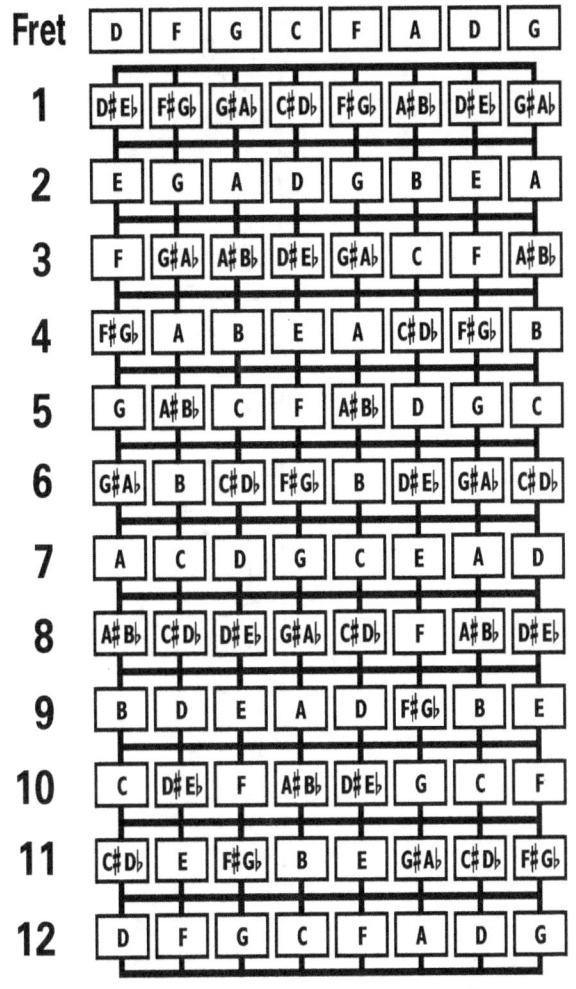

Fingerboard note layout for an 8-course Renaissance lute.

For 7 or 6-course instruments, ignore one or both of the courses on the right (i.e. D and F)

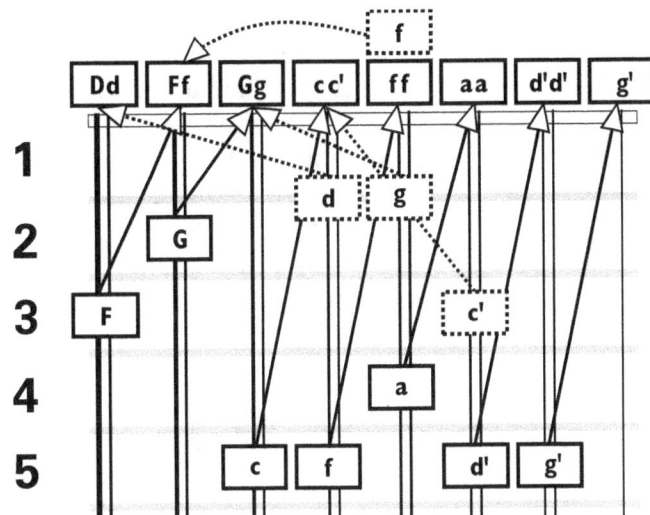

Tuning the Renaissance lute by fretting at given intervals on the fingerboard. The broken lines and boxes indicate the fretting location for the higher octave strings.

Note:
A classical guitar can be utilised as a makeshift lute by tuning the 3rd string down a semitone to F# and capoing at the 3rd fret. This will allow you to use the chords in this book and to follow standard lute notation.

Renaissance lute tuning notation
(written an octave higher than sounded)

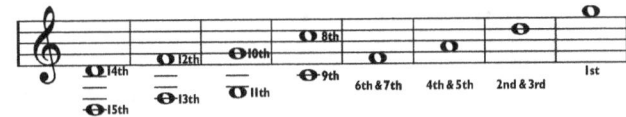

To tune your lute accurately, it's best to use an electronic chromatic tuner, but if there isn't one available, you can tune it to a guitar or piano/electronic keyboard. The following tuning grid gives the correct fingering positions on the guitar fingerboard and piano keyboard.

Renaissance Lute	Guitar	Piano
1st string (*or chanterelle*) (g')	1st string (E) fretted at the 3rd fret	1st G above middle C
2nd & 3rd string (d')	2nd string (B) fretted at the 3rd fret	1st D above middle C
4th & 5th string (a)	3rd string (G) fretted at the 2nd fret	1st A below middle C
6th & 7th string (f)	4th string (D) fretted at the 3rd fret	1st F below middle C
8th octave string (c')	2nd string (B) fretted at the 1st fret	Middle C
9th string (c)	2nd string (A) fretted at 3rd fret	1st C below middle C
10th octave string (g)	3rd open string (G)	1st G below middle C
11th string (G)	6th string (E) fretted at the 3rd fret	2nd G below middle C
12th octave string (f)	4th string (D) fretted at the 3rd fret	1st F below middle C
13th string (F)	6th string (E) fretted at the 1st fret	2nd F below middle C
14th octave string (d)	4th open string (D)	1st D below middle C
15th string (D)	6th open string (E) and fret lute on 2nd fret whilst tuning	2nd D above middle C

THE CHORDS COVERED IN THIS BOOK

Chord	Chord Name in Full	Harmonic Interval
C	Major	1–3–5
Cm	Minor	1–F3–5
C-5	Major Diminished Fifth	1–3–F5
C°	Diminished	1–F3–F5
C4	Fourth	1–4
C5	Fifth or Power Chord	1–5
Csus2	Suspended Second	1–2–5
Csus4	Suspended Fourth	1–4–5
Csus4add9	Suspended Fourth Added Ninth	1–4–5–9
C+	Augmented	1–3–S5
C6	Major Sixth	1–3–5–6
Cadd9	Major Added Ninth	1–3–5–9
Cadd11	Major Added Eleventh	1–3–5–11
Cm6	Minor Sixth	1–F3–5–6
Cm-6	Minor Diminished Sixth	1–F3–5–F6
Cmadd9	Minor Added Ninth	1–F3–5–9
C6add9	Major Sixth Added Ninth	1–3–5–6–9
Cm6add9	Minor Sixth Added Ninth	1–F3–5–6–9
C°7	Diminished Seventh	1–F3–F5–DF7
C7	Seventh	1–3–5–F7
C7sus2	Seventh Suspended Second	1–2–5–F7
C7sus4	Seventh Suspended Fourth	1–4–5–F7
C7-5	Seventh Diminished Fifth	1–3–F5–F7
C7+5	Seventh Augmented Fifth	1–3–S5–F7
C7-9	Seventh Minor Ninth	1–3–5–F7–F9
C7+9	Seventh Augmented Ninth	1–3–5–F7–S9
C7-5-9	Seventh Diminished Fifth Minor Ninth	1–3–F5–F7–F9
C7-5+9	Seventh Diminished Fifth Augmented Ninth	1–3–F5–F7–S9
C7+5-9	Seventh Augmented Fifth Minor Ninth	1–3–S5–F7–F9
C7+5+9	Seventh Augmented Fifth Augmented Ninth	1–3–S5–F7–S9
C7add11	Seventh Added Eleventh	1–3–5–F7–11
C7+11	Seventh Augmented Eleventh	1–3–5–F7–S11
C7add13	Seventh Added Thirteenth	1–3–5–F7–13
Cm7	Minor Seventh	1–F3–5–F7
Cm7-5	Minor Seventh Diminished Fifth	1–F3–F5–F7
Cm7-5-9	Minor Seventh Diminished Fifth Minor Ninth	1–F3–F5–F7–F9
Cm7-9	Minor Seventh Minor Ninth	1–F3–5–F7–F9
Cm7add11	Minor Seventh Added Eleventh	1–F3–5–F7–11
Cm(maj7)	Minor Major Seventh	1–F3–5–7
Cmaj7	Major Seventh	1–3–5–7
Cmaj7-5	Major Seventh Diminished Fifth	1–3–F5–7
Cmaj7+5	Major Seventh Augmented Fifth	1–3–S5–7
Cmaj7+11	Major Seventh Augmented Eleventh	1–3–5–7–S11
C9	Ninth	1–3–5–F7–9
C9sus4	Ninth Suspended Fourth	1–4–5–F7–9
C9-5	Ninth Diminished Fifth	1–3–F5–F7–9
C9+5	Ninth Augmented Fifth	1–3–S5–F7–9
C9+11	Ninth Augmented Eleventh	1–3–5–F7–9–S11
Cm9	Minor Ninth	1–F3–5–F7–9

Chord	Chord Name in Full	Harmonic Interval
Cm9-5	Minor Ninth Diminished Fifth	1–F3–F5–F7–9
Cm(maj9)	Minor Major Ninth	1–F3–5–7–9
Cmaj9	Major Ninth	1–3–5–7–9
Cmaj9-5	Major Ninth Diminished Fifth	1–3–F5–7–9
Cmaj9+5	Major Ninth Augmented Fifth	1–3–S5–7–9
Cmaj9add6	Major Ninth Added Sixth	1–3–5–6–7–9
Cmaj9+11	Major Ninth Augmented Eleventh	1–3–5–7–9–S11
C11	Eleventh	1–3–5–F7–9–11
C11-9	Eleventh Diminished Ninth	1–3–5–F7–F9–11
Cm11	Minor Eleventh	1–F3–5–F7–9–11
Cmaj11	Major Eleventh	1–3–5–7–9–11
C13	Thirteenth	1–3–5–F7–9–11–13
C13sus4	Thirteenth Suspended Fourth	1–4–5–F7–9–11–13
C13-5-9	Thirteenth Diminished Fifth Minor Ninth	1–3–F5–F7–F9–11–13
C13-9	Thirteenth Minor Ninth	1–3–5–F7–F9–11–13
C13+9	Thirteenth Augmented Ninth	1–3–5–F7–S9–11–13
C13+11	Thirteenth Augmented Eleventh	1–3–5–F7–9–S11–13
Cm13	Minor Thirteenth	1–F3–5–F7–9–11–13
Cmaj13	Major Thirteenth	1–3–5–7–9–11–13

Key: F = Flat   S = Sharp   DF = Double Flat

SLASH CHORDS

What is a slash chord? Put simply, they're standard chords with an added note in the bass. *So what differentiates a C chord from a C/G when the G is already part of that chord, in this case, the fifth?* Theoretically, nothing, but the difference is very apparent when you actually sound the chord. The G bass is emphasised to provide a different feel to the harmonics. Slashes are also commonly found when the music calls for a descending bassline. For example; C, C/B, C/A and C/G.

The note after the slash indicates the bass note being played. For instance C/D would be an instruction to play a C chord with a D bass.

Slash Note. Generally found on the 4th, 5th or 6th courses, but sometimes on the lower courses of 7-10 course instruments

How do I play a slash chord that isn't listed in this book? Well, firstly, it would be an almost impossible task to cover every possible slash chord in existence, because the variations are potentially even greater than with standard chords. What you can do, within the confines of this guide, is to find the part of the chord before the slash in the main body of the book and then look for the nearest bass note on the fifth or sixth courses and beyond. To find the right bass note, consult the fingerboard layout on *page 11*.

USING A CAPO (OR *CAPO D'ASTRA*)

Using a capo on a lute isn't really a viable option because of the extra wide fingerboard. If however, you've decided to tune your classical guitar to lute tuning, there are many different capos available for flat or convex fingerboards.

C Chords

C	Cm	C7	Cm7
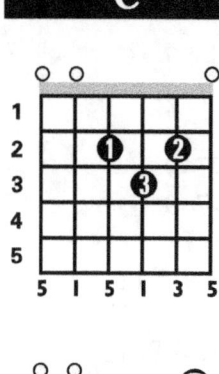	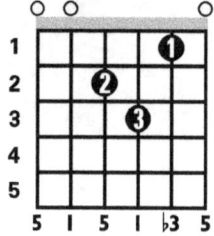	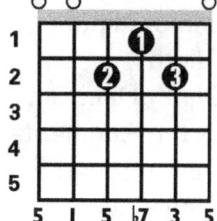	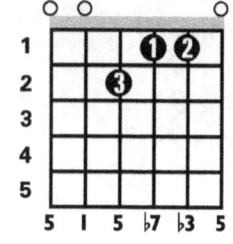
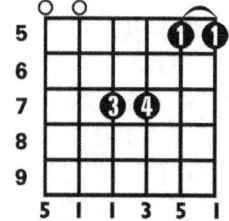	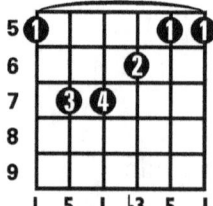	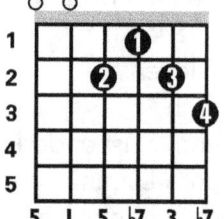	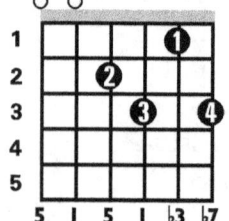
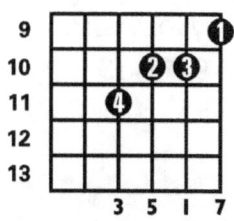	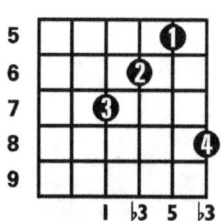	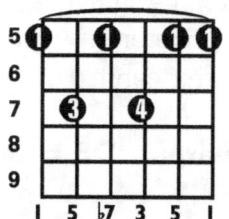	

C5	C6	Cm6	Cmaj7
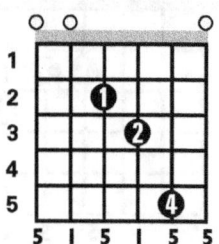	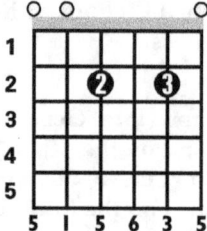	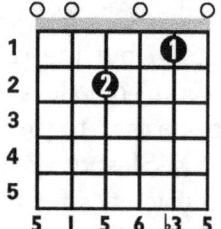	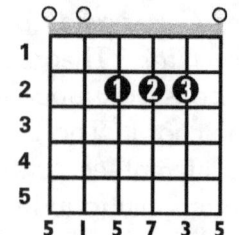
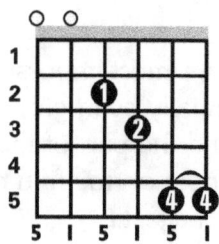	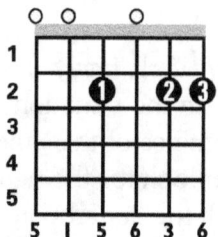	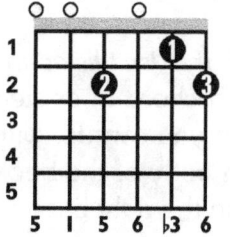	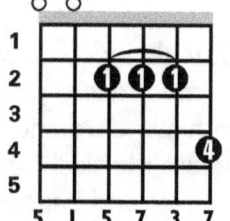
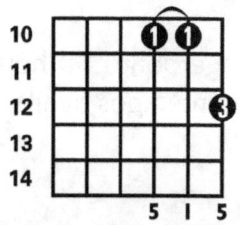	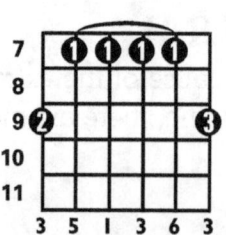	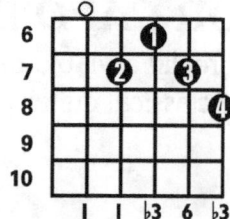	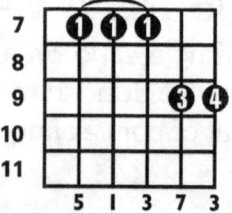

C Chords

C°
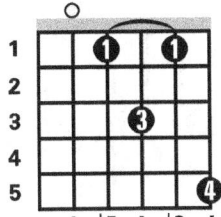
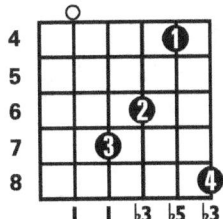
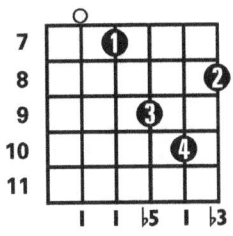

C°7
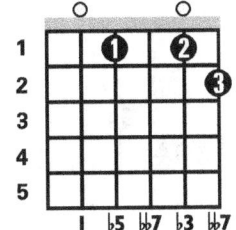
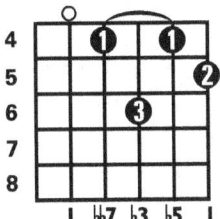
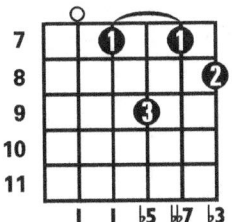

C-5
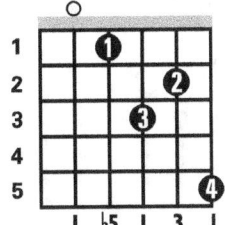
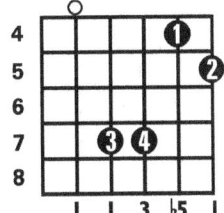
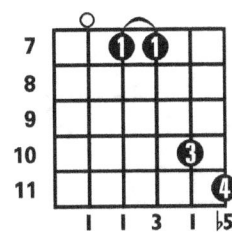

C+
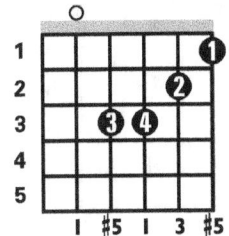
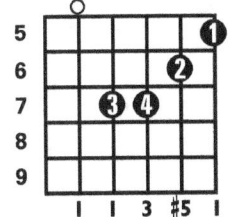
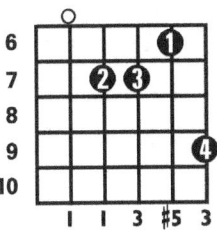

Csus2
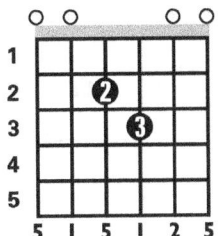
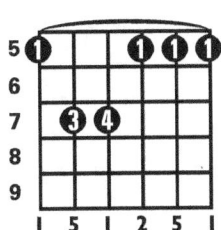
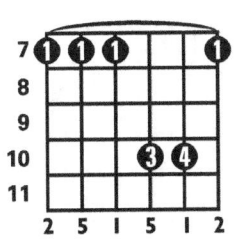

Csus4
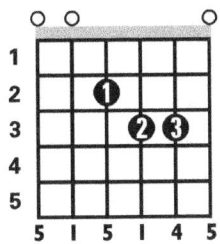
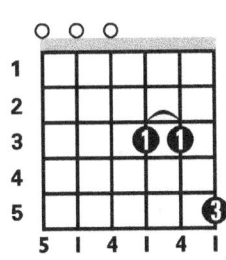
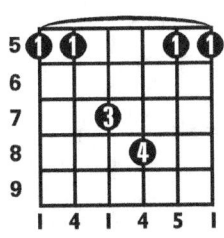

C7sus4
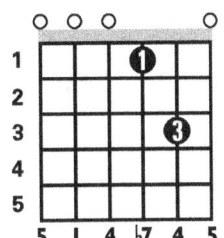
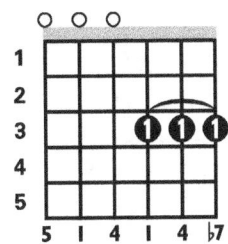
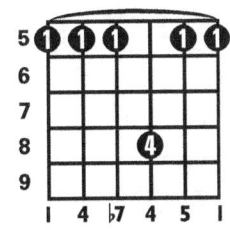

Cm7-5
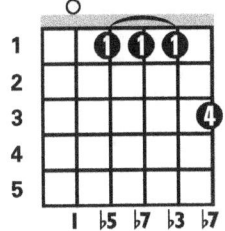
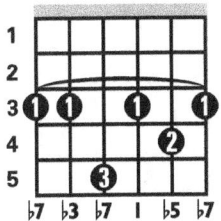
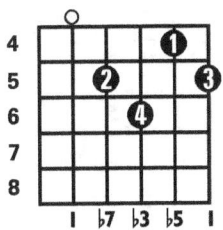

C Chords

Cadd9	Cmadd9	C6add9	Cm6add9
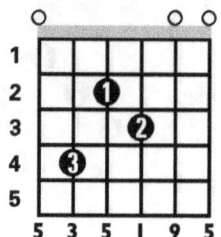	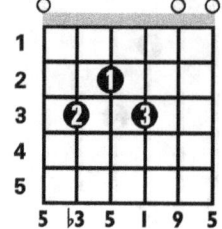	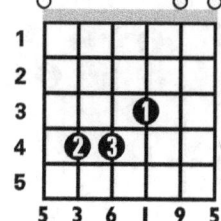	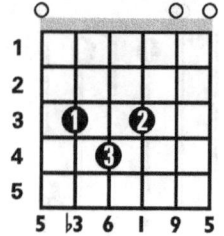
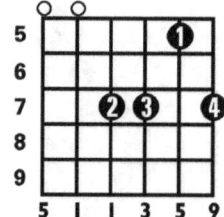	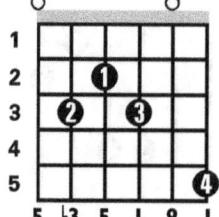	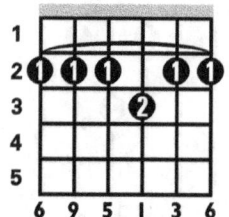	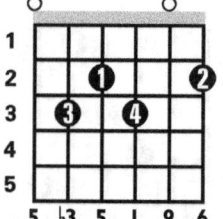
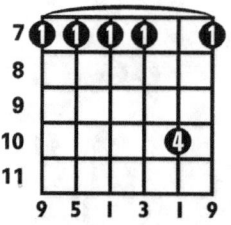	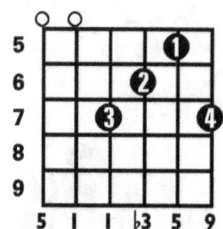	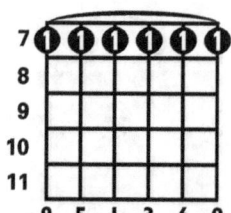	

C7-5	C7+5	C7-9	C7+9
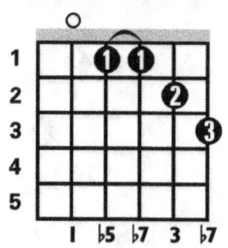	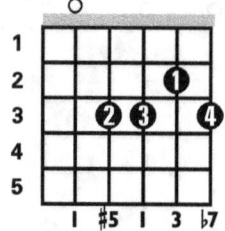	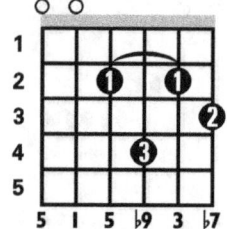	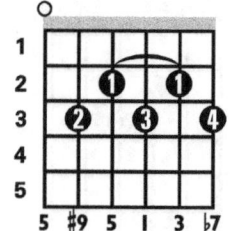
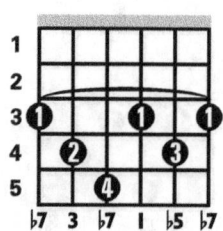	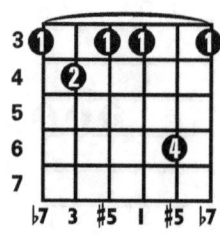	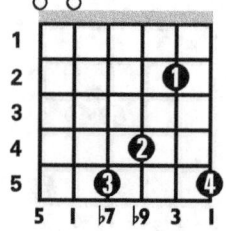	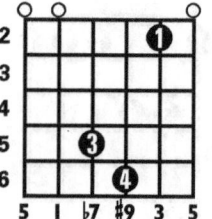
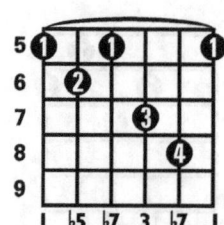	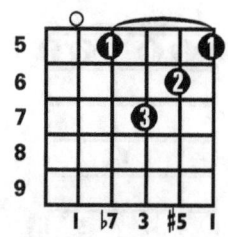	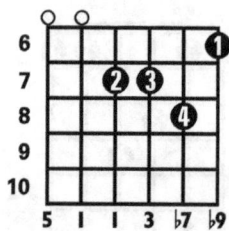	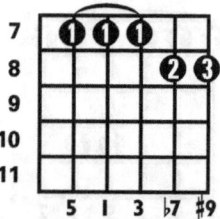

C Chords

Cm(maj7)
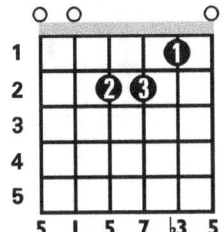
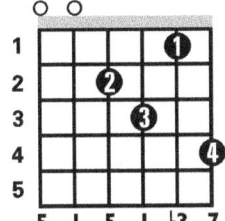
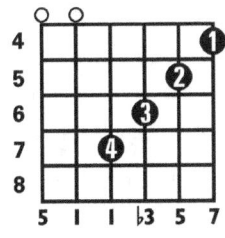

Cmaj7-5
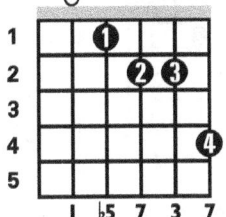
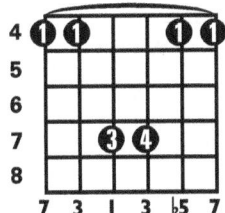
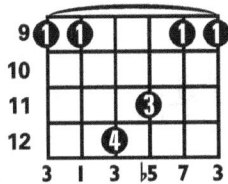

Cmaj7+5
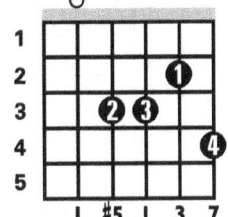
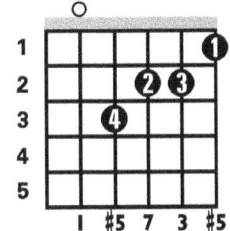
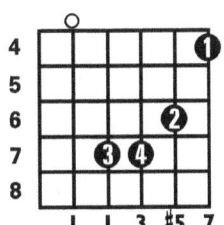

C9
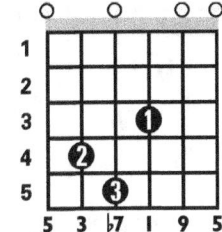
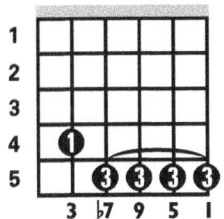
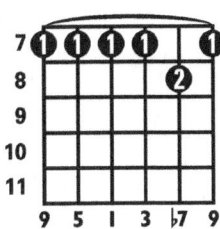

Cm9
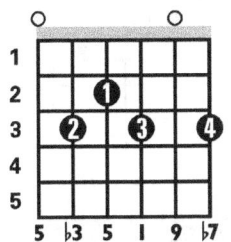
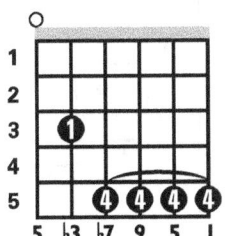
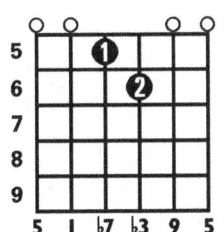

Cmaj9
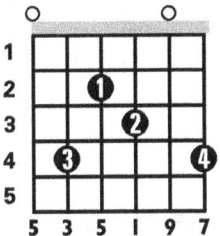
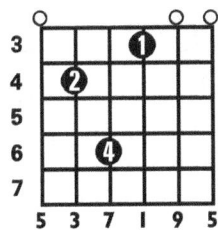
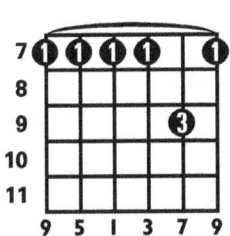

C11
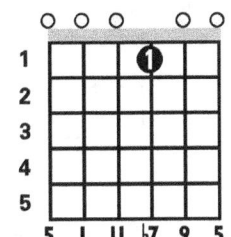
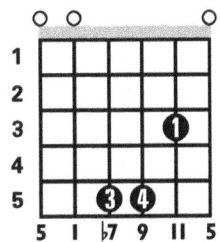
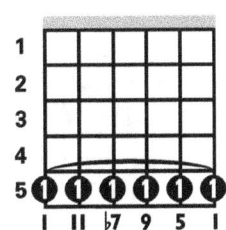

C13
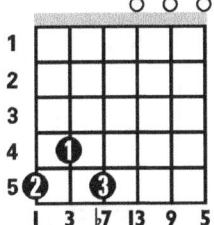
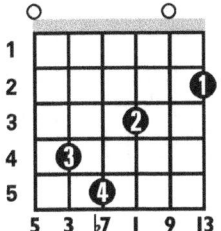
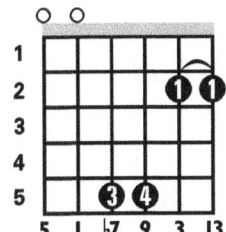

C Chords (Advanced)

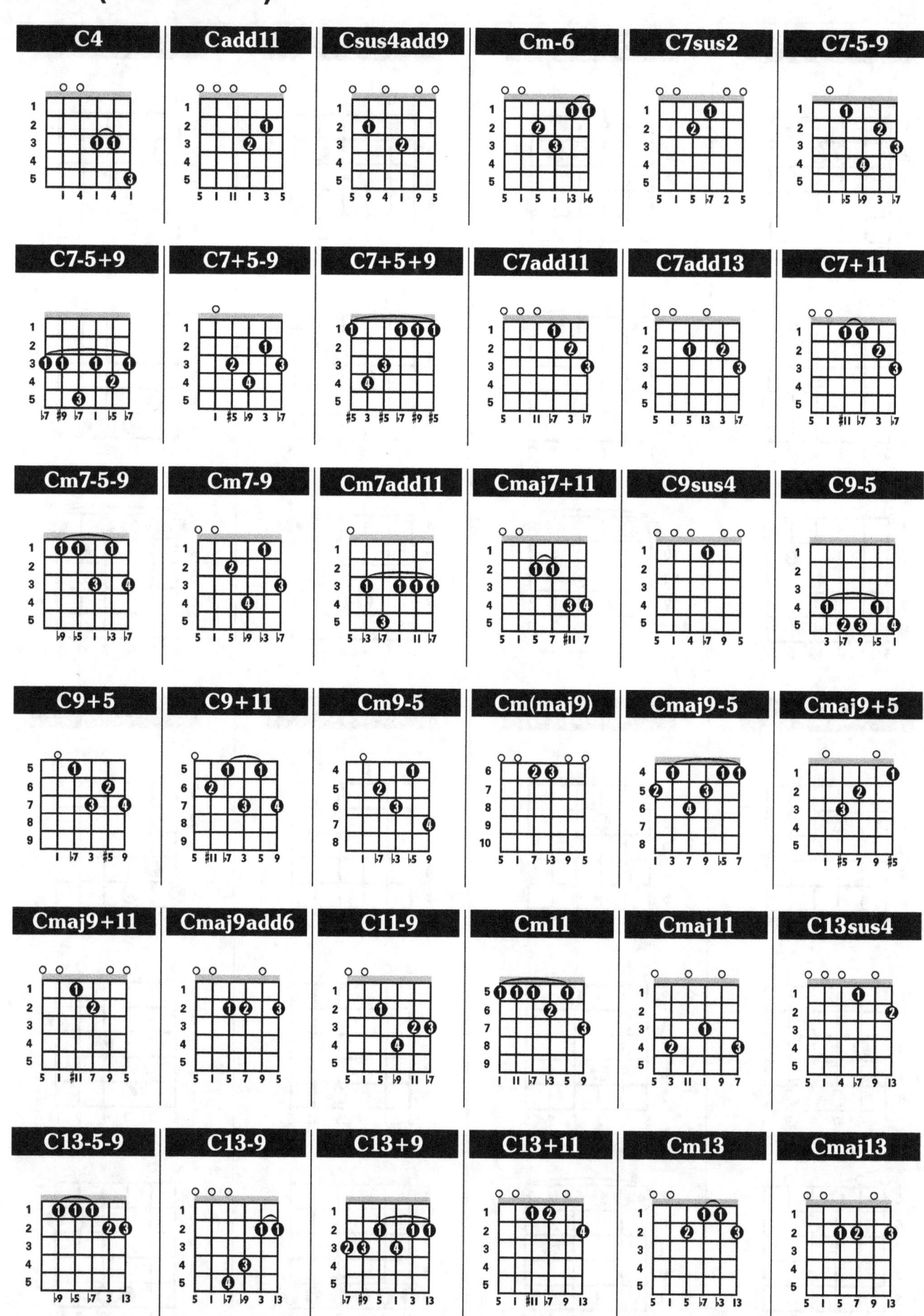

C#/D♭ Chords

D♭
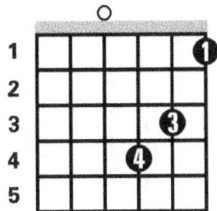
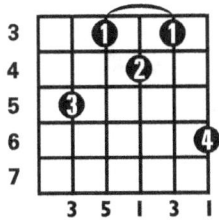
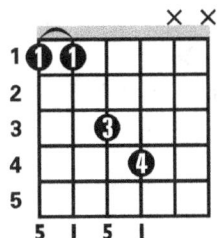

D♭m
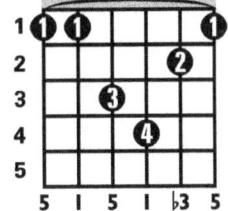
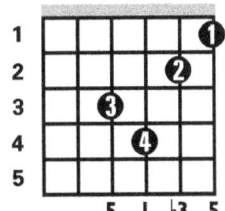
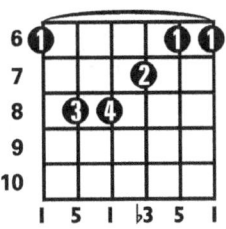

D♭7
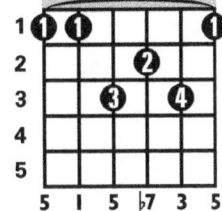

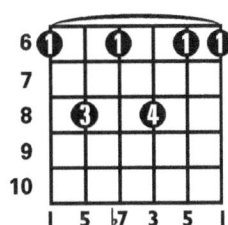

D♭m7
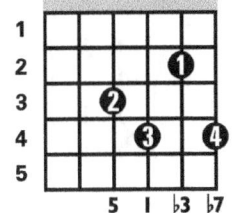
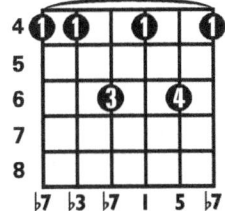
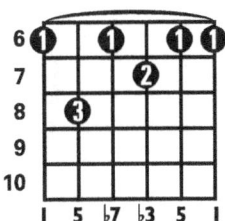

D♭5
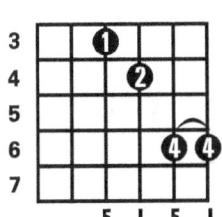
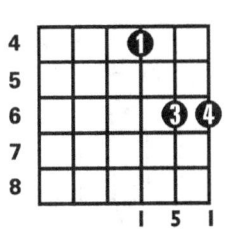

D♭6
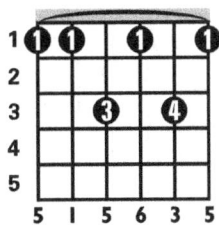
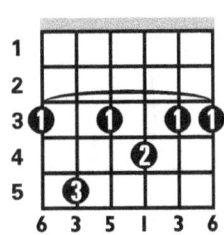
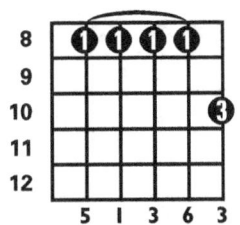

D♭m6
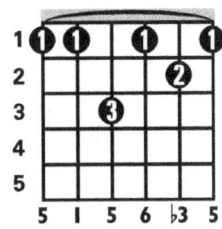
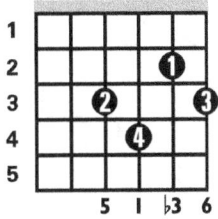
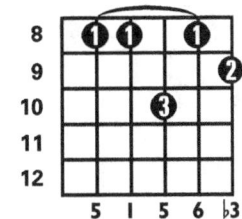

D♭maj7
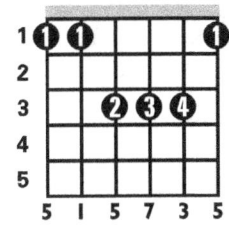
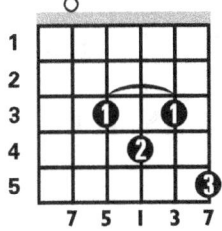
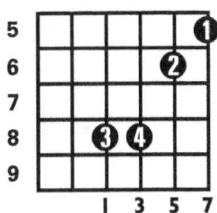

C#/ D♭ Chords

D♭°	D♭°7	D♭-5	D♭+
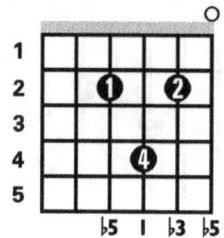	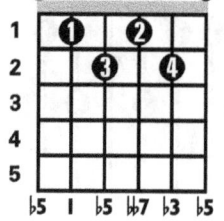	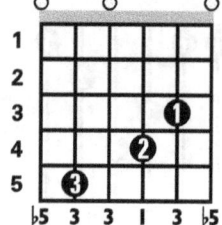	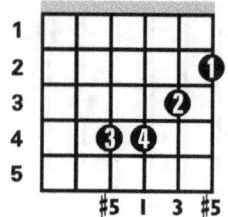
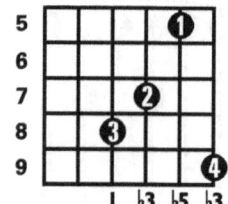	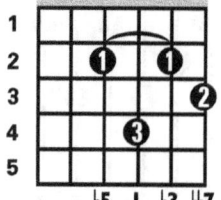	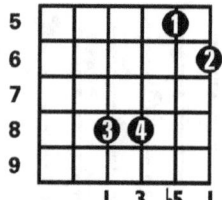	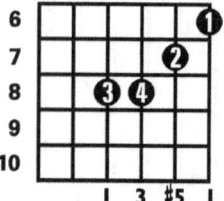
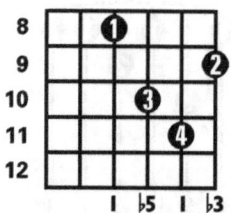	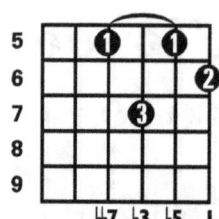	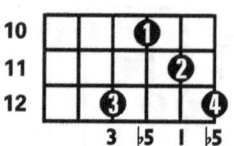	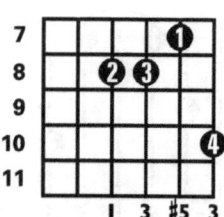

D♭sus2	D♭sus4	D♭7sus4	D♭m7-5
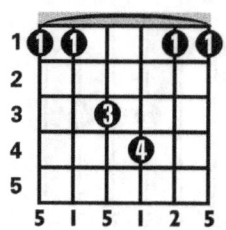	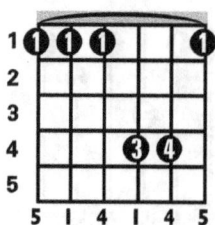		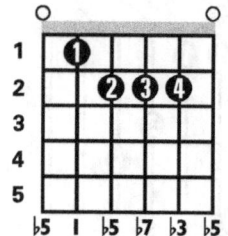
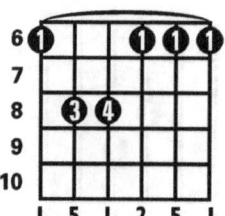	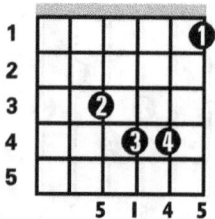	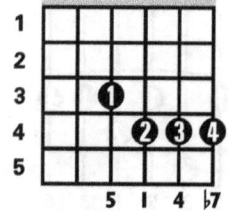	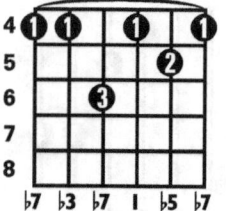
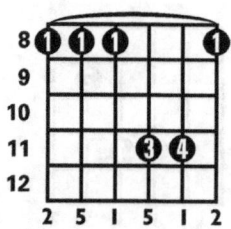	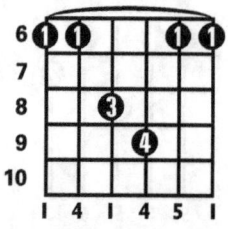	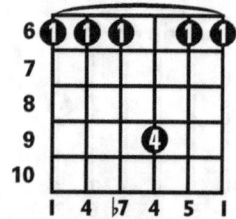	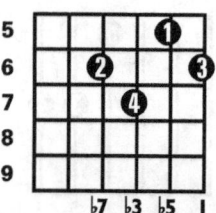

C#/D♭ Chords

D♭add9
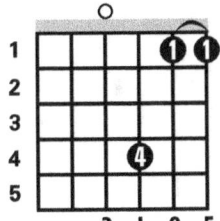
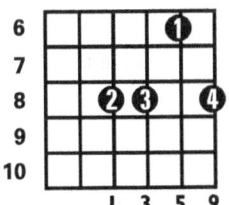
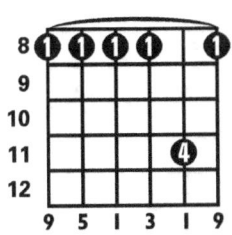

D♭madd9
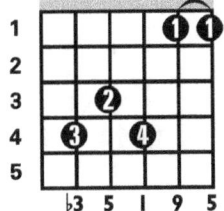
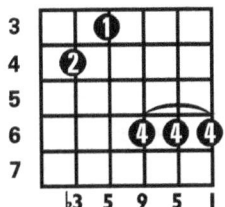
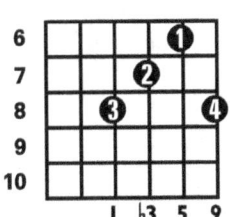

D♭6add9
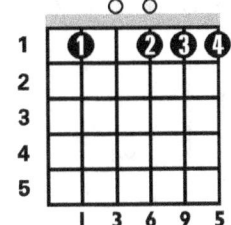
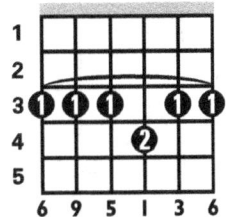
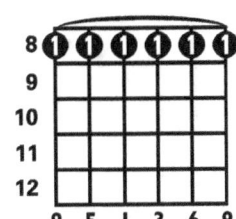

D♭m6add9
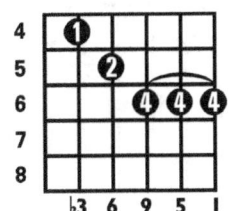
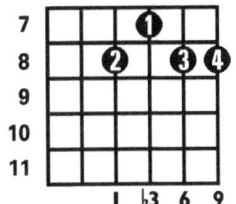
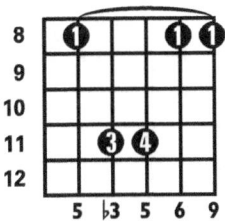

D♭7-5
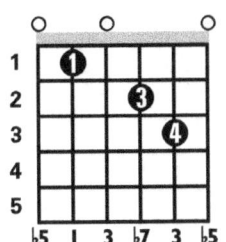
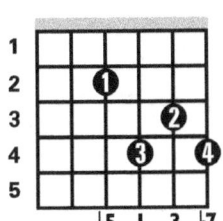
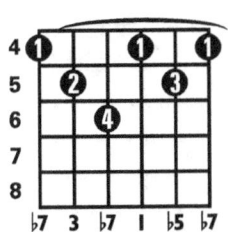

D♭7+5
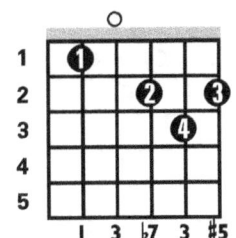
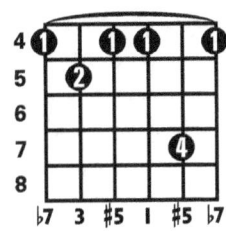
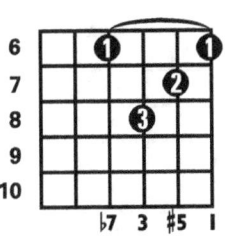

D♭7-9
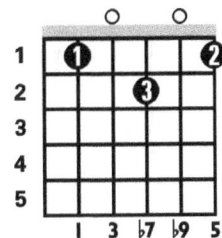
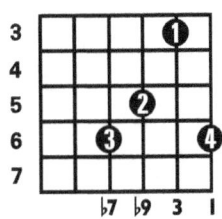
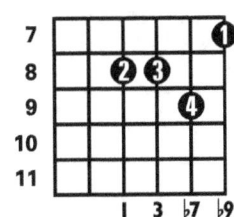

D♭7+9
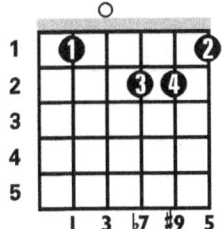
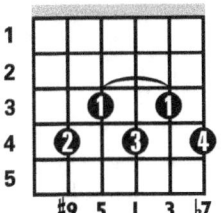
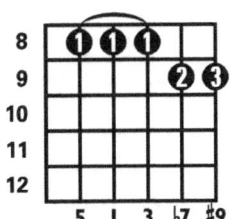

C#/ D♭ Chords

D♭m(maj7)	D♭maj7-5	D♭maj7+5	D♭9
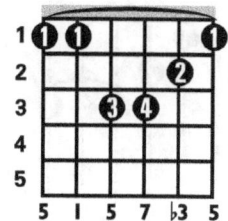	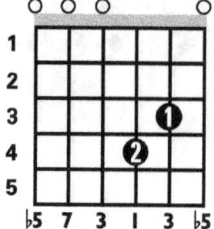	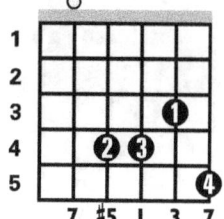	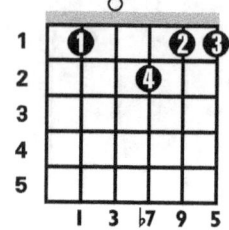
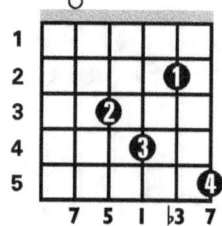	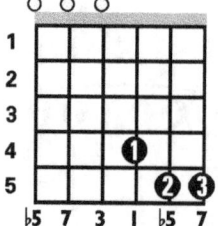	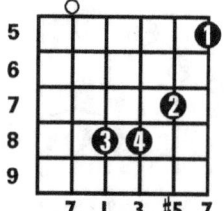	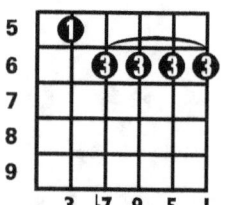
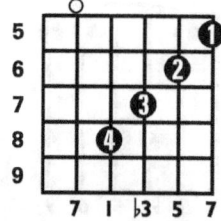	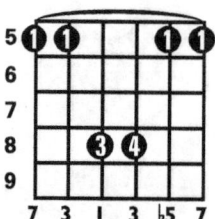	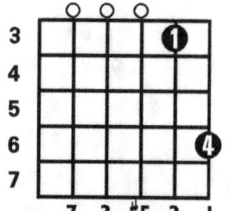	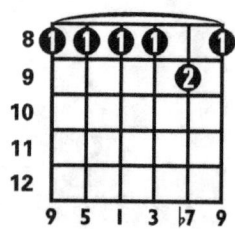

D♭m9	D♭maj9	D♭11	D♭13
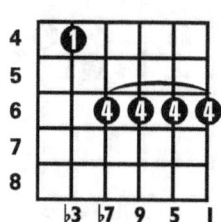	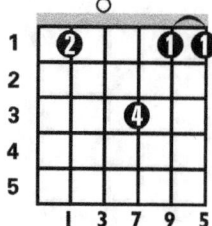		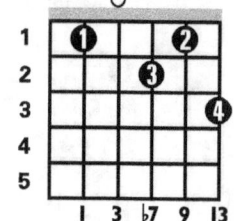
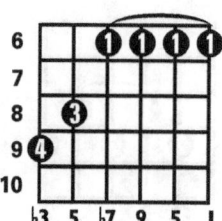	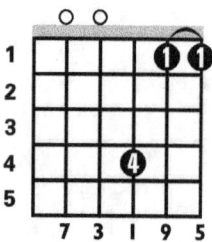	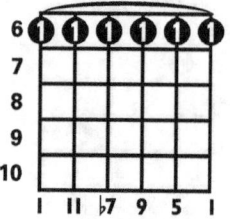	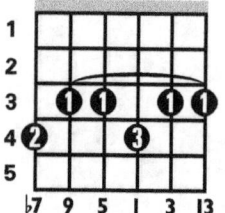
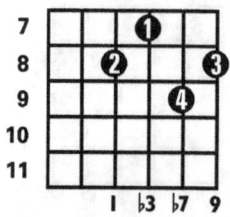	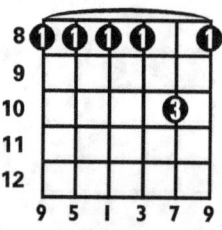	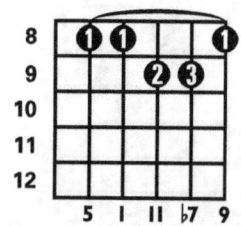	

C#/ D♭ Chords (Advanced)

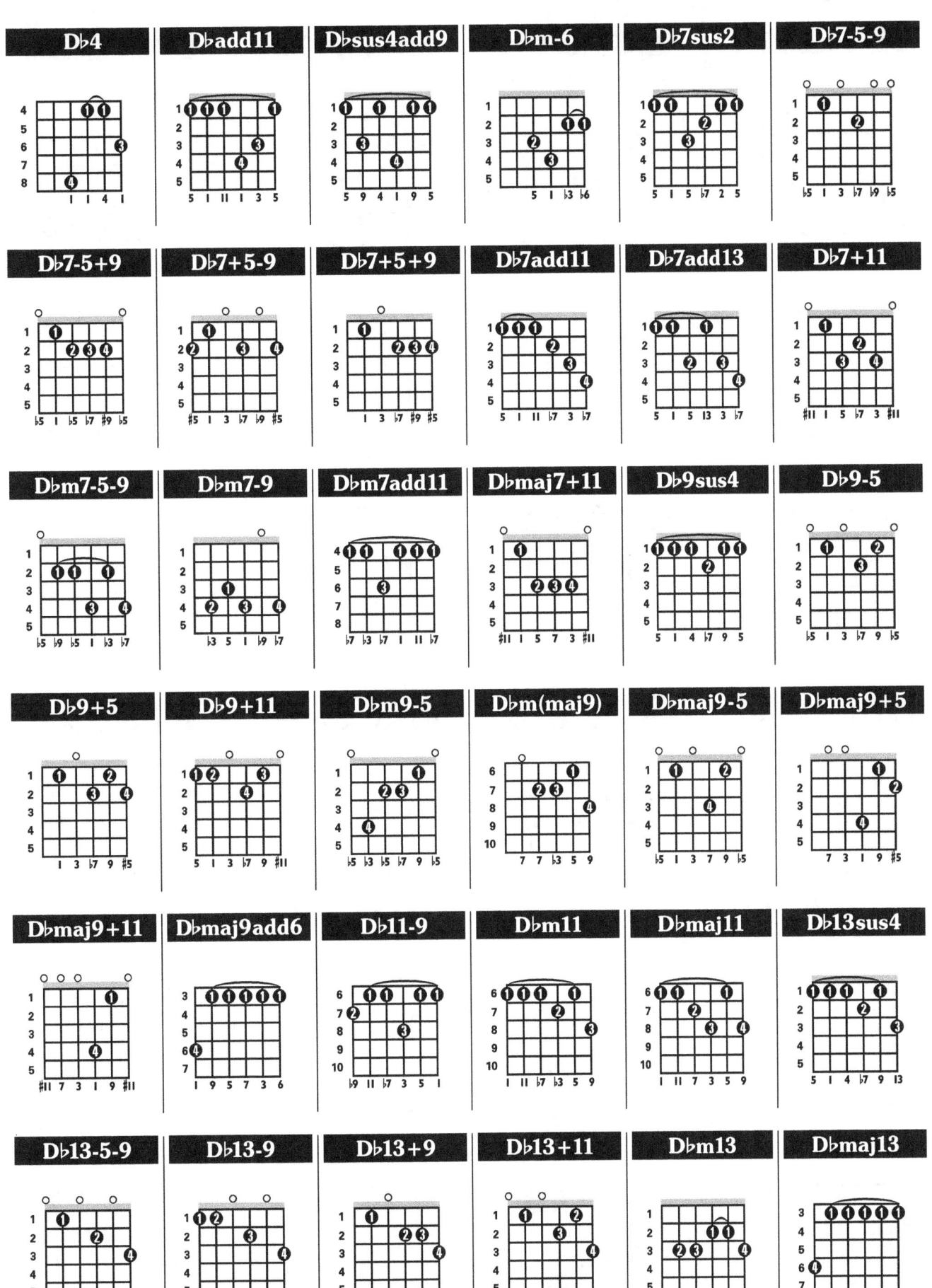

D Chords

D	Dm	D7	Dm7
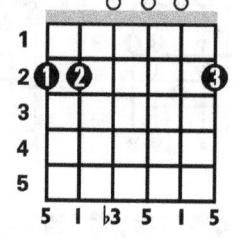	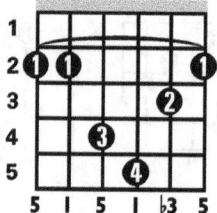	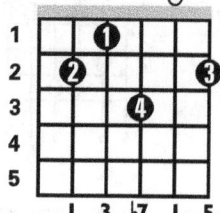	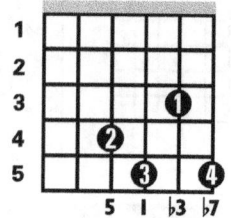
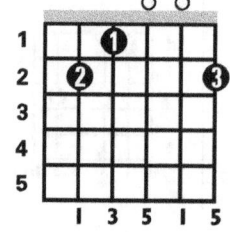	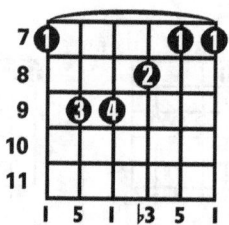	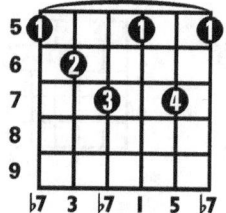	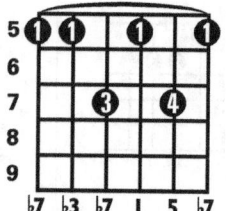
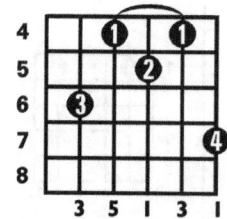	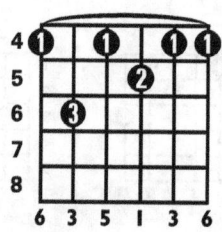	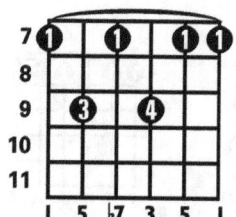	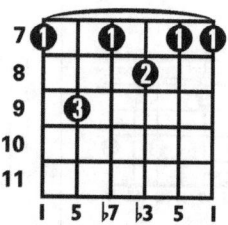

D5	D6	Dm6	Dmaj7
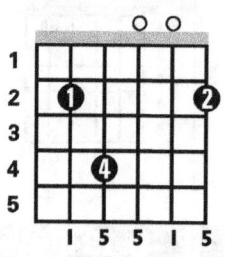	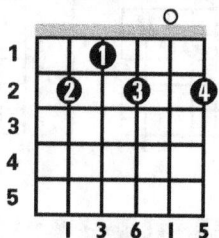	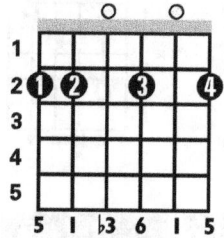	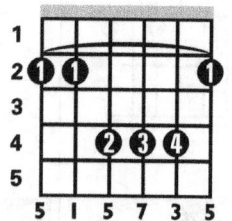
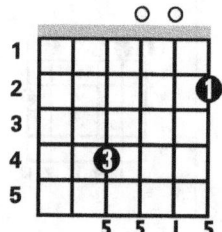	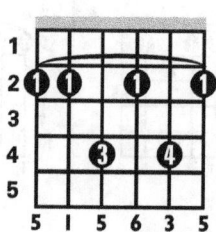	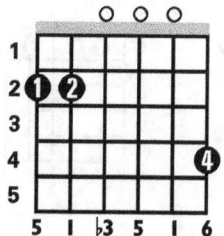	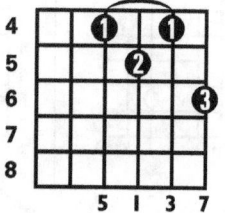
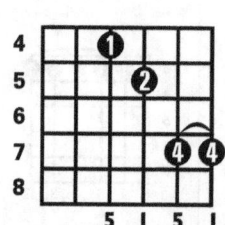	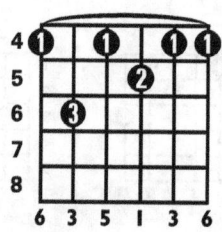	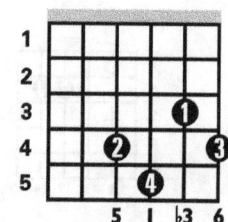	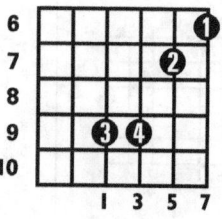

D Chords

D°
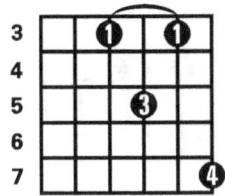
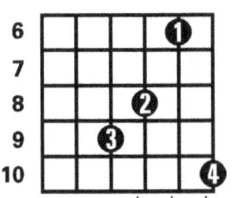
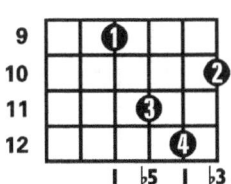

D°7
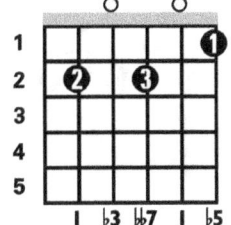
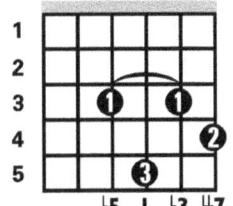
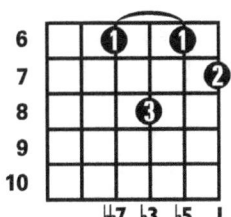

D-5
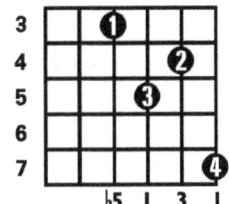
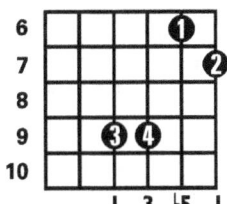
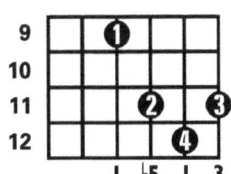

D+
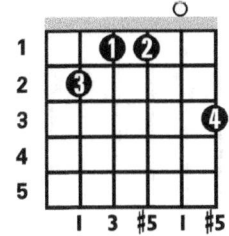
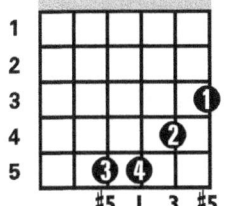
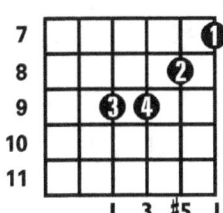

Dsus2
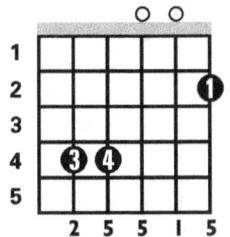
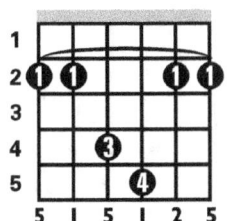
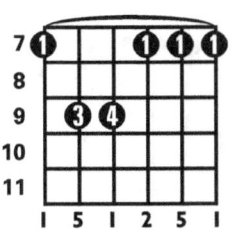

Dsus4
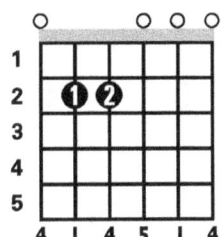
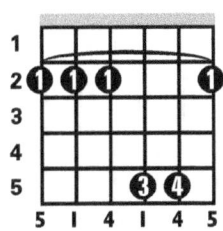
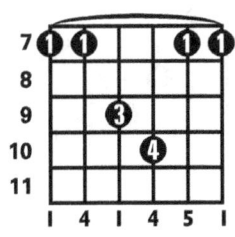

D7sus4
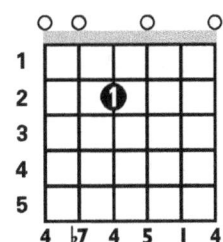
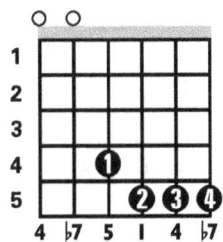
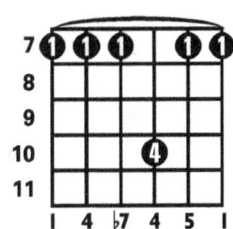

Dm7-5
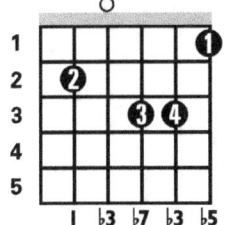
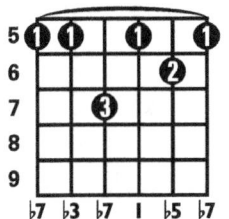
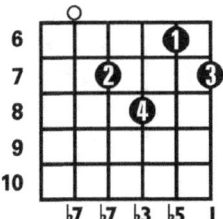

D Chords

Dadd9
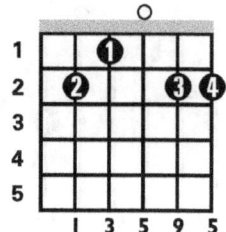
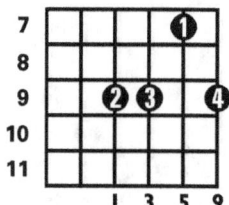
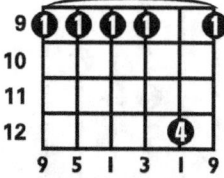

Dmadd9
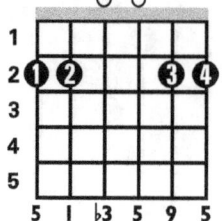
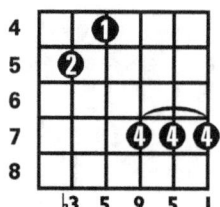
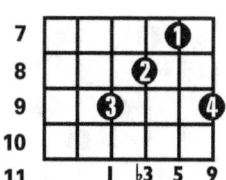

D6add9
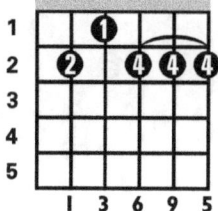
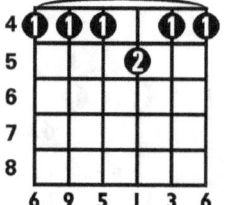
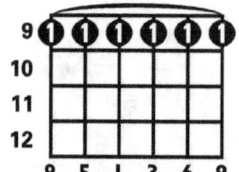

Dm6add9
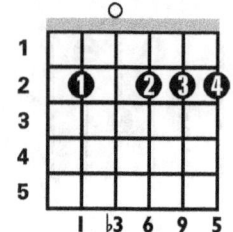
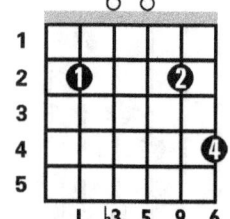
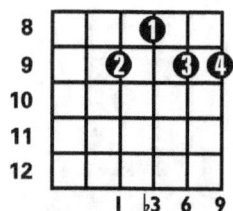

D7-5
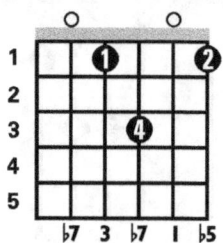
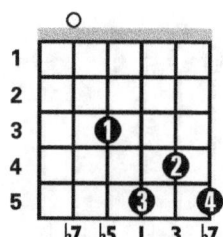
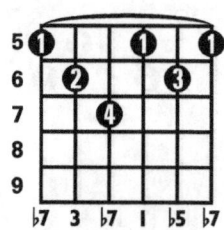

D7+5
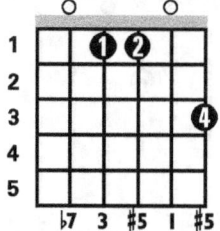
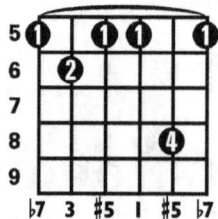
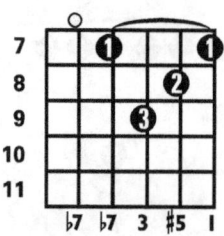

D7-9
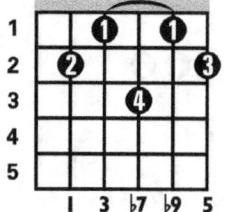
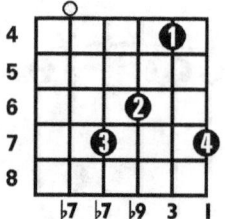
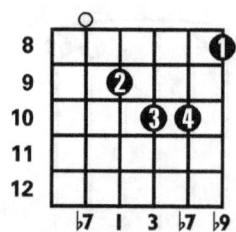

D7+9
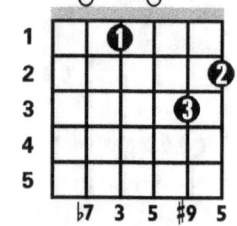
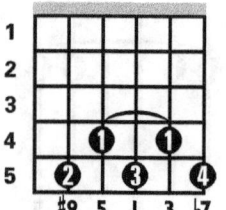
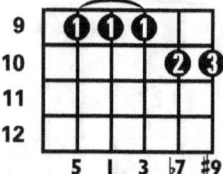

D Chords

Dm(maj7)
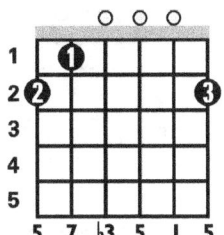
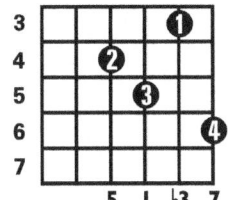
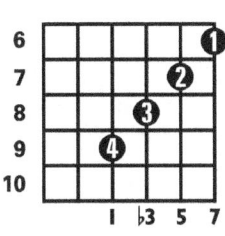

Dmaj7-5
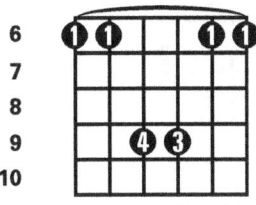
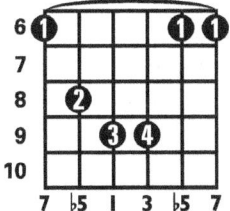
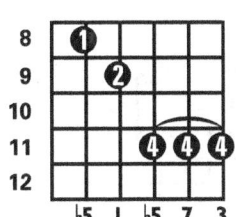

Dmaj7+5
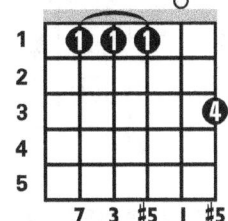
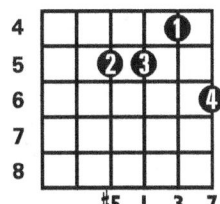
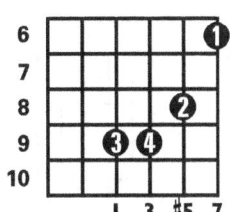

D9
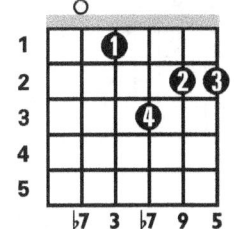
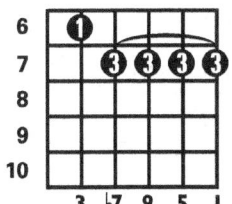
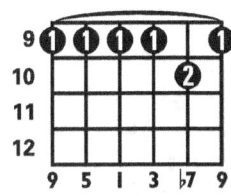

Dm9
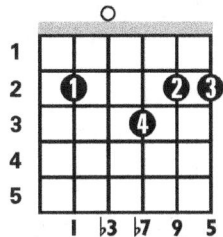
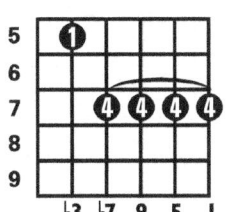
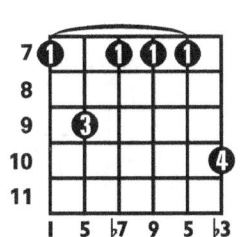

Dmaj9
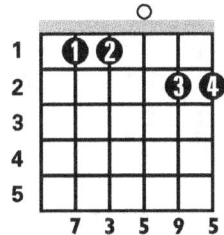
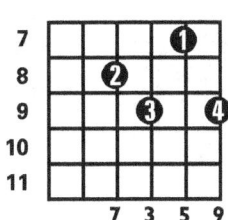
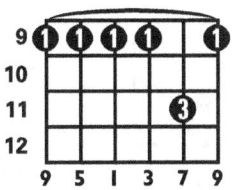

D11
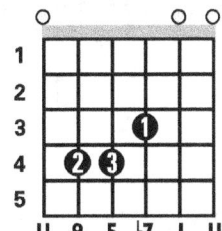
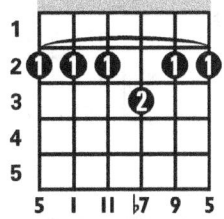
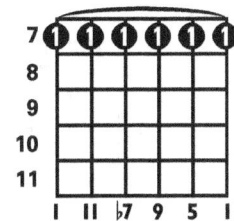

D13
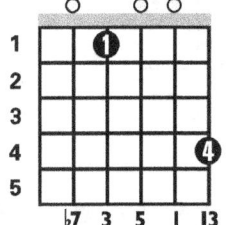
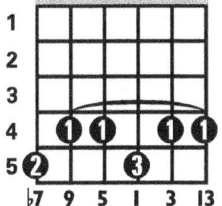
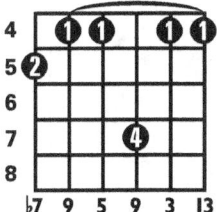

D Chords (Advanced)

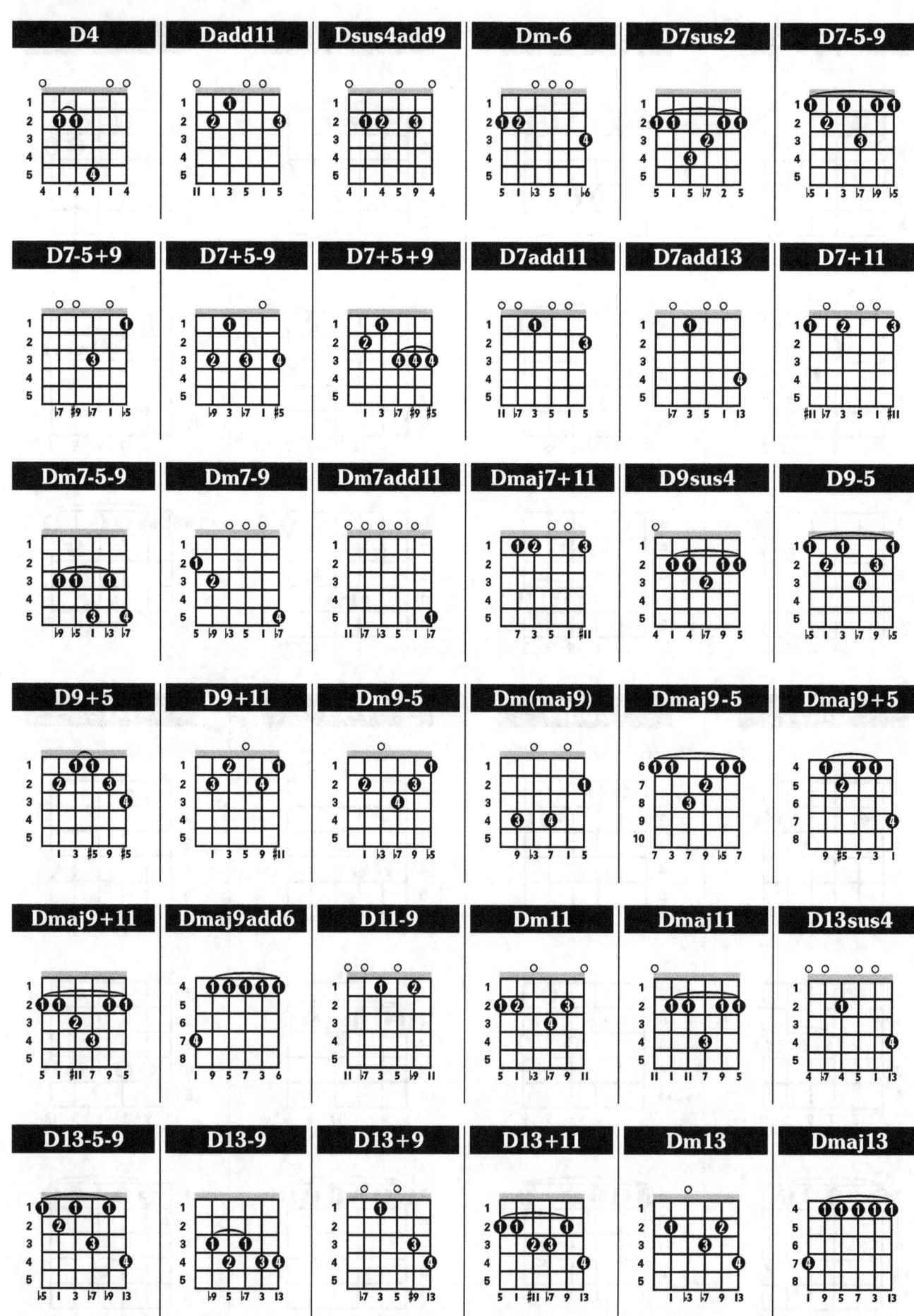

D#/ E♭ Chords

E♭
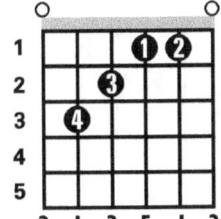
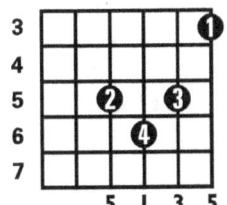
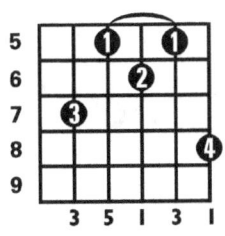

E♭m
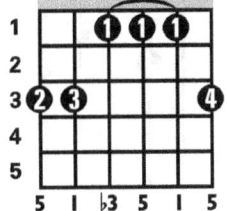
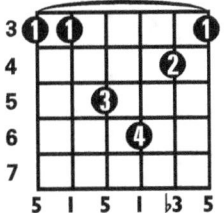
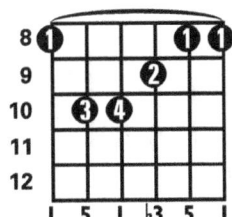

E♭7
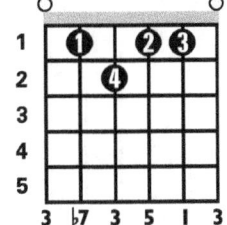
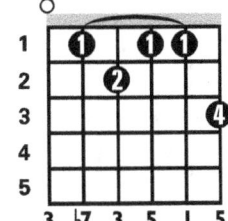
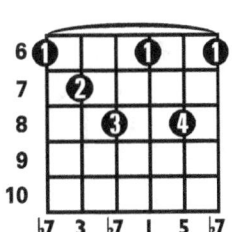

E♭m7
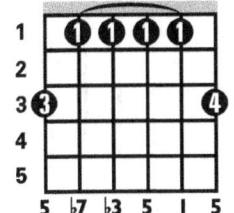
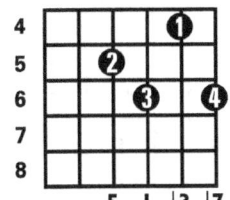
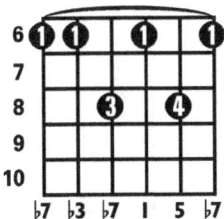

E♭5
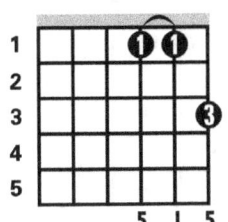
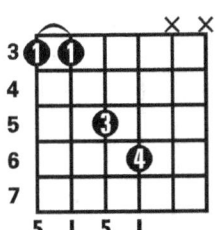
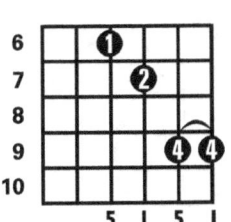

E♭6
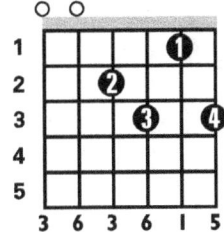
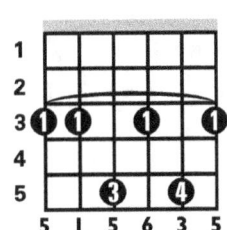
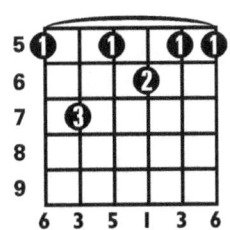

E♭m6
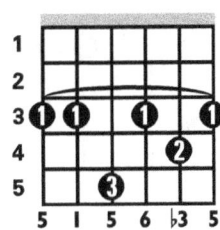
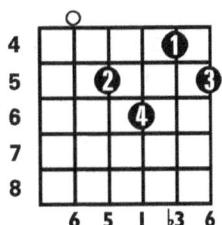
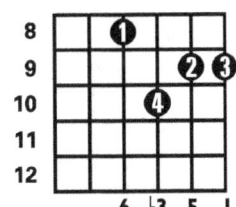

E♭maj7
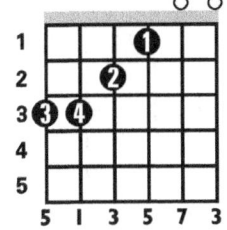
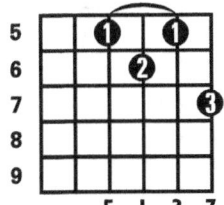
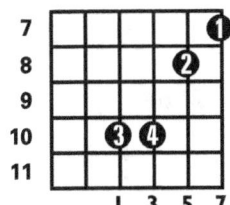

D#/ E♭ Chords

E♭°	E♭°7	E♭-5	E♭+
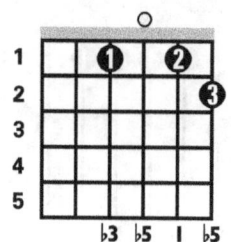	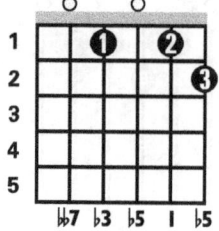	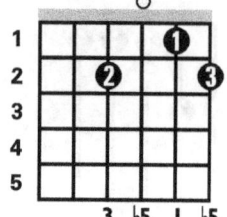	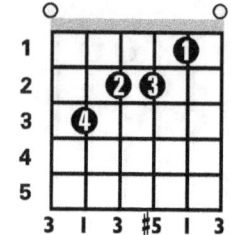
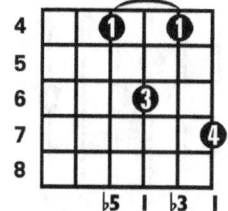	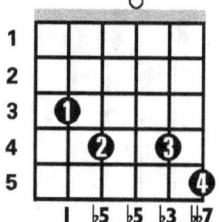	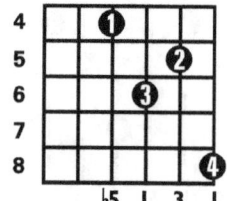	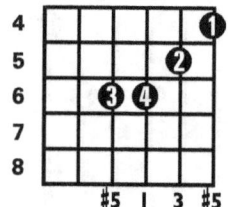
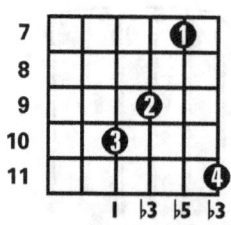	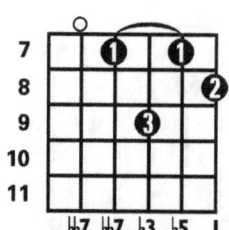	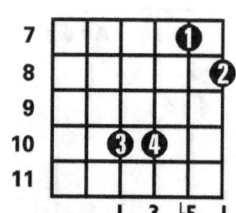	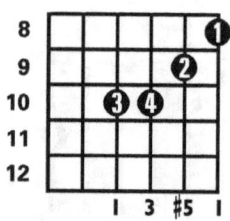

E♭sus2	E♭sus4	E♭7sus4	E♭m7-5
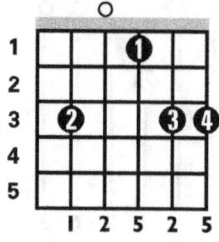	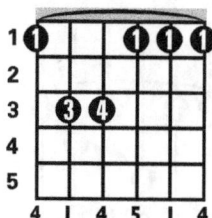	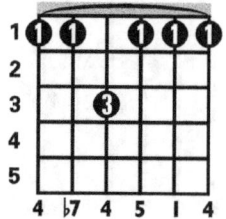	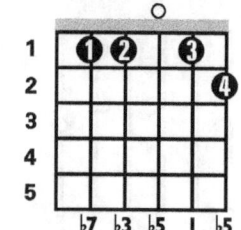
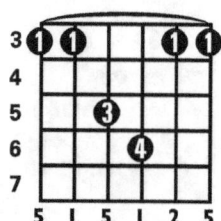	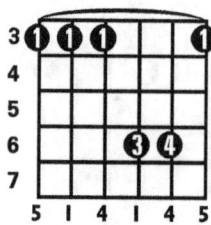	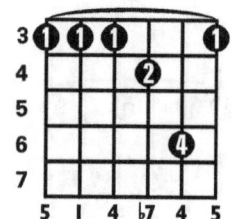	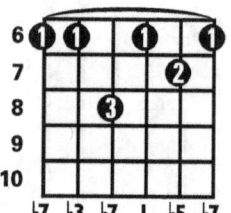
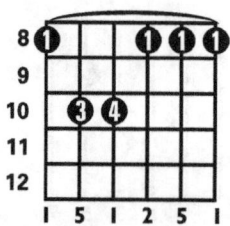	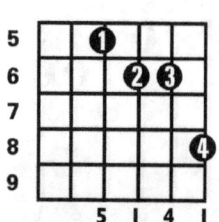	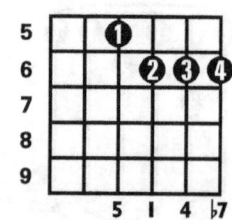	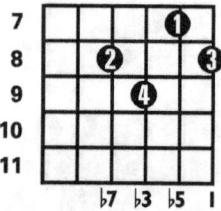

D#/ E♭ Chords

E♭add9
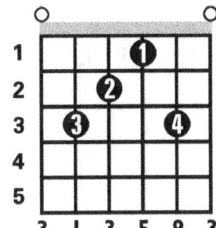
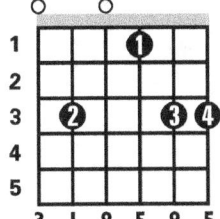
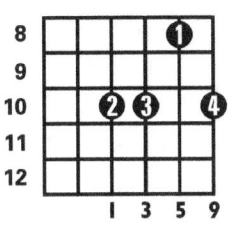

E♭madd9
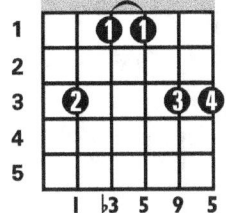
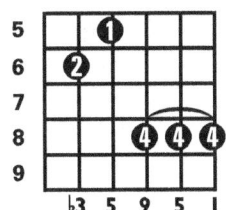
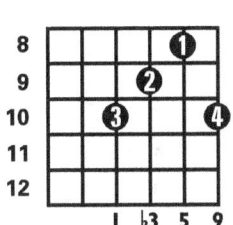

E♭6add9
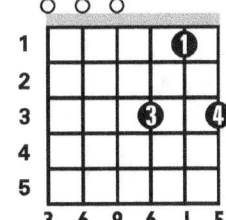
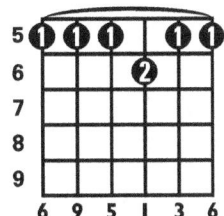
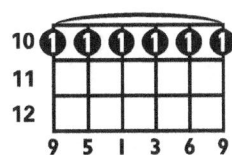

E♭m6add9
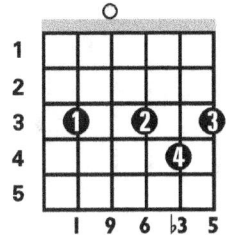
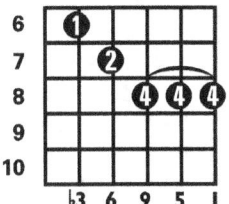
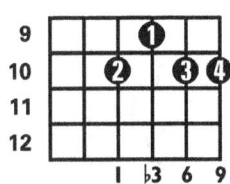

E♭7-5
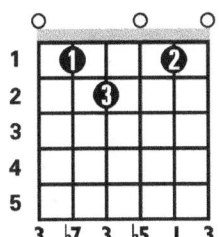
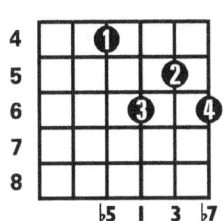
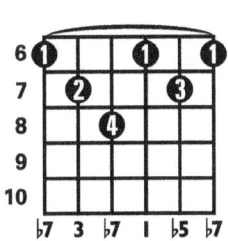

E♭7+5
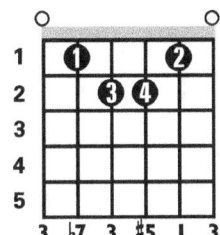
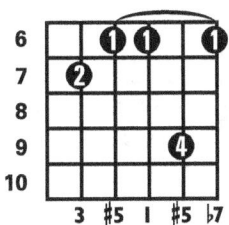
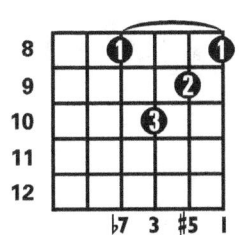

E♭7-9
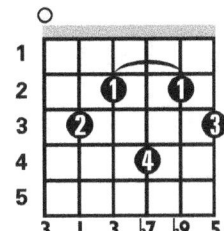
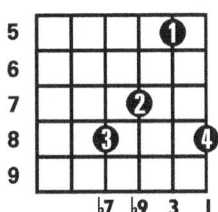
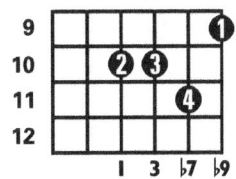

E♭7+9
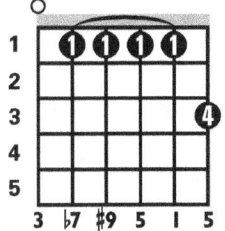
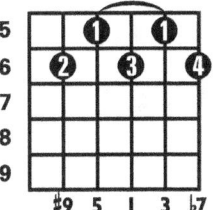
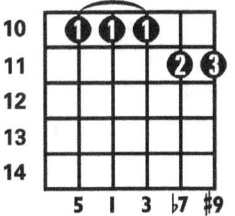

D#/ E♭ Chords

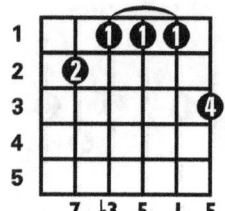
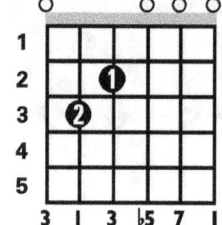
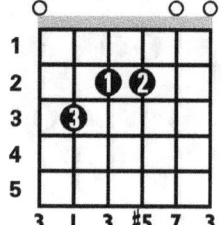
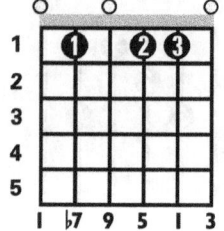

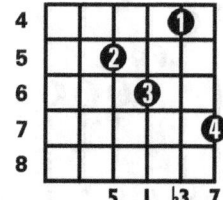
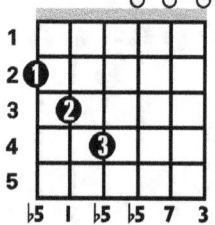
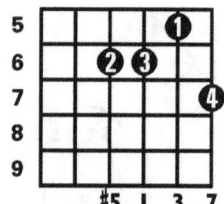
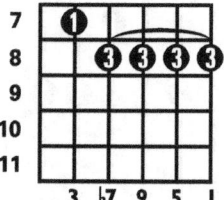

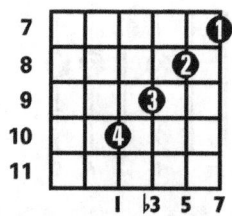
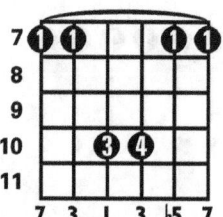
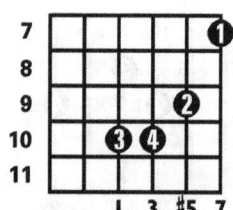
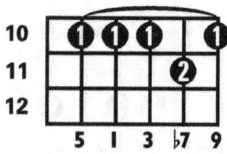

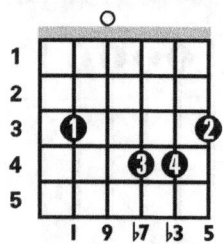
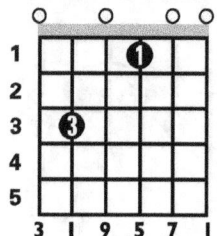
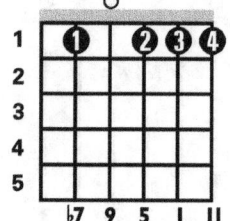
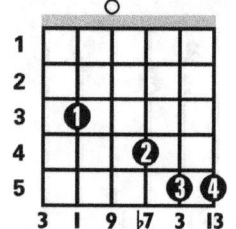

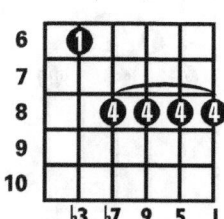
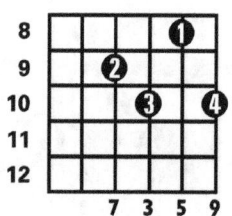
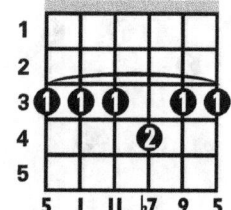
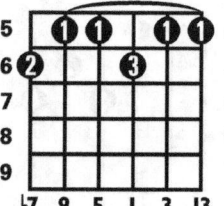

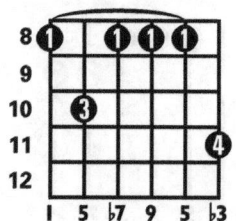
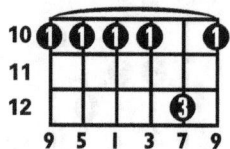
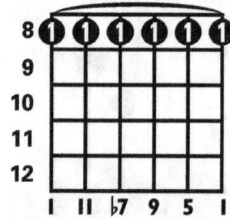
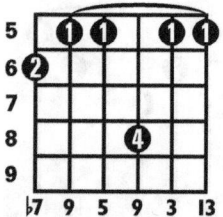

D#/ E♭ Chords (Advanced)

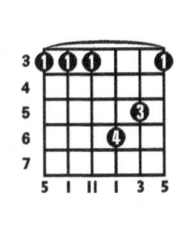 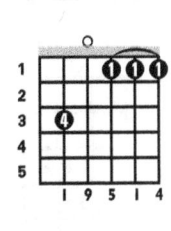 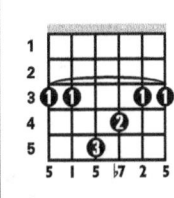 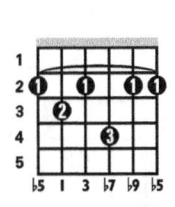

E Chords

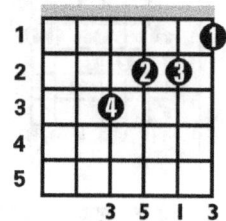 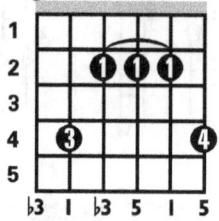 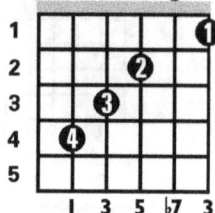 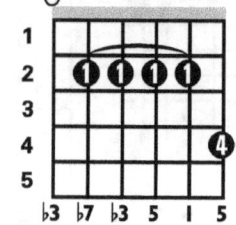

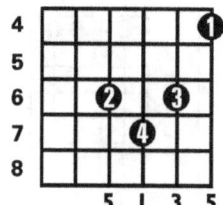 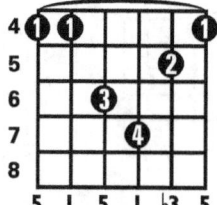 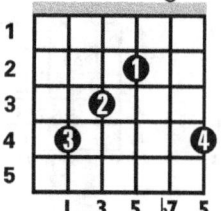 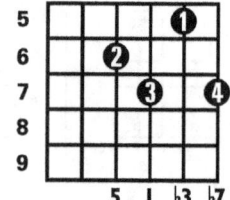

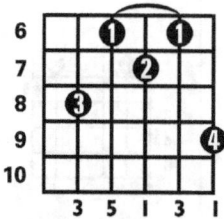 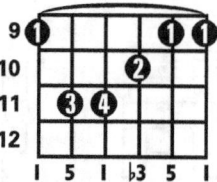 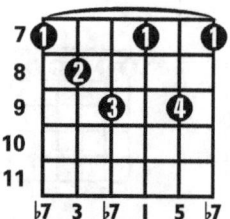 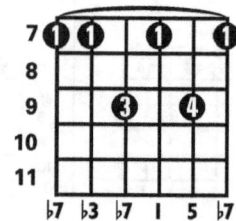

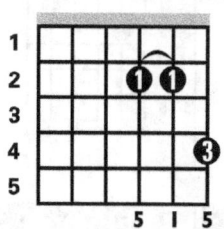 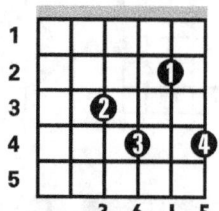 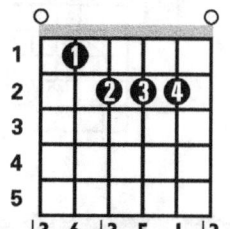 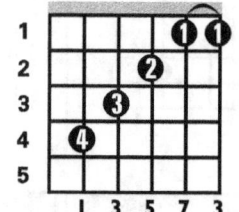

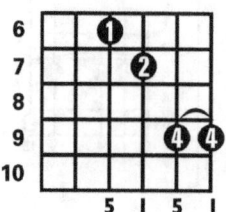 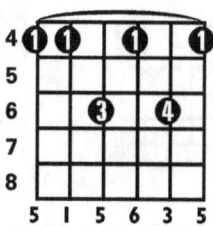 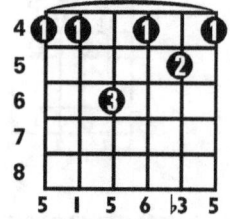 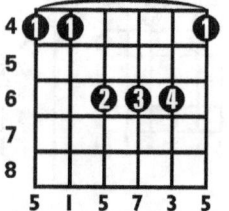

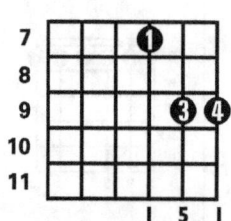 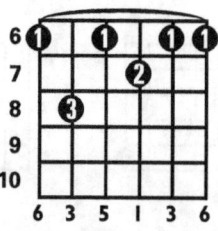 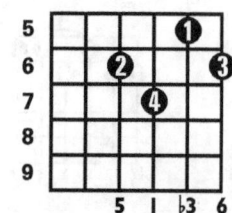 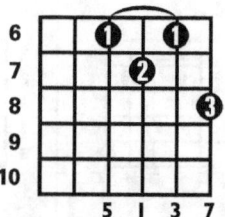

E Chords

E°
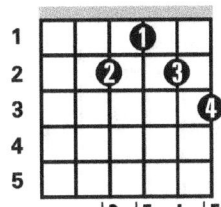
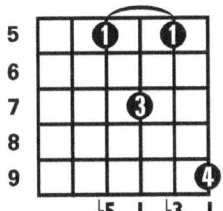
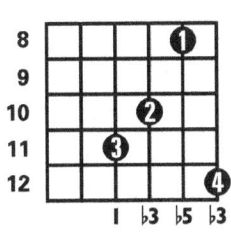

E°7
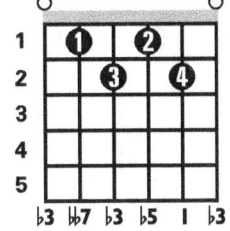
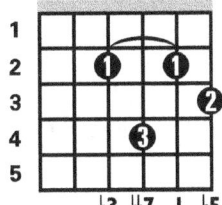
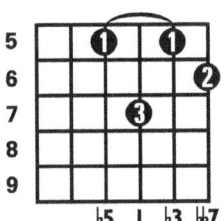

E-5
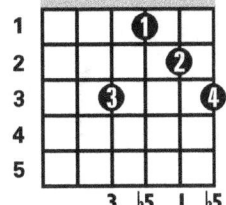
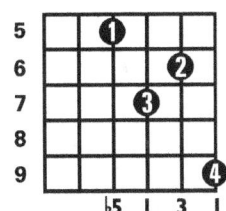
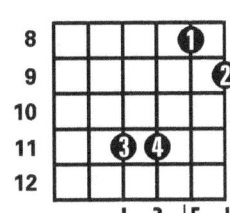

E+
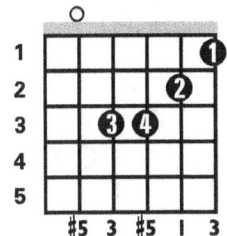
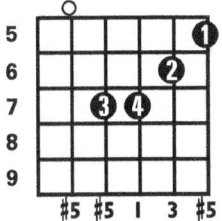
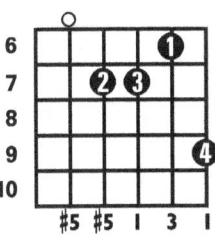

Esus2
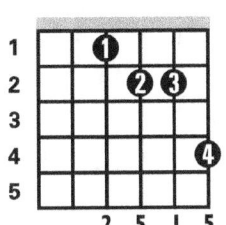
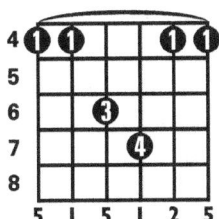
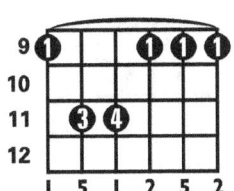

Esus4
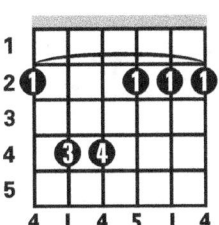
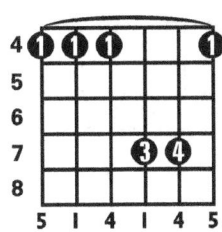
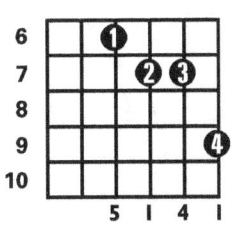

E7sus4
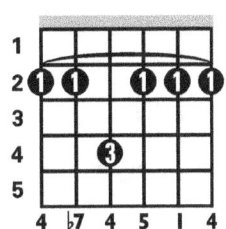
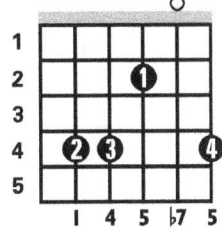
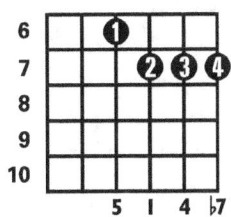

Em7-5
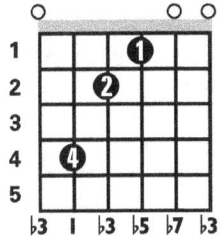
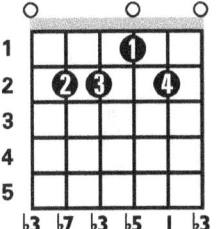
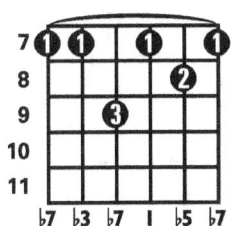

E Chords

Eadd9	Emadd9	E6add9	Em6add9
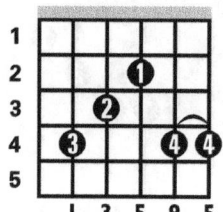	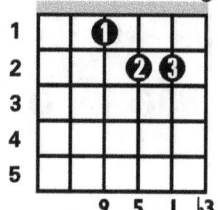	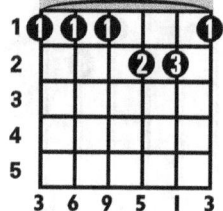	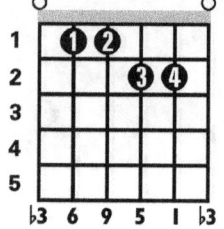
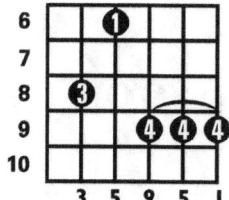	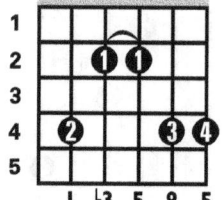	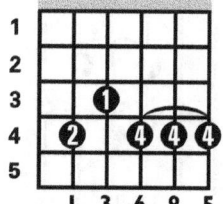	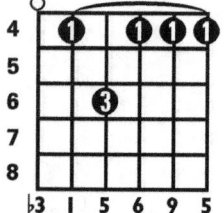
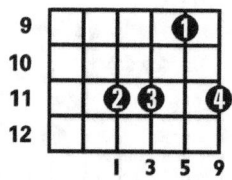	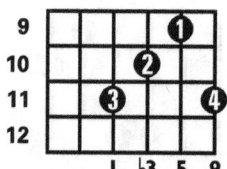	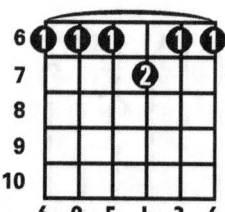	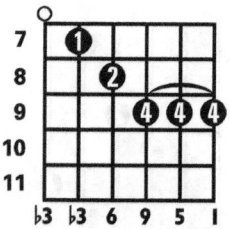

E7-5	E7+5	E7-9	E7+9
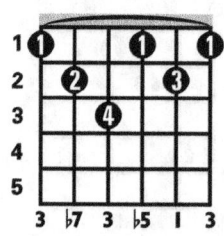	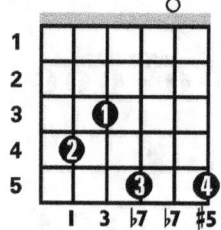	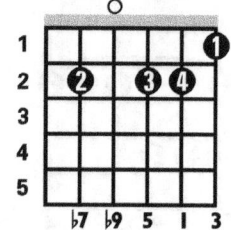	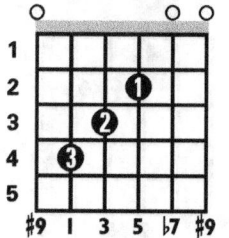
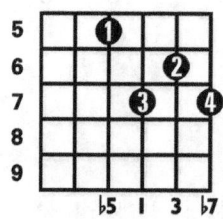	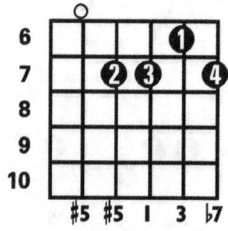	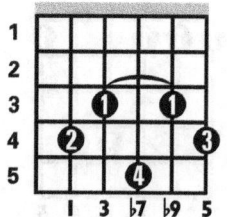	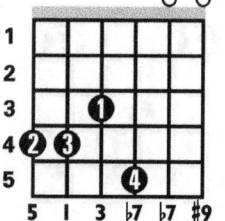
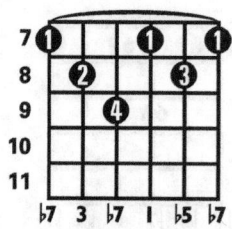	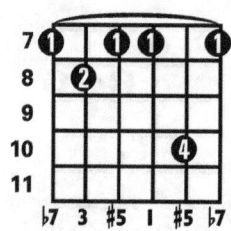	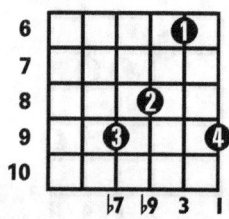	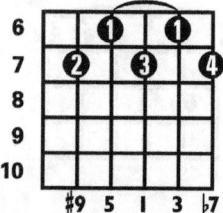

E Chords

Em(maj7)
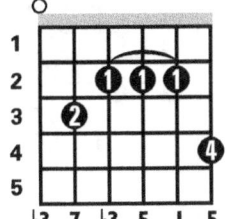
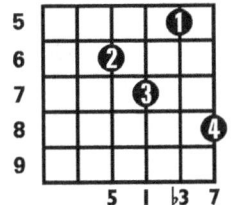
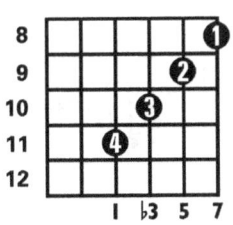

Emaj7-5
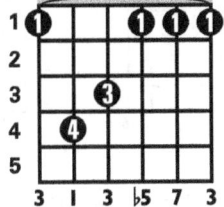
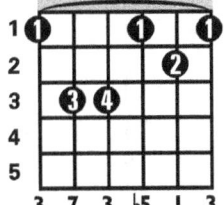
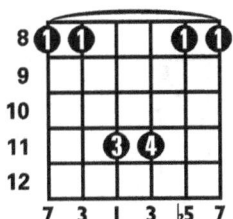

Emaj7+5
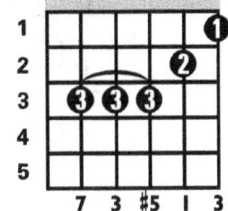
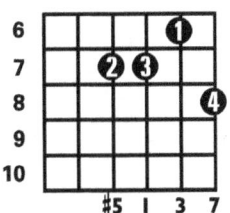
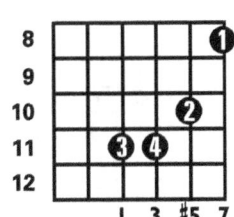

E9
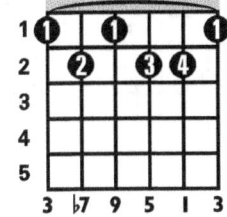
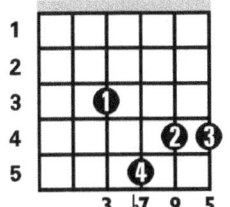
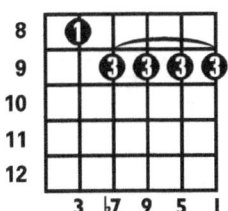

Em9
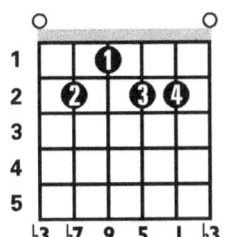
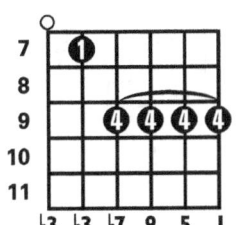
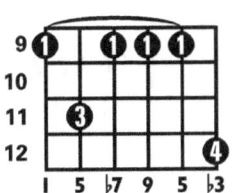

Emaj9
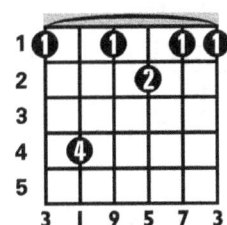
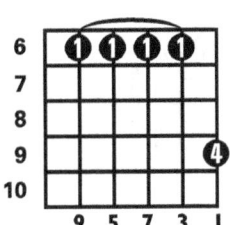
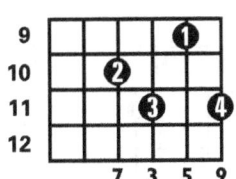

E11
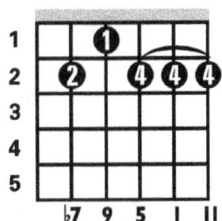
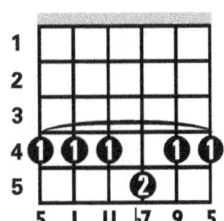
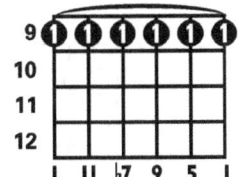

E13
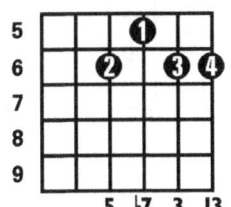
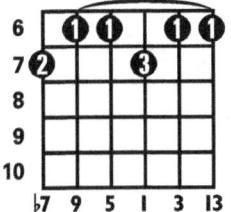
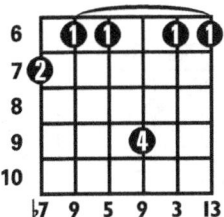

E Chords (Advanced)

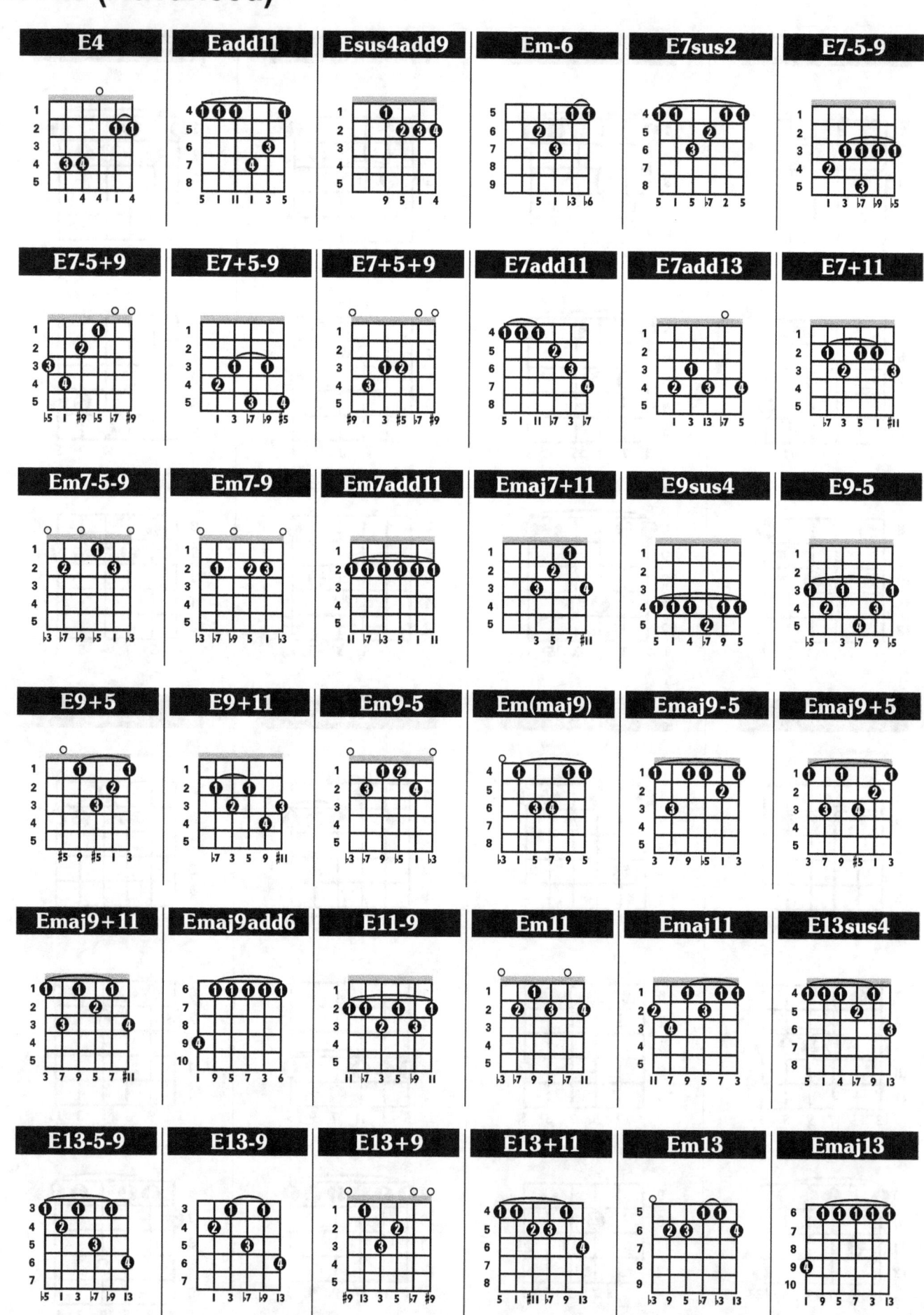

F Chords

F
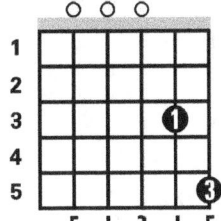
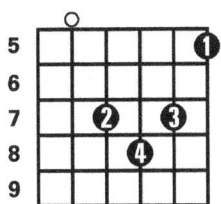
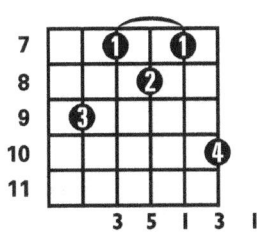

Fm
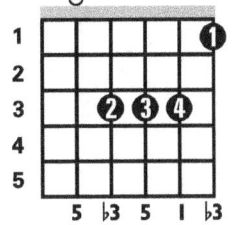
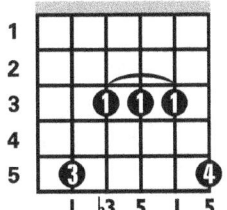
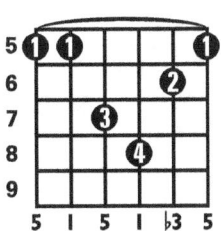

F7
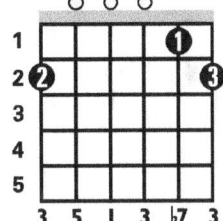
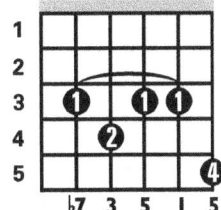
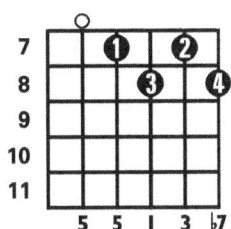

Fm7
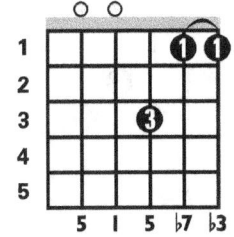
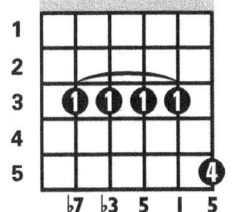
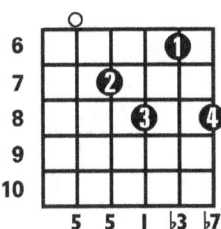

F5
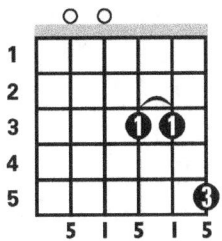
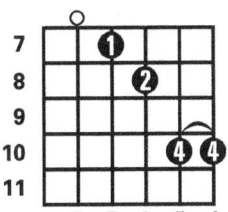
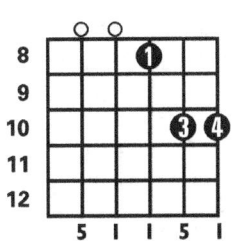

F6
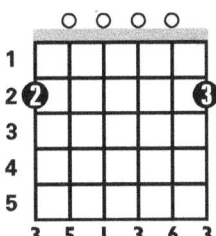
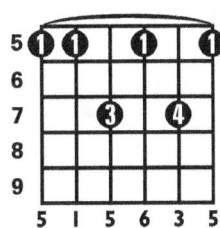
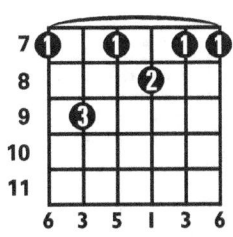

Fm6
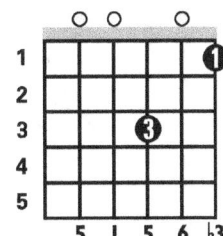
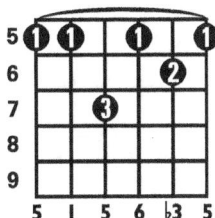
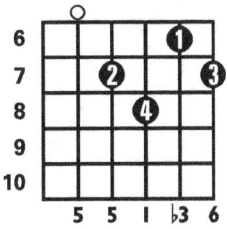

Fmaj7
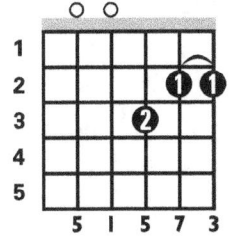
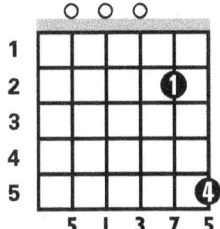
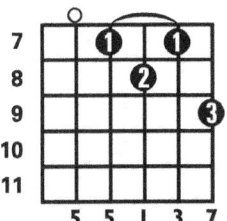

F Chords

F°	F°7	F-5	F+
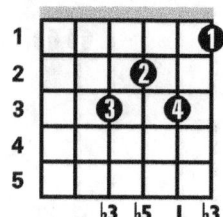	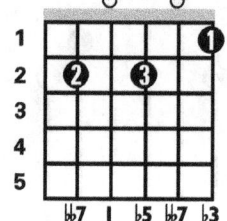	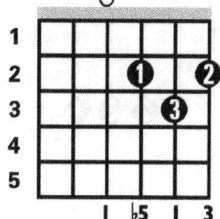	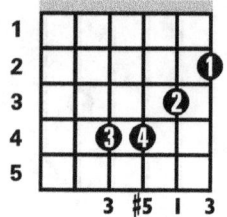
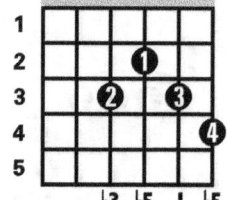	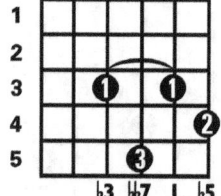	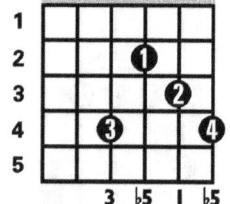	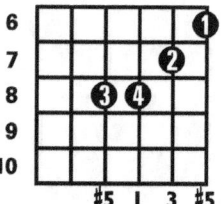
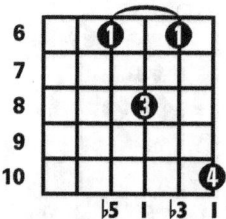	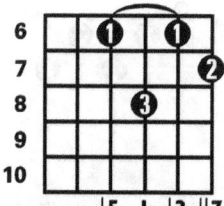	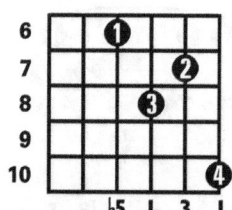	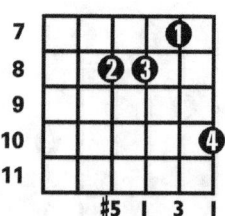

Fsus2	Fsus4	F7sus4	Fm7-5
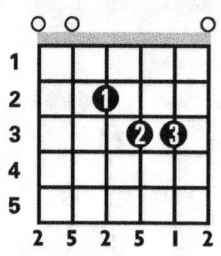	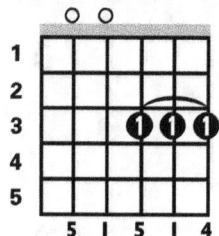	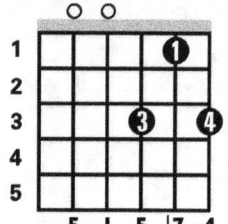	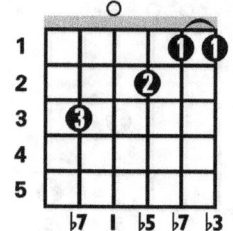
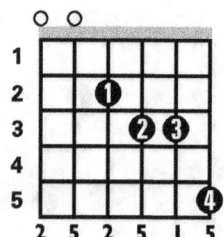	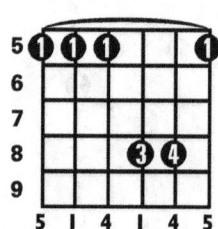	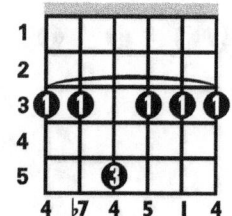	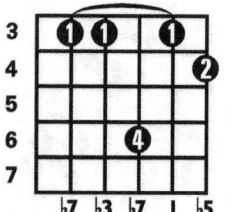
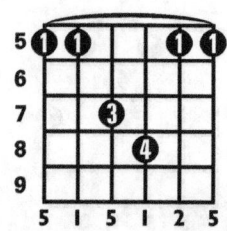	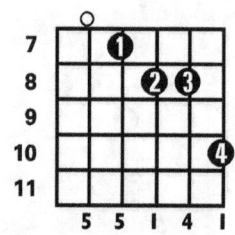	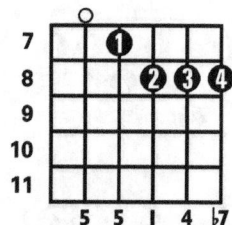	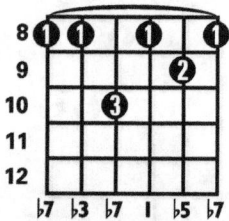

F Chords

Fadd9
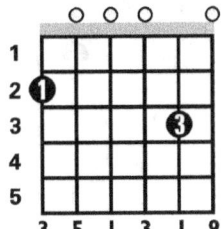
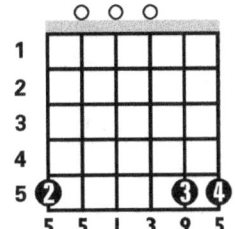
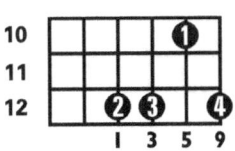

Fmadd9
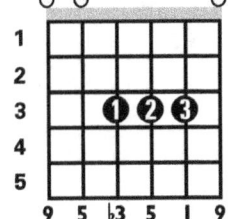
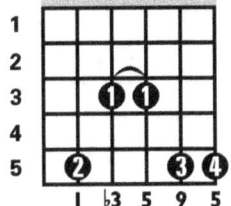
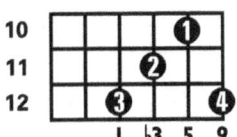

F6add9
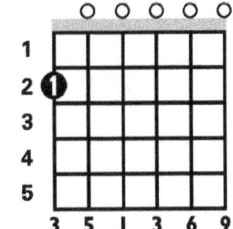
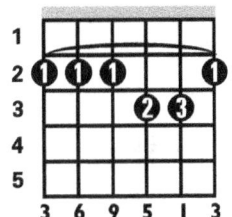
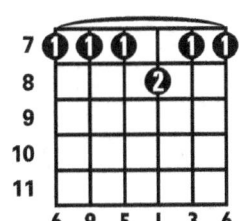

Fm6add9
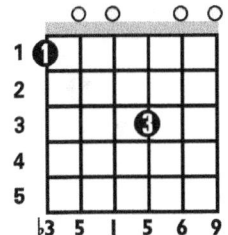
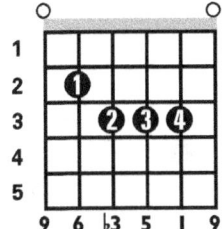
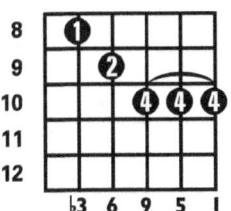

F7-5
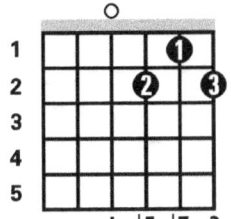
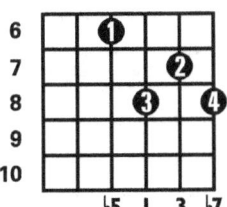
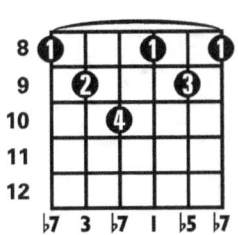

F7+5
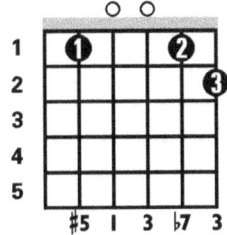
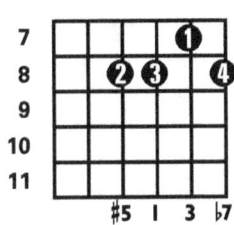
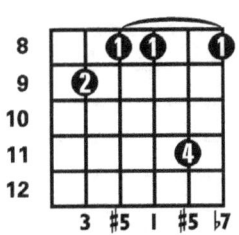

F7-9
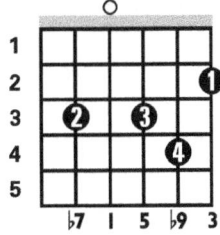
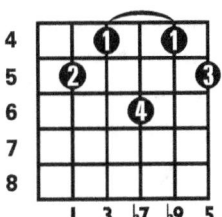
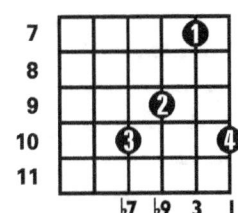

F7+9
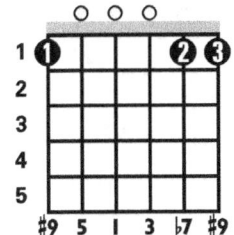
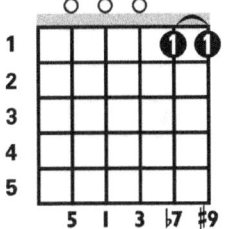
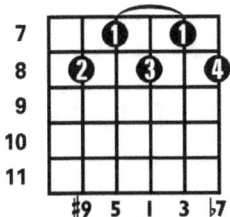

F Chords

Fm(maj7)
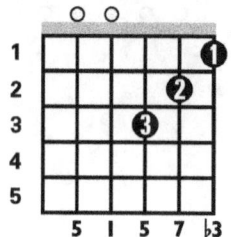
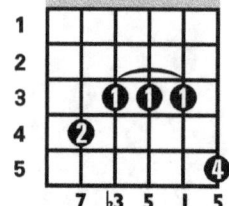
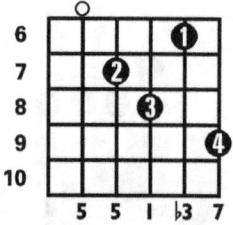

Fmaj7-5
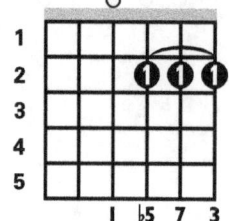
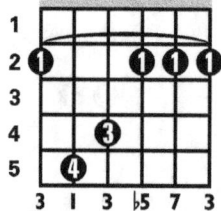
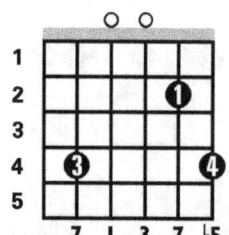

Fmaj7+5
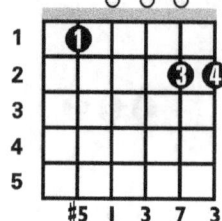
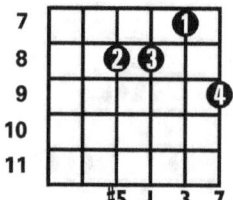
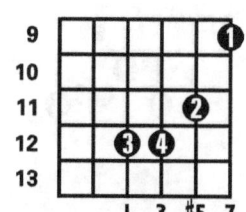

F9
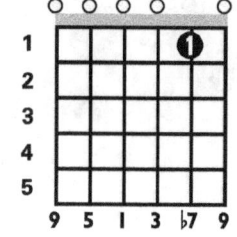
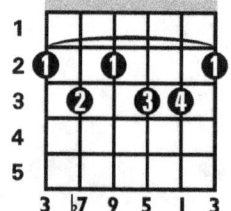
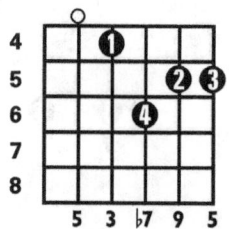

Fm9
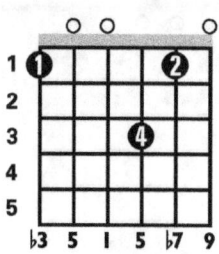
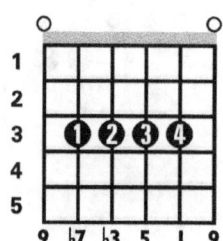
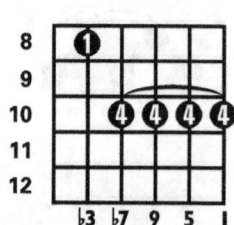

Fmaj9
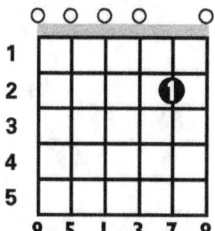
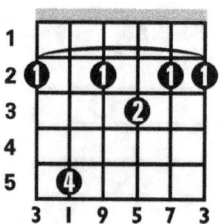
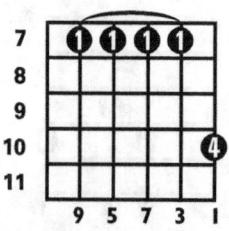

F11
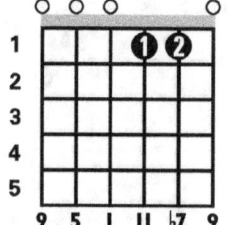
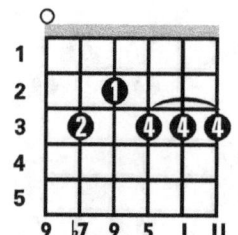
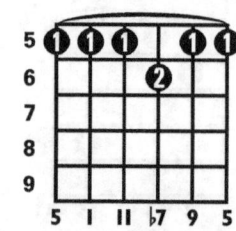

F13
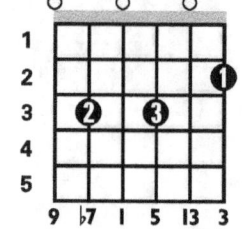
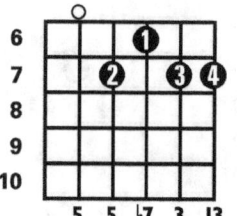
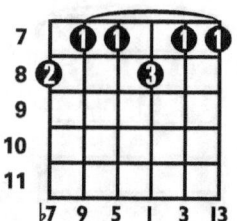

F Chords (Advanced)

F4 | Fadd11 | Fsus4add9 | Fm-6 | F7sus2 | F7-5-9

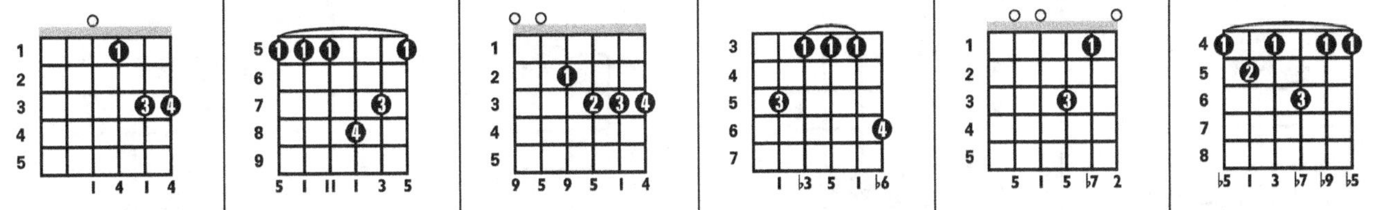

F7-5+9 | F7+5-9 | F7+5+9 | F7add11 | F7add13 | F7+11

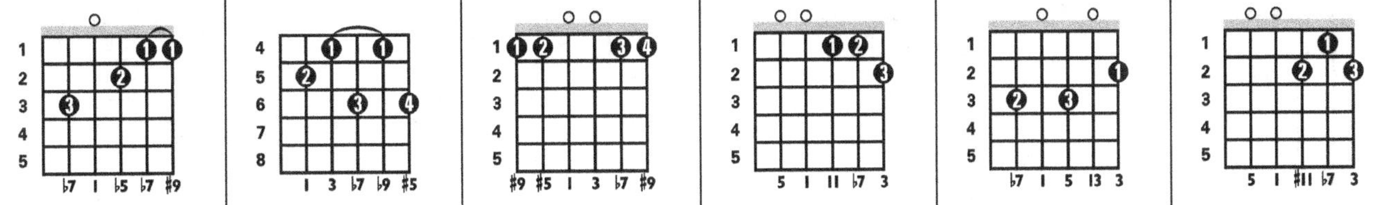

Fm7-5-9 | Fm7-9 | Fm7add11 | Fmaj7+11 | F9sus4 | F9-5

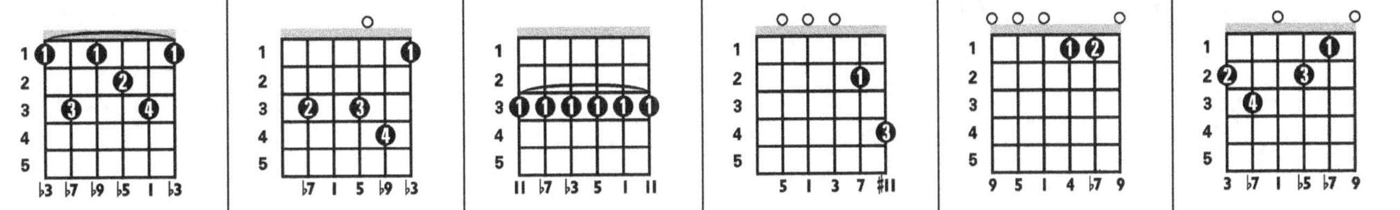

F9+5 | F9+11 | Fm9-5 | Fm(maj9) | Fmaj9-5 | Fmaj9+5

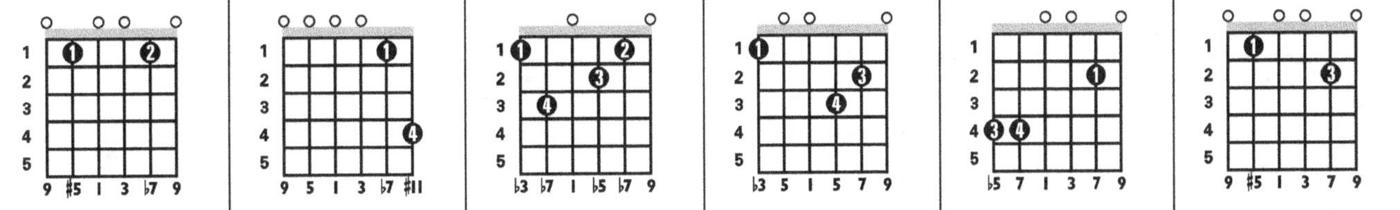

Fmaj9+11 | Fmaj9add6 | F11-9 | Fm11 | Fmaj11 | F13sus4

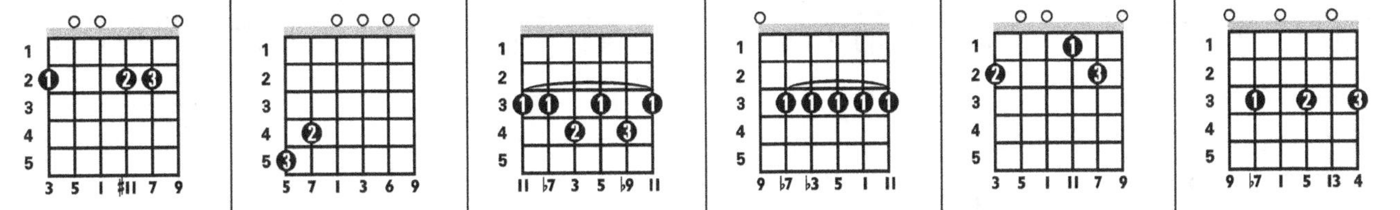

F13-5-9 | F13-9 | F13+9 | F13+11 | Fm13 | Fmaj13

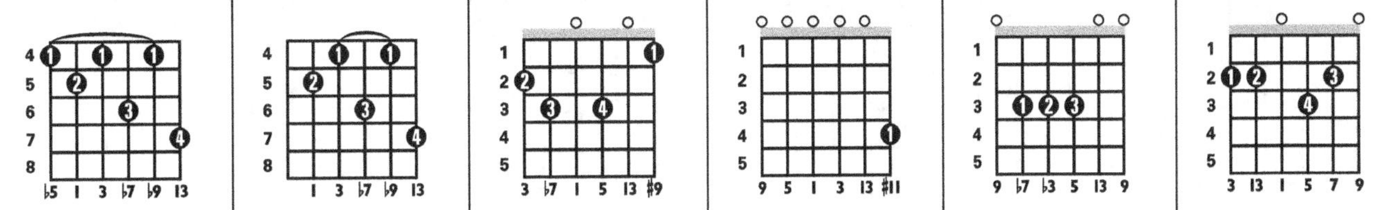

F#/G♭ Chords

F#/Gb Chords

F#°
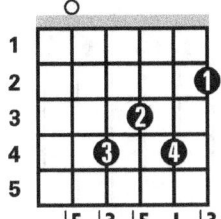
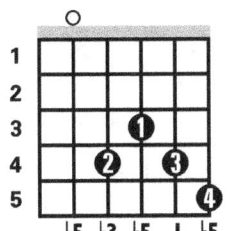
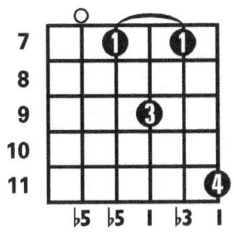

F#°7
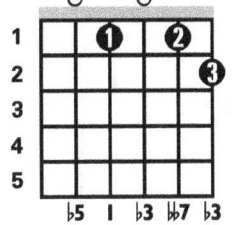
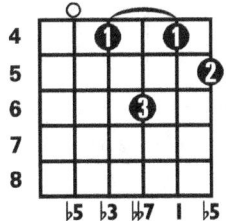
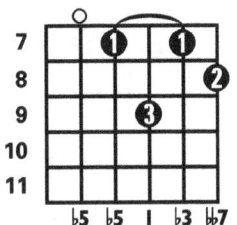

F#-5
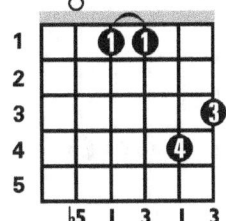
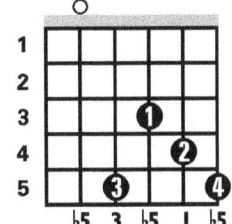
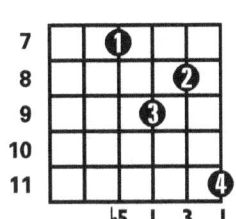

F#+
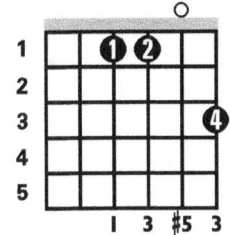
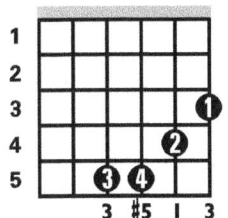
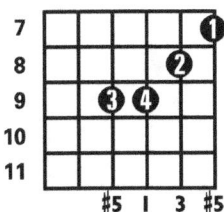

F#sus2
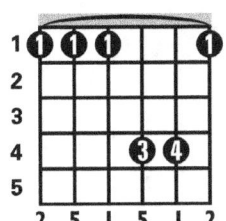
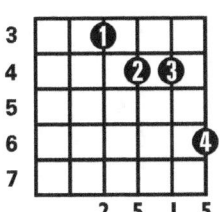
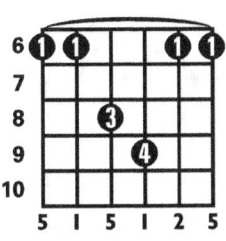

F#sus4

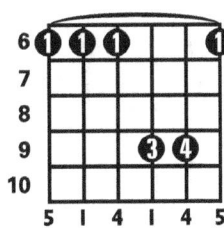
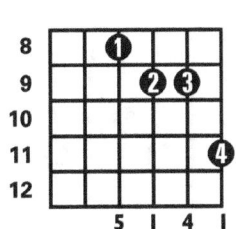

F#7sus4
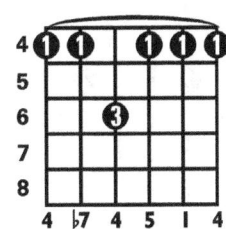
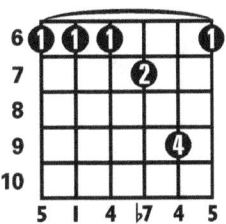
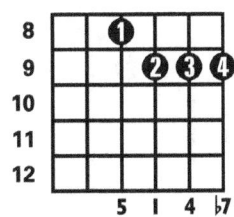

F#m7-5
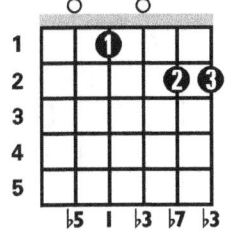
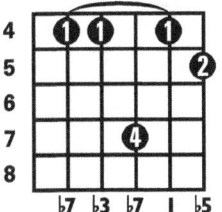
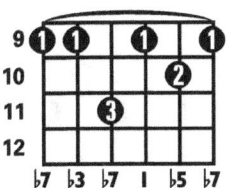

F#/G♭ Chords

F#add9	F#madd9	F#6add9	F#m6add9
	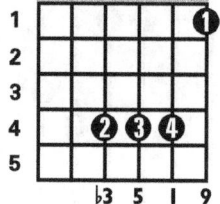	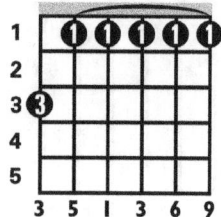	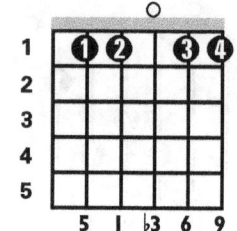
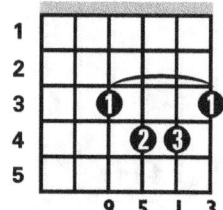	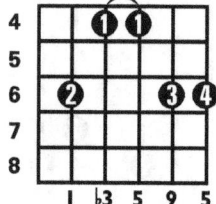	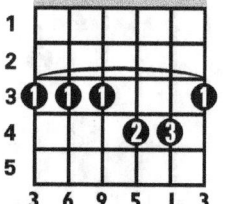	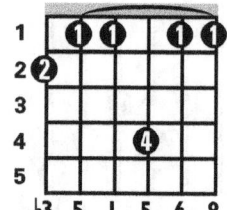
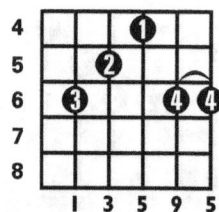	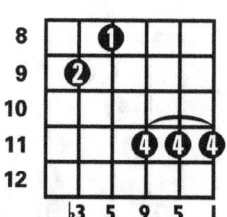	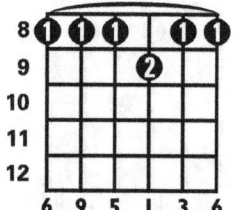	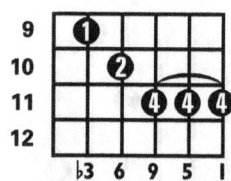

F#7-5	F#7+5	F#7-9	F#7+9
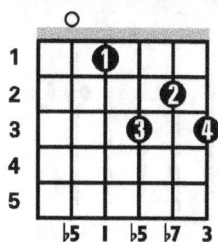	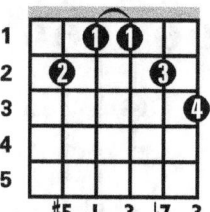	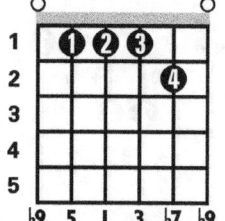	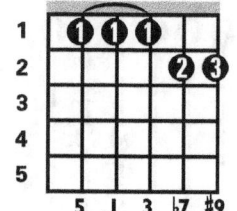
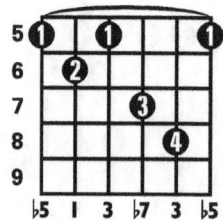	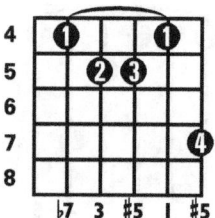	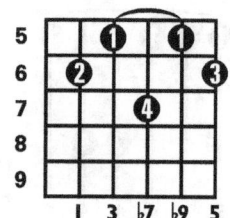	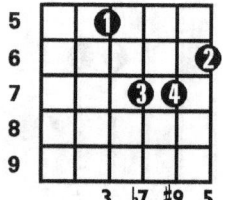
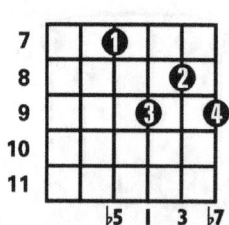	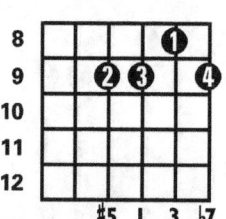	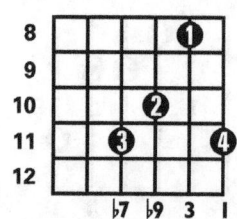	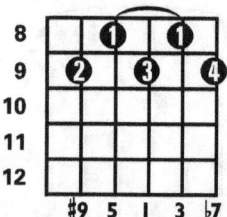

F#/Gb Chords

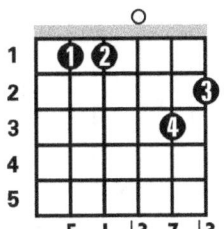 F#m(maj7)
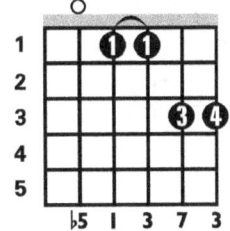 F#maj7-5
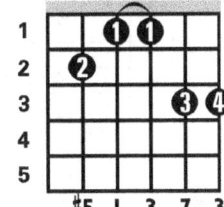 F#maj7+5
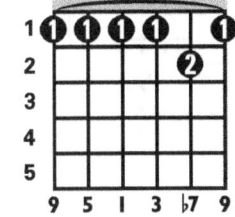 F#9

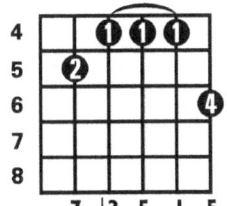
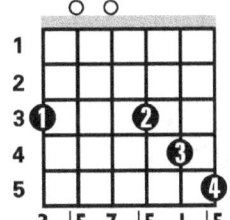
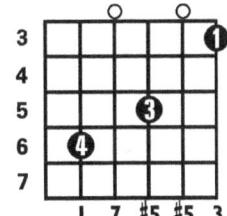
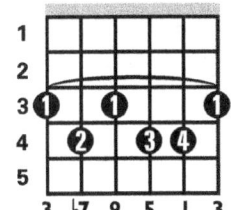

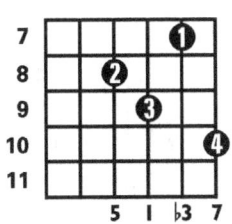
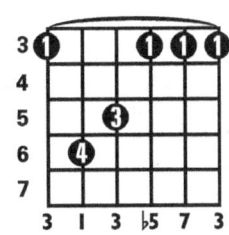
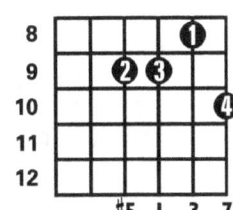
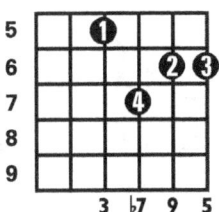

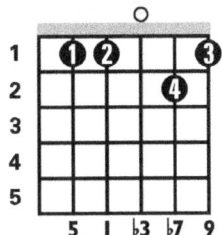 F#m9
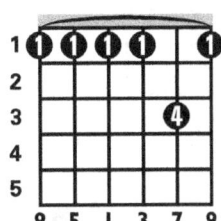 F#maj9
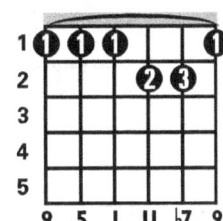 F#11
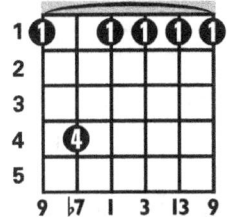 F#13

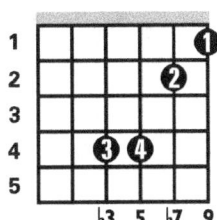
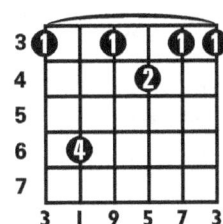
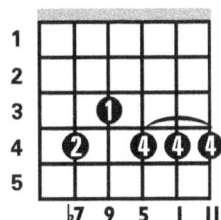
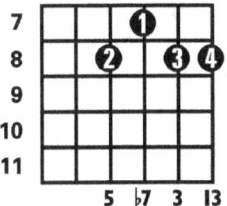

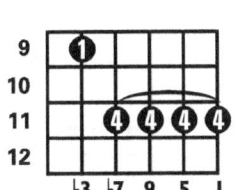
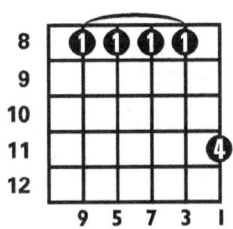
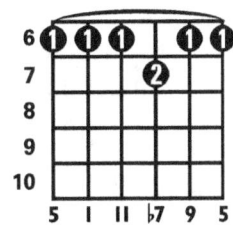
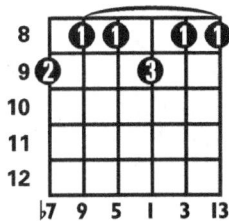

F#/Gb Chords (Advanced)

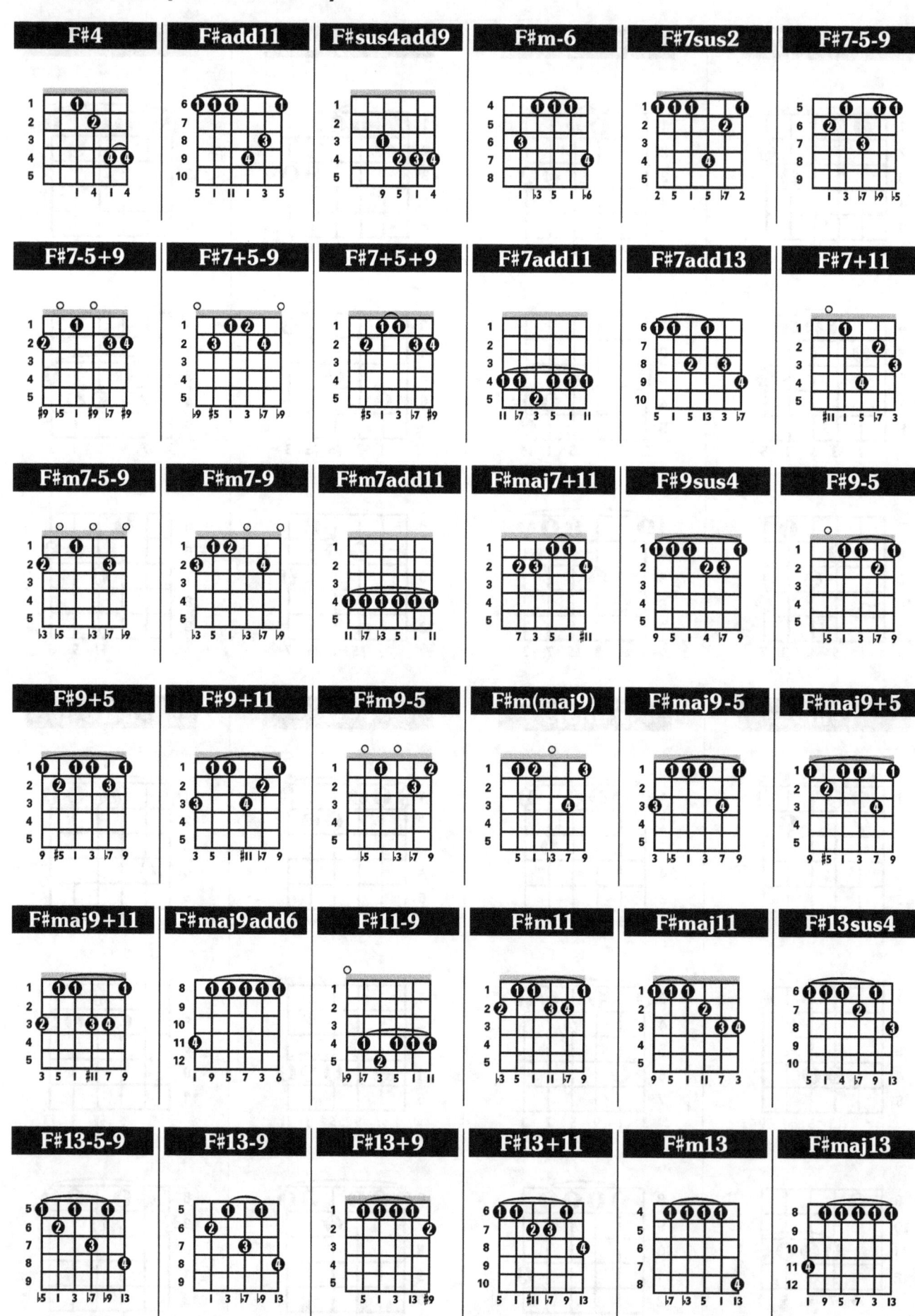

G Chords

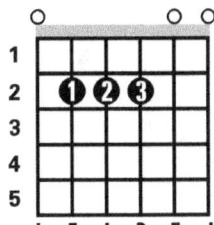 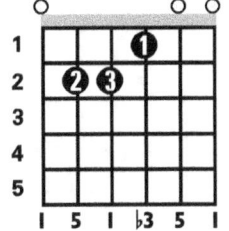 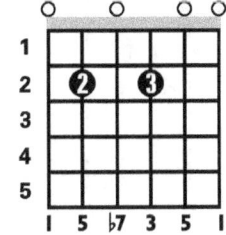 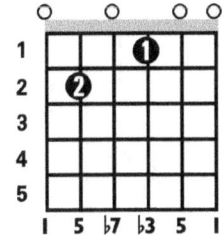

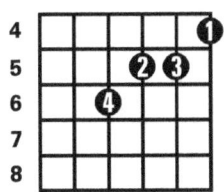 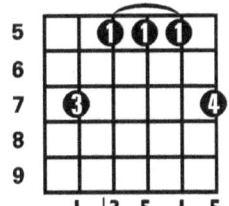 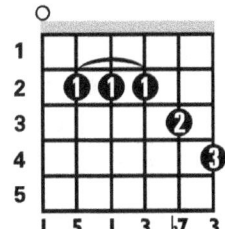 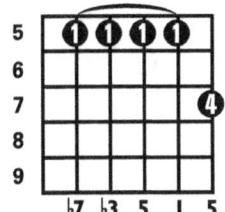

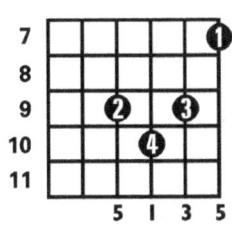 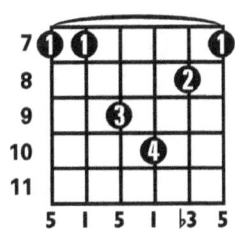 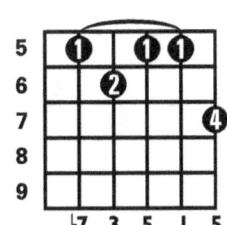 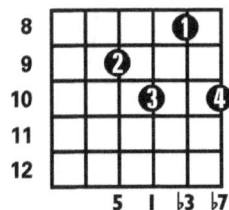

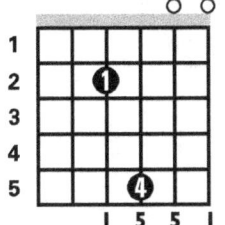 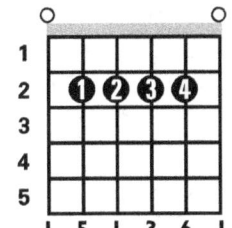 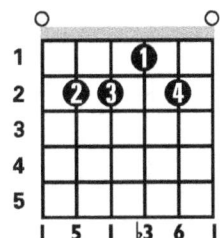 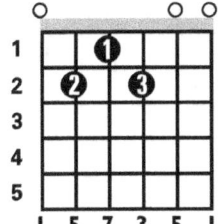

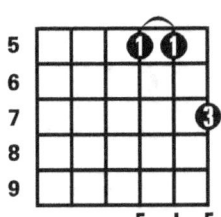 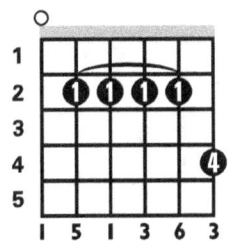 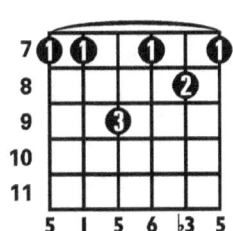 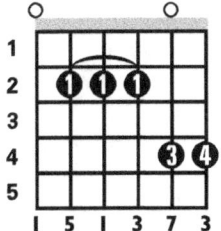

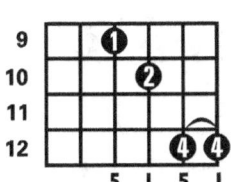 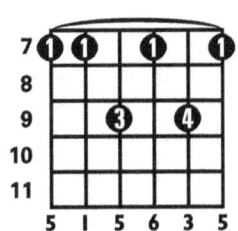 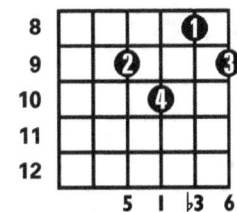 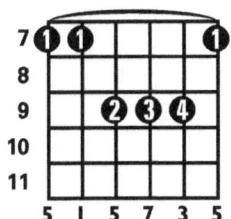

G Chords

G°
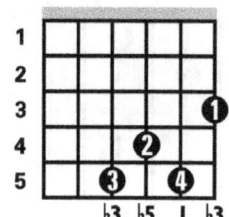
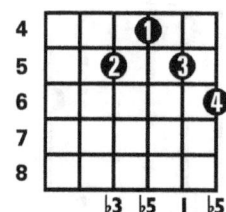
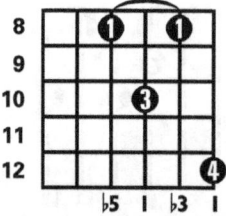

G°7
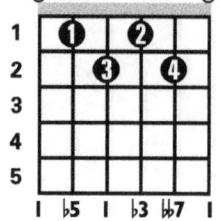
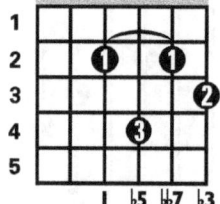
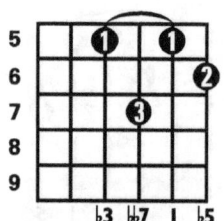

G-5
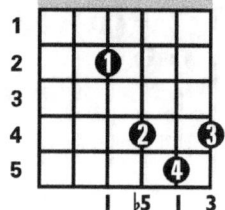
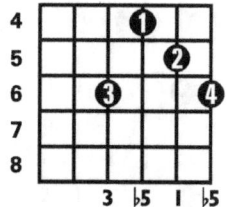
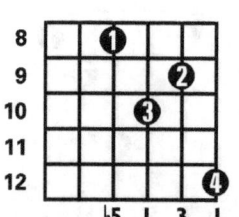

G+
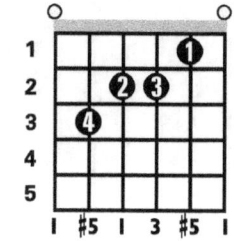
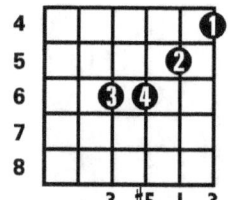
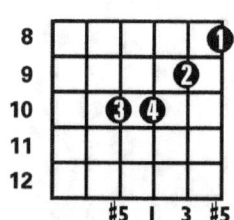

Gsus2
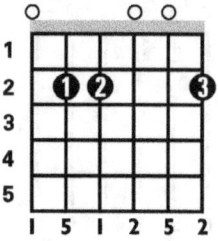
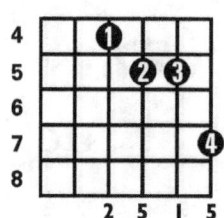
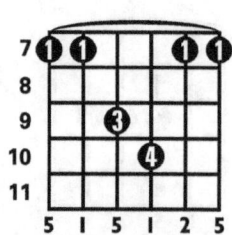

Gsus4
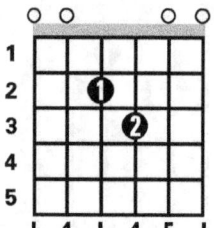
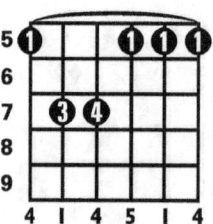
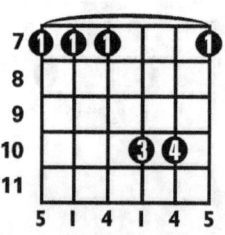

G7sus4
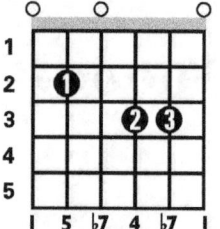
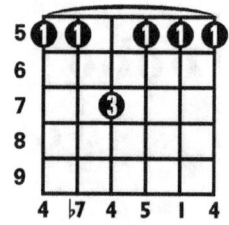
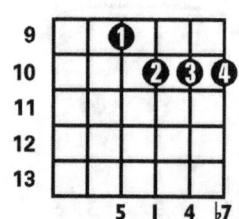

Gm7-5
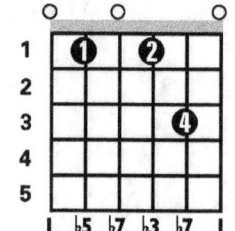
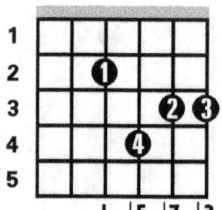
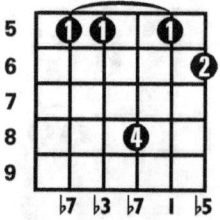

G Chords

Gadd9
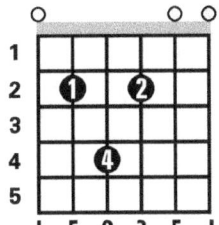
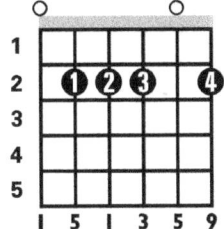
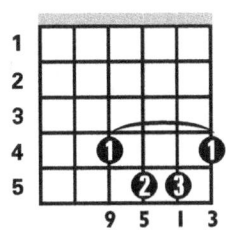

Gmadd9
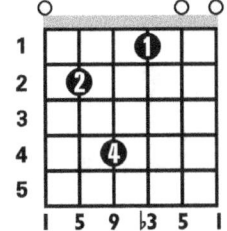
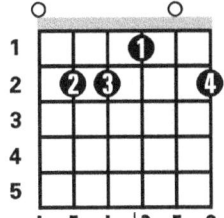
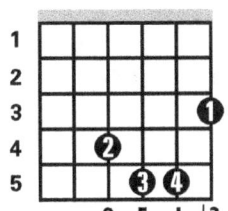

G6add9
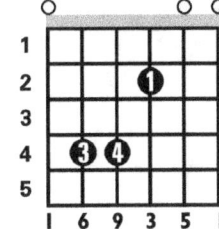
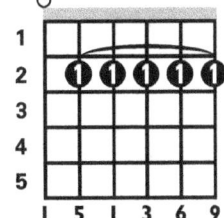
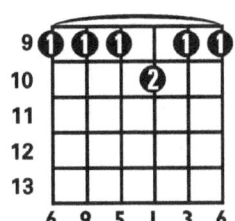

Gm6add9
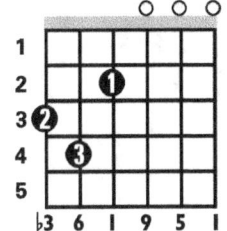
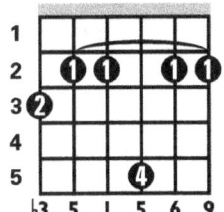
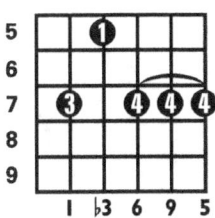

G7-5
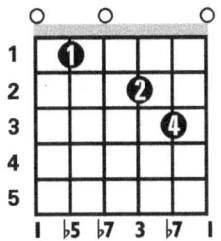
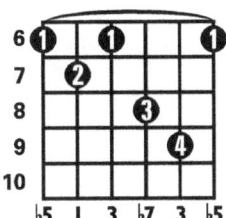
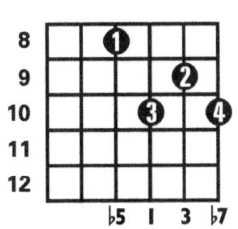

G7+5
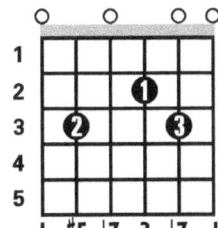
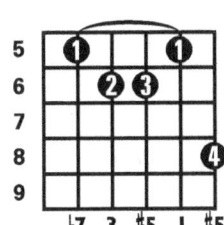
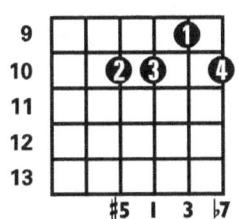

G7-9
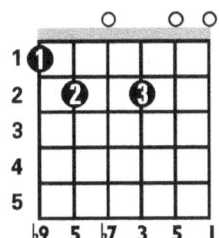
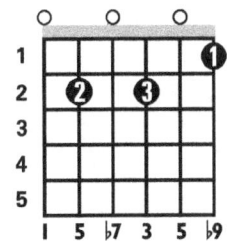
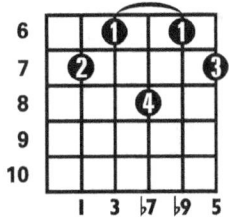

G7+9
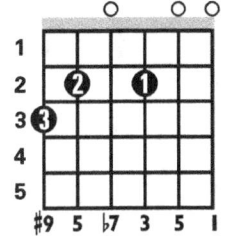
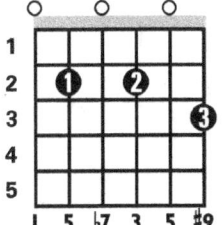
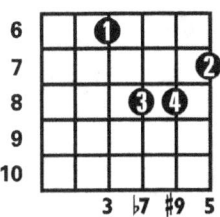

51

G Chords

Gm(maj7)
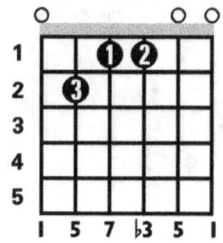
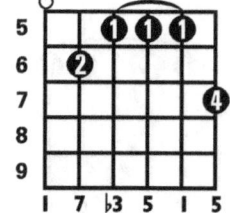
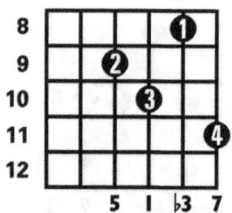

Gmaj7-5
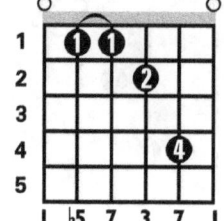
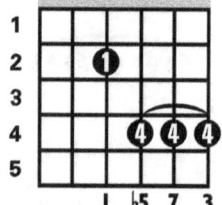
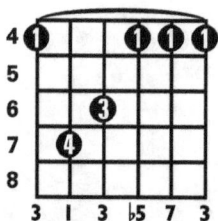

Gmaj7+5
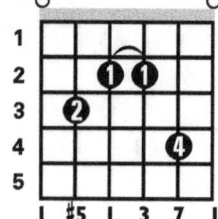
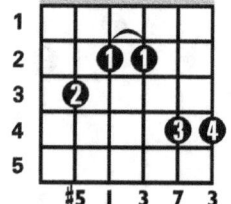
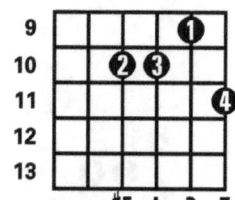

G9
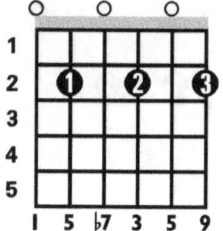
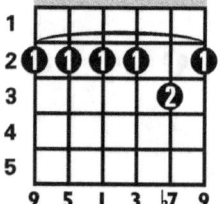
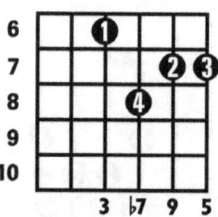

Gm9
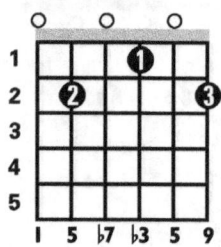
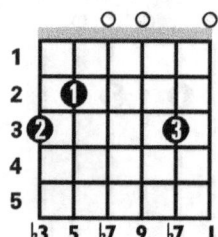
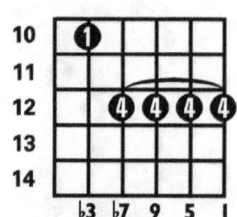

Gmaj9
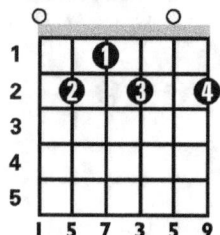
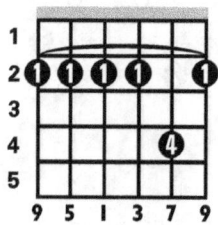
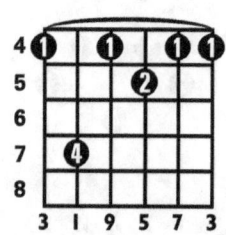

G11
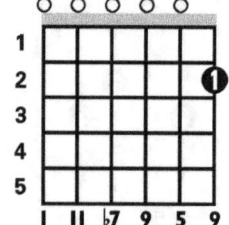
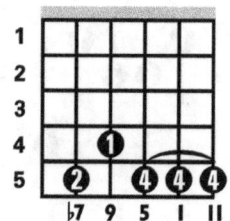
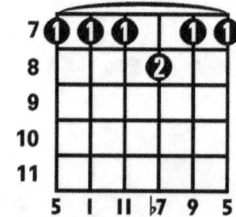

G13
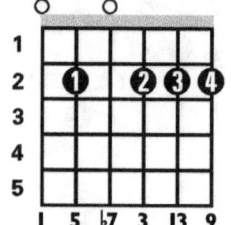
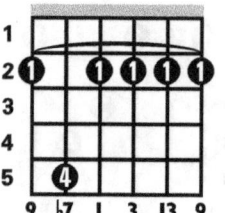
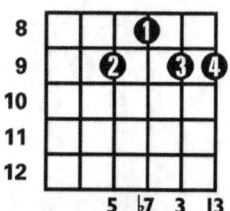

G Chords (Advanced)

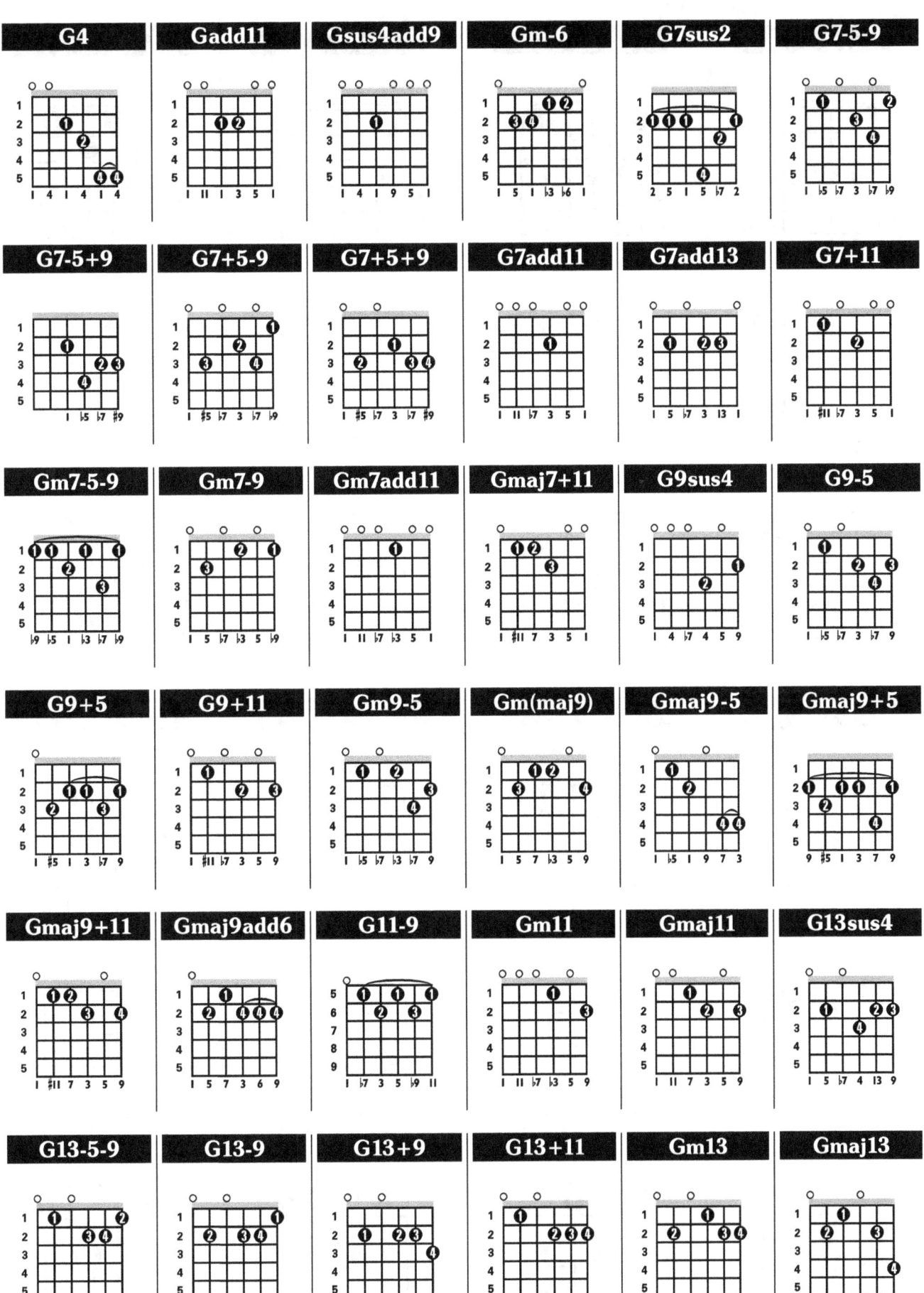

G# / A♭ Chords

A♭	A♭m	A♭7	A♭m7
	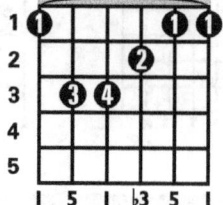	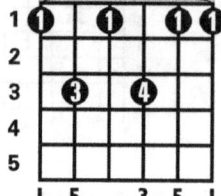	
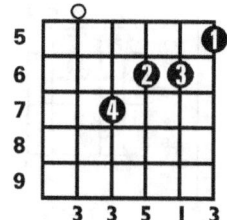	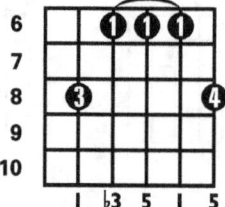	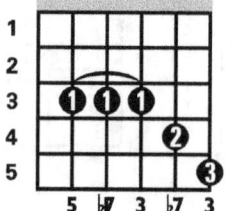	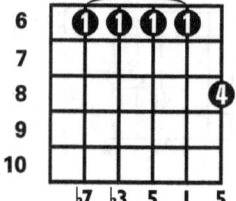
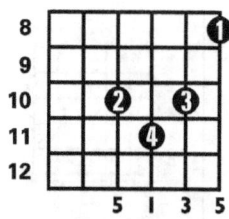	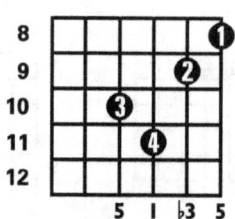	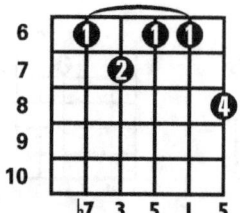	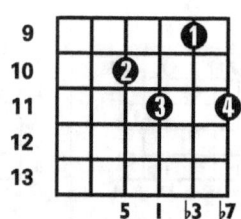

A♭5	A♭6	A♭m6	A♭maj7
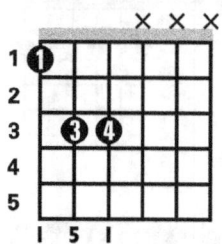	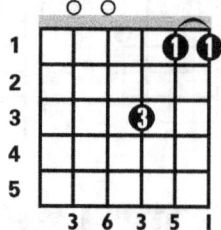	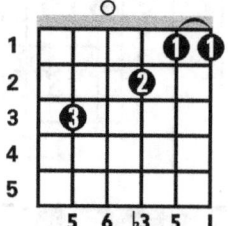	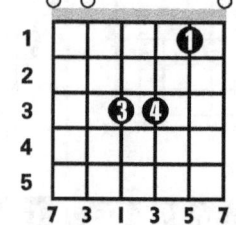
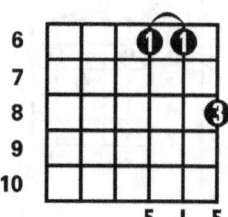	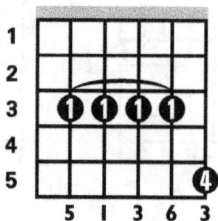	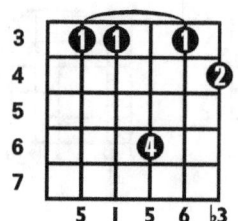	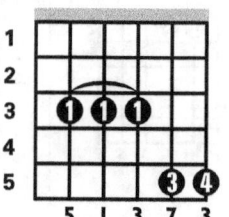
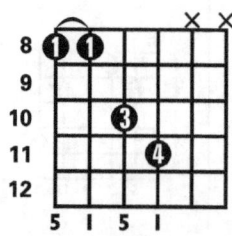	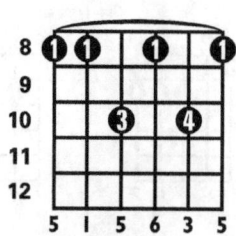	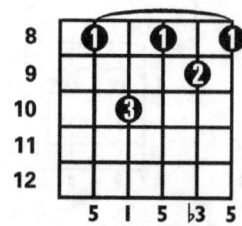	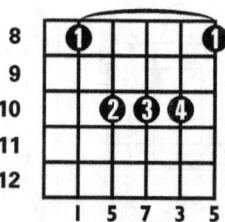

G#/A♭ Chords

A♭°
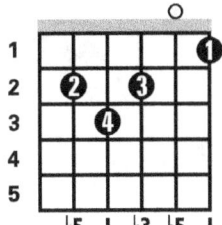
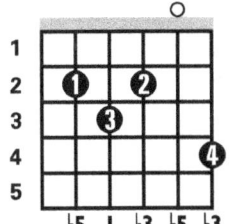
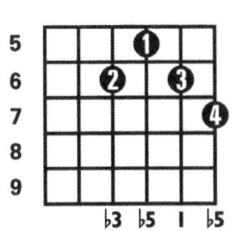

A♭°7
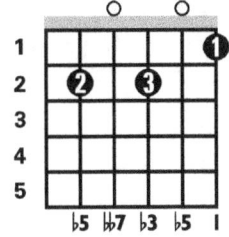
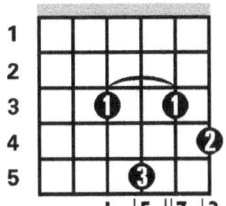
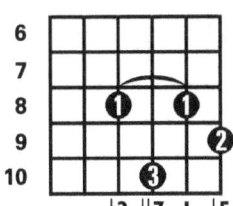

A♭-5
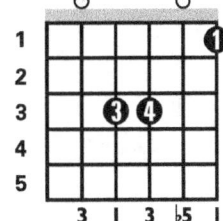
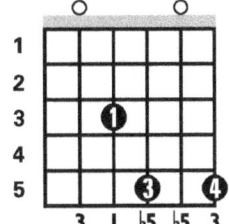
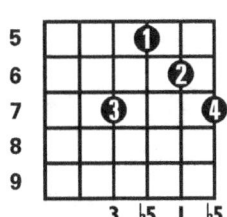

A♭+
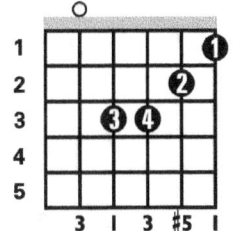
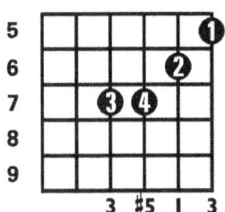
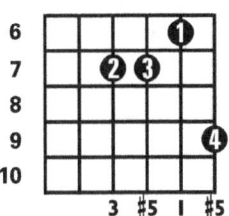

A♭sus2
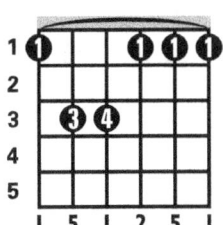
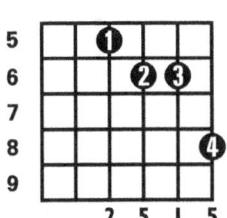
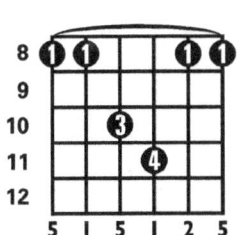

A♭sus4
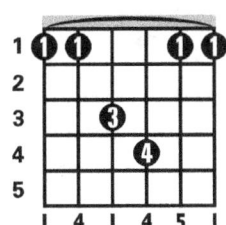
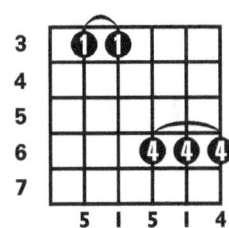
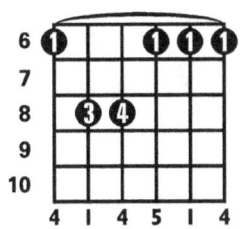

A♭7sus4
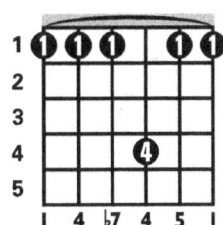
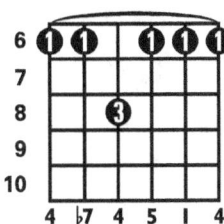
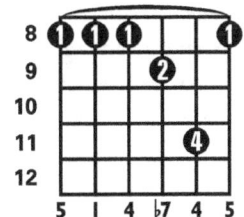

A♭m7-5
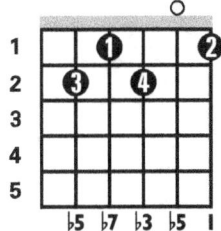
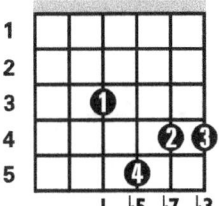
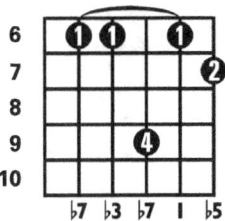

G♯ / A♭ Chords

A♭add9	A♭madd9	A♭6add9	A♭m6add9
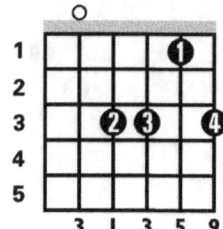	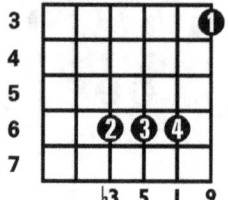	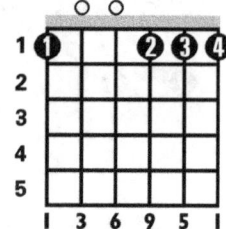	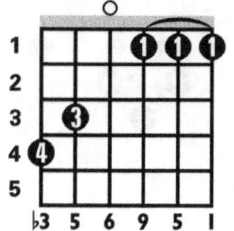
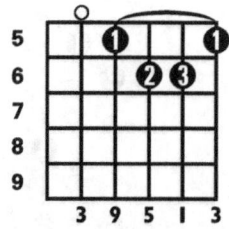	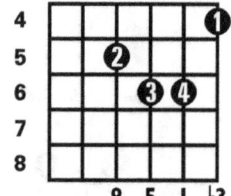	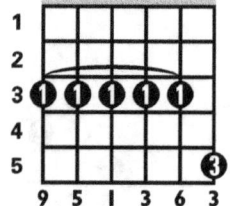	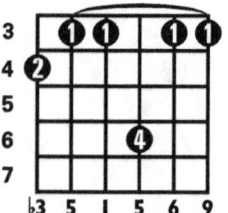
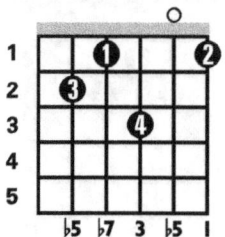	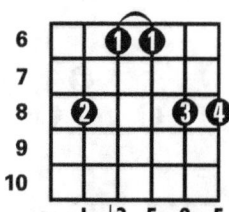	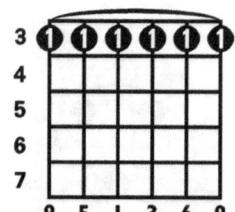	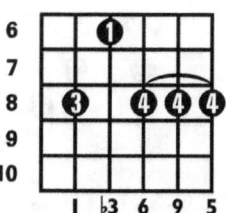

A♭7-5	A♭7+5	A♭7-9	A♭7+9
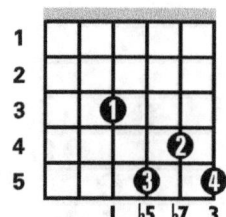	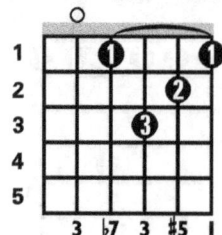	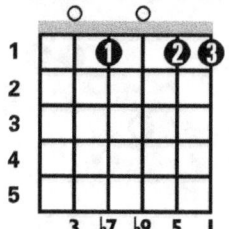	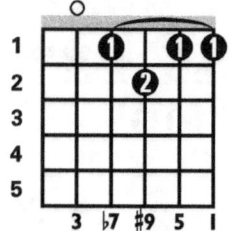
	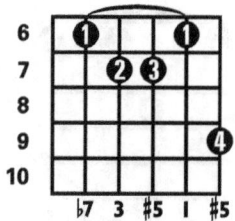	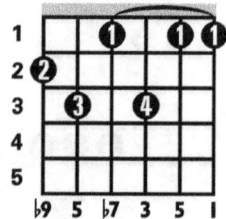	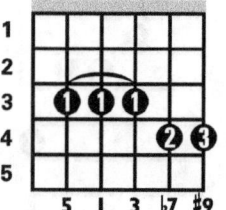
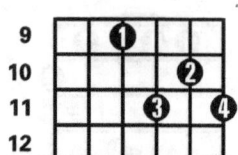	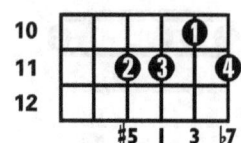	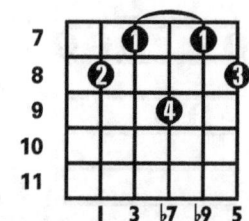	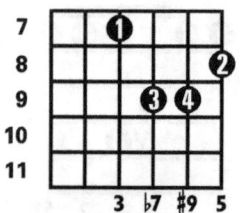

G#/A♭ Chords

A♭m(maj7)
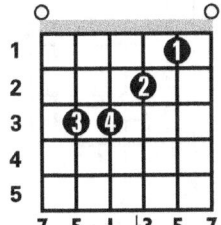
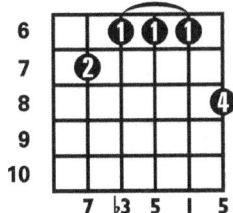
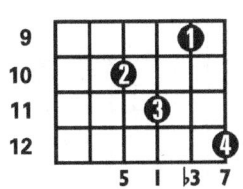

A♭maj7-5
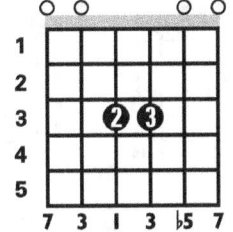
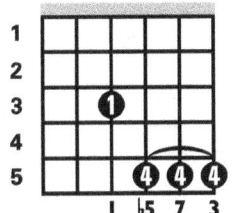
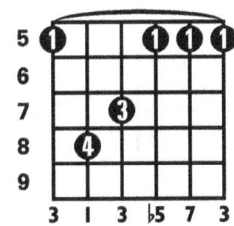

A♭maj7+5
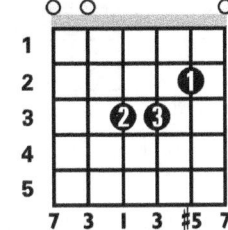
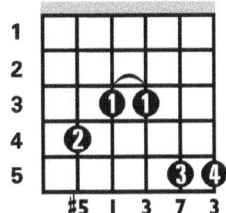
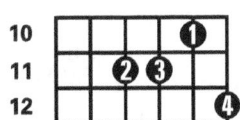

A♭9
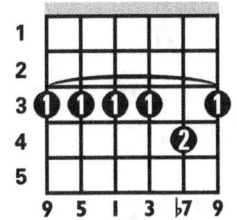
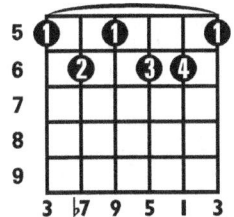
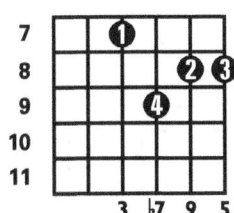

A♭m9
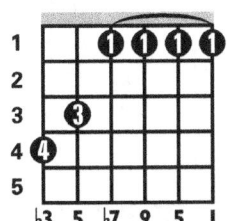
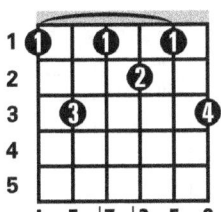
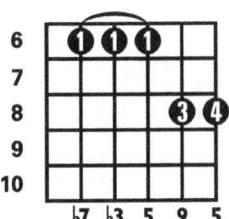

A♭maj9
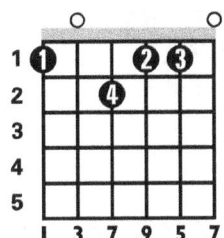
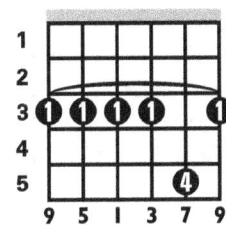
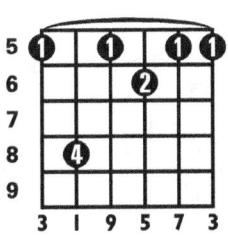

A♭11
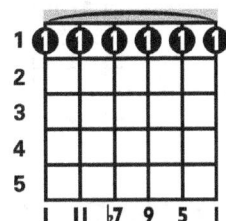
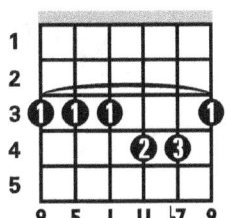
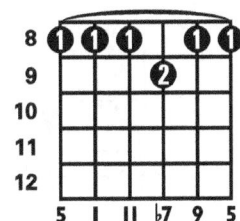

A♭13

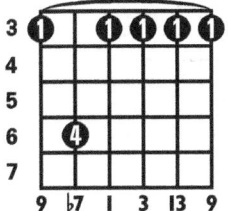
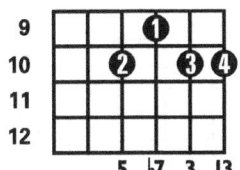

G♯ / A♭ Chords (Advanced)

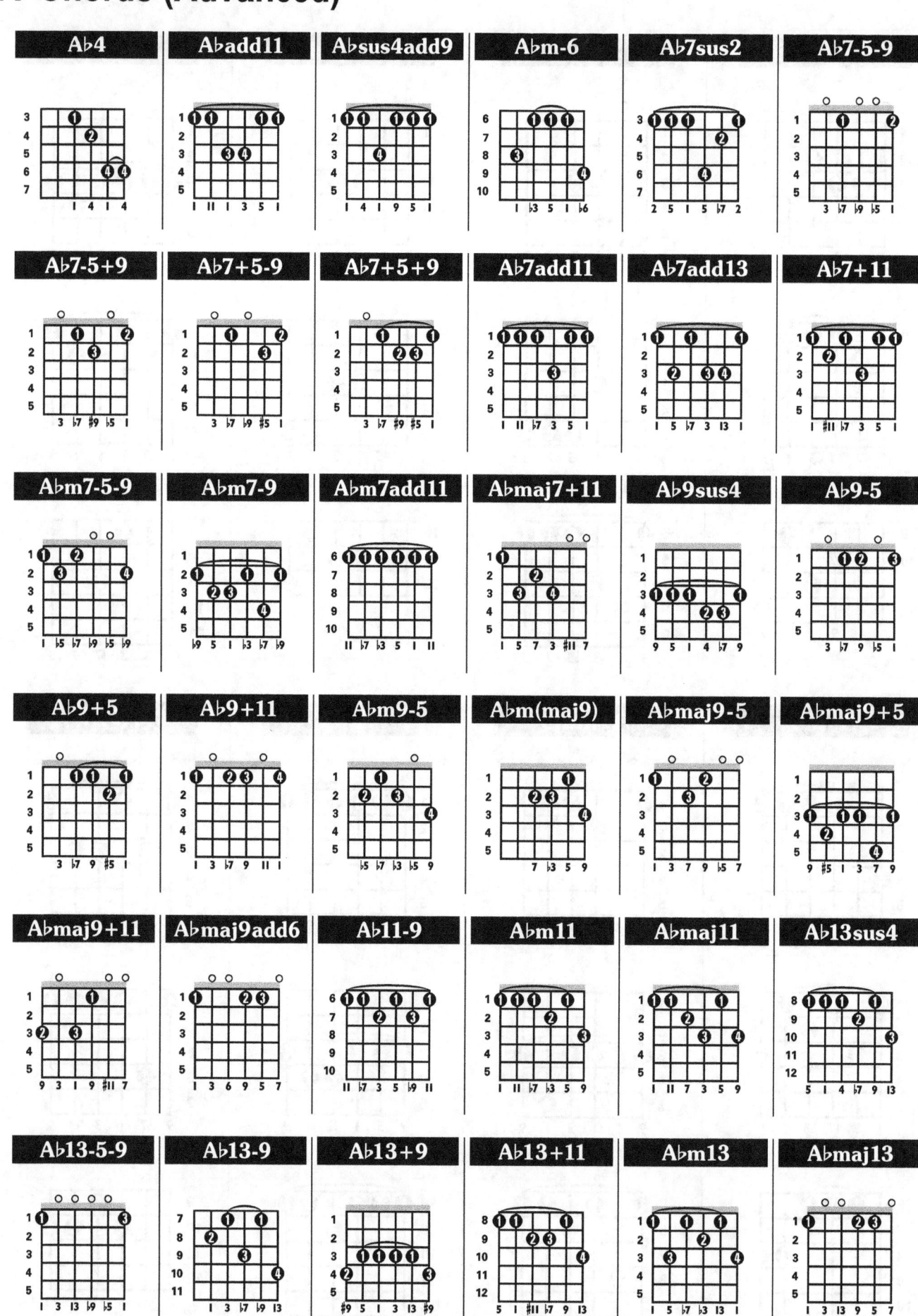

A Chords

A
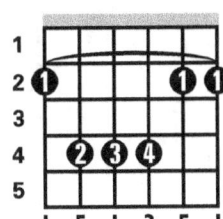
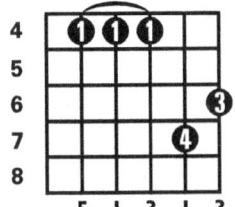
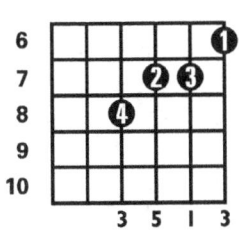

Am
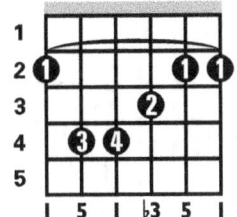
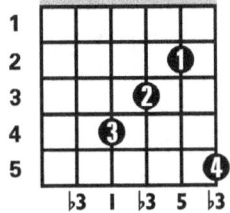
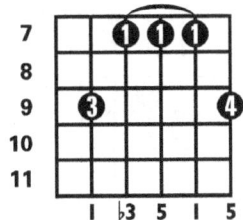

A7
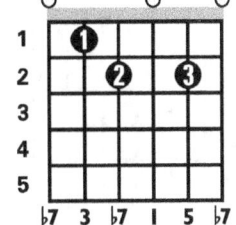
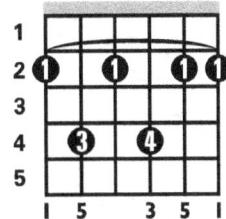
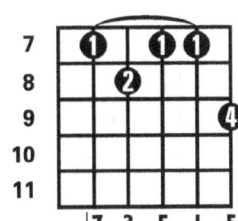

Am7
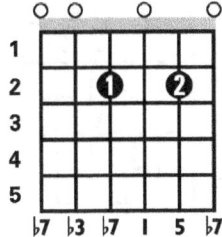
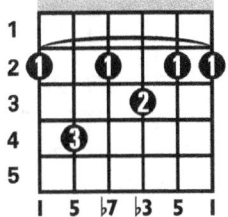
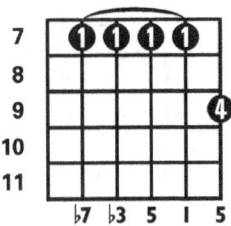

A5
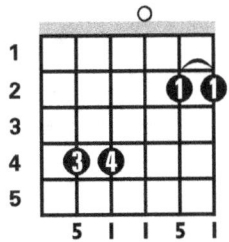
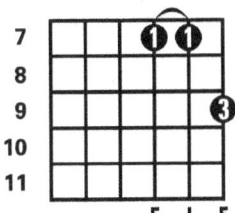
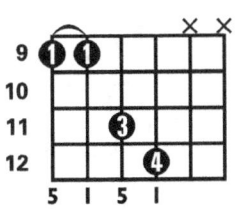

A6
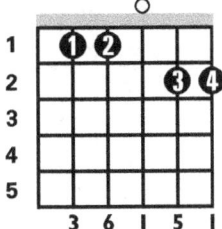
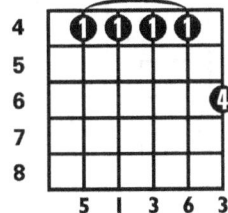
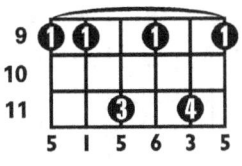

Am6
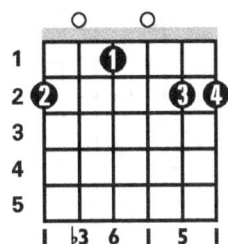
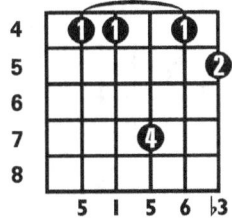
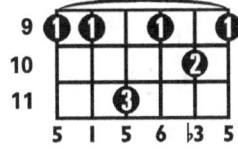

Amaj7
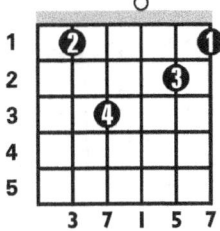
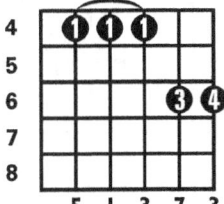
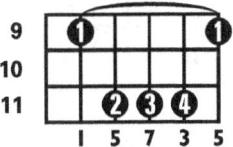

A Chords

A°	A°7	A-5	A+
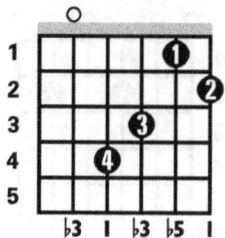	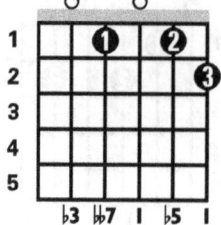	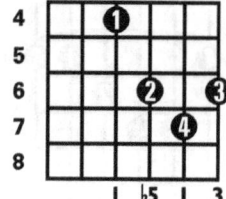	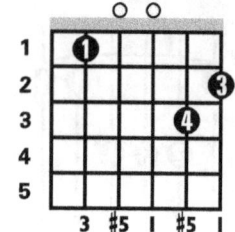
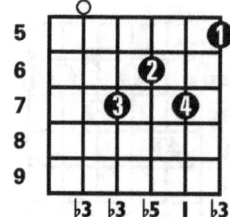	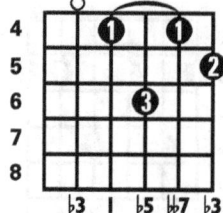	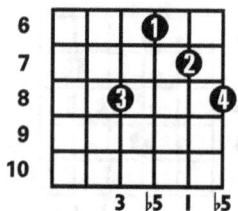	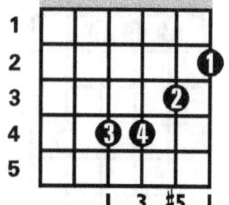
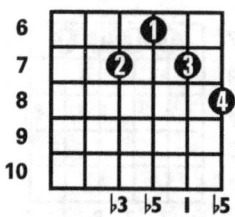	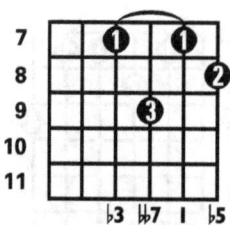	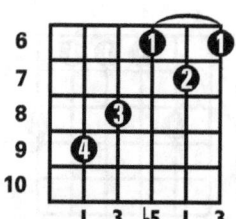	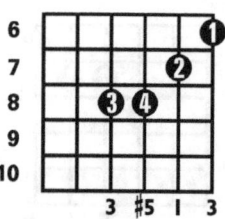

Asus2	Asus4	A7sus4	Am7-5
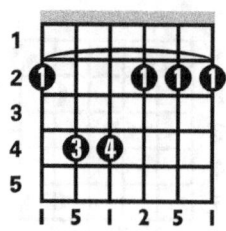	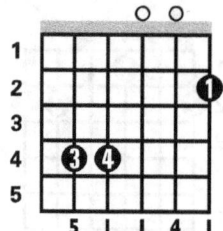	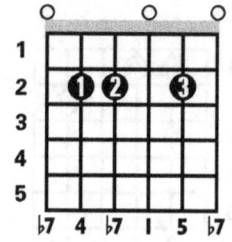	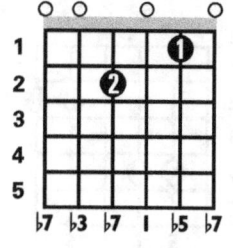
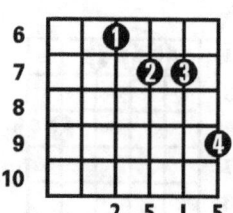	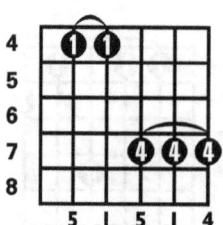	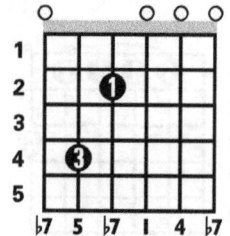	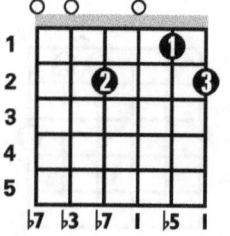
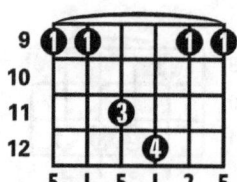	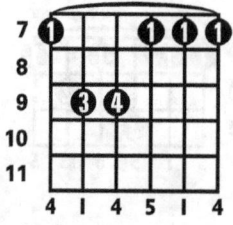	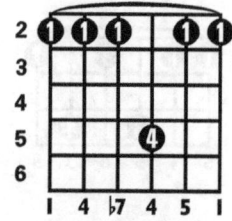	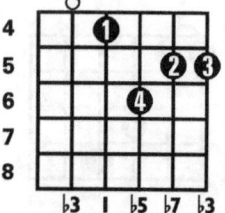

A Chords

Aadd9
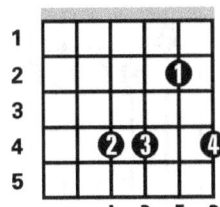
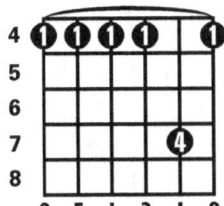
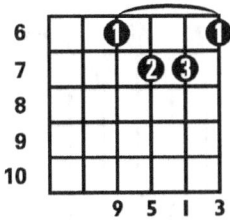

Amadd9
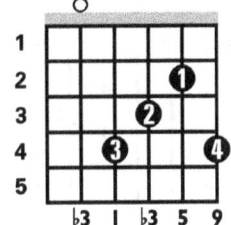
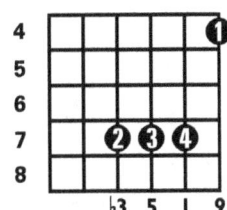
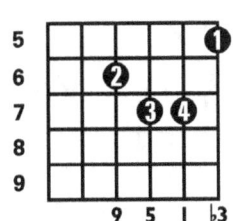

A6add9
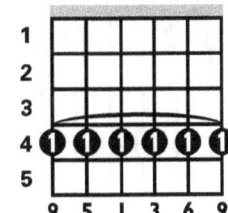
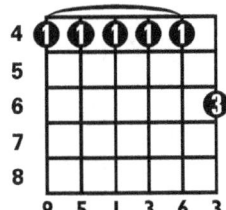
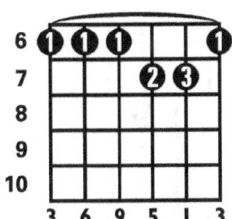

Am6add9
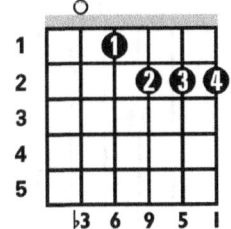
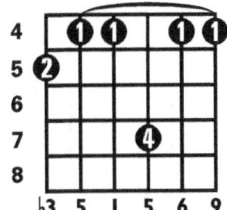
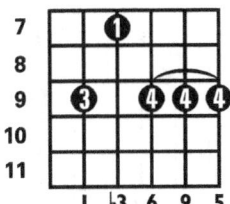

A7-5
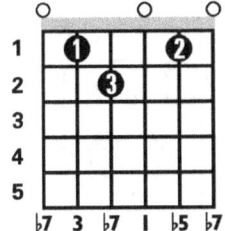
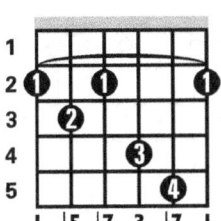
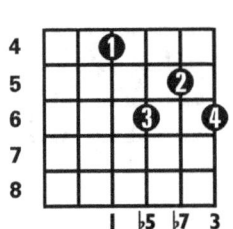

A7+5
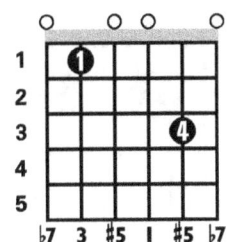
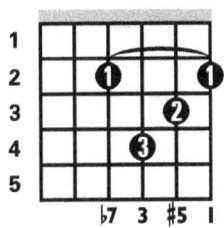
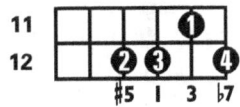

A7-9
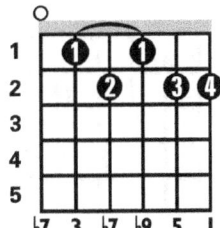
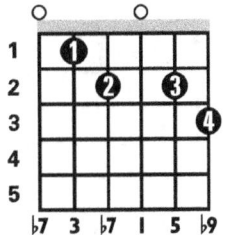
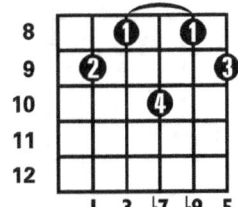

A7+9
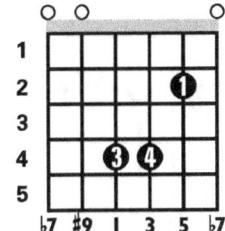
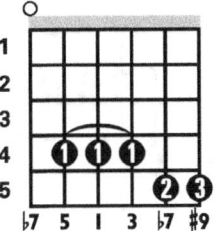
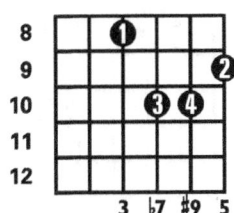

A Chords

Am(maj7)
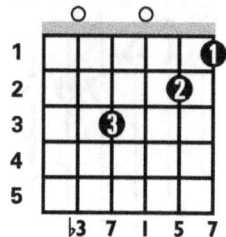
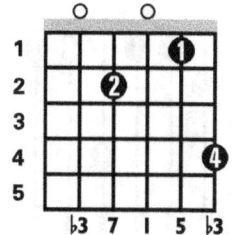
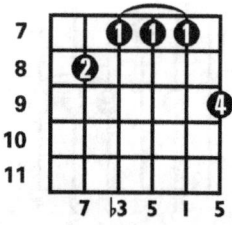

Amaj7-5
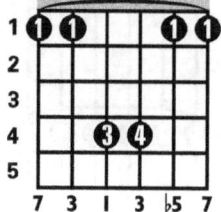
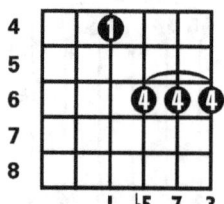
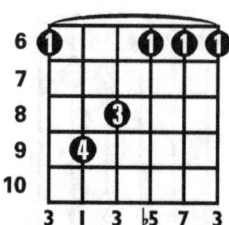

Amaj7+5
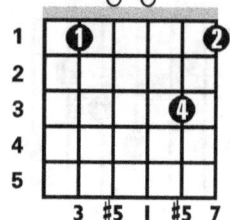
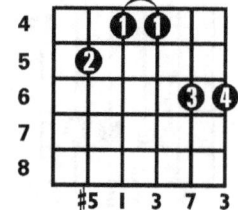
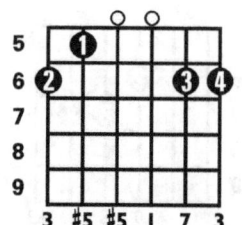

A9
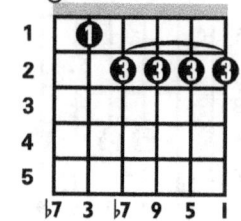
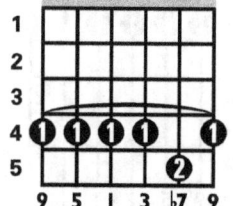
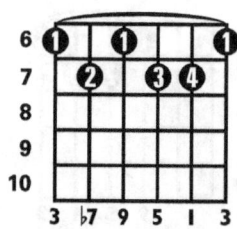

Am9
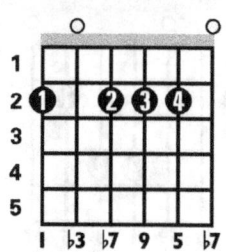
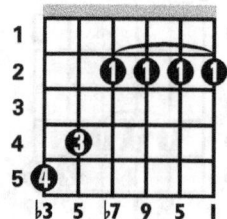
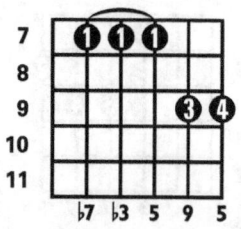

Amaj9
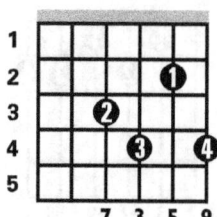
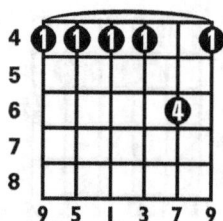
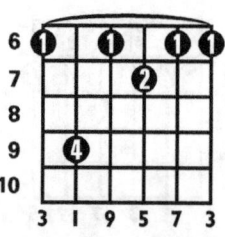

A11
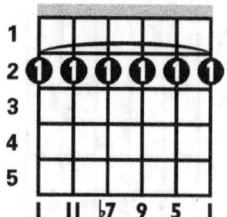
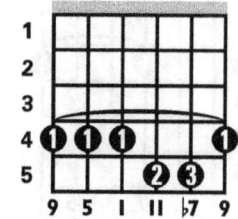
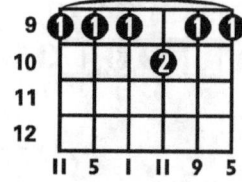

A13
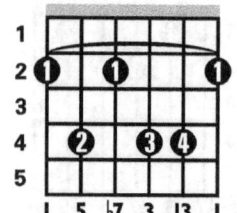
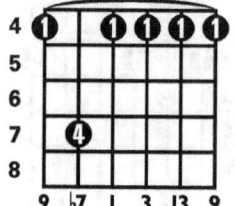
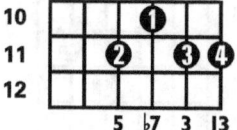

A Chords (Advanced)

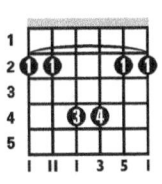 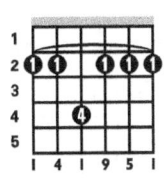 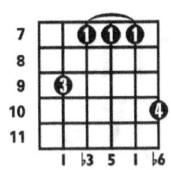 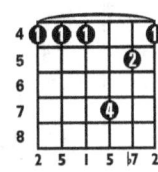 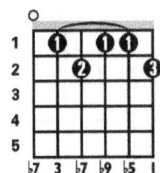
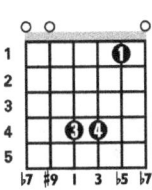 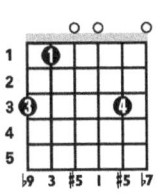 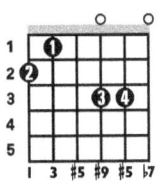 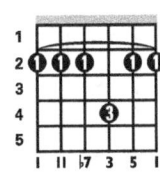 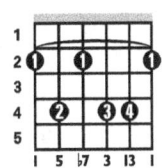 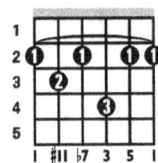
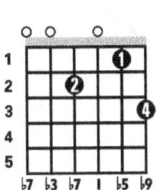 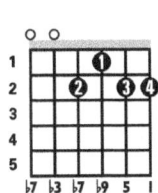 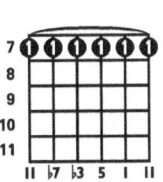 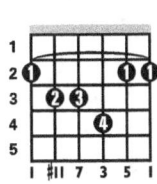 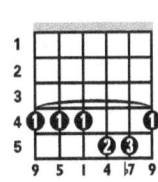 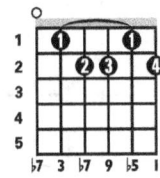
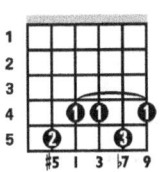 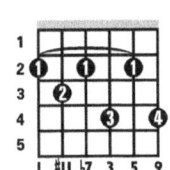 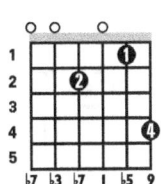 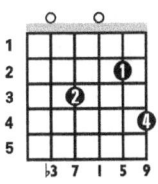 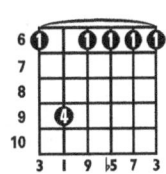 
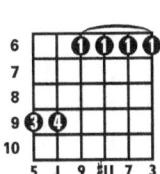 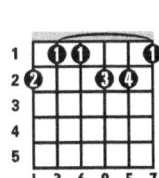 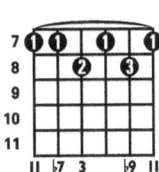 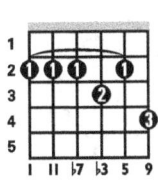 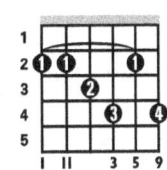 
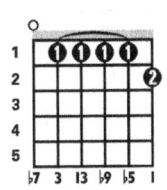 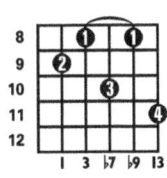 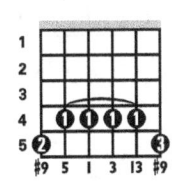 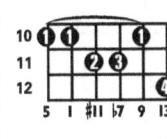 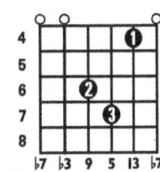 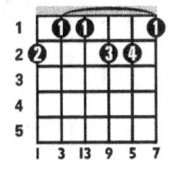

A# / B♭ Chords

B♭
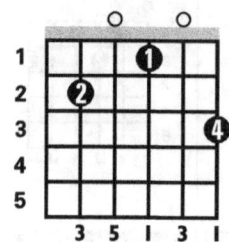
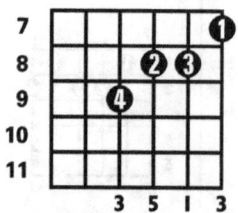
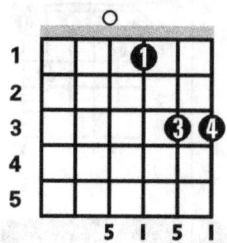

B♭m
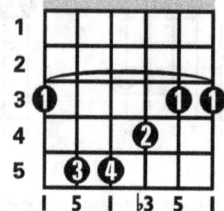
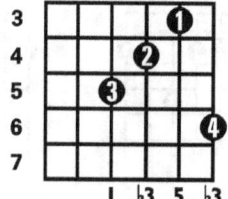
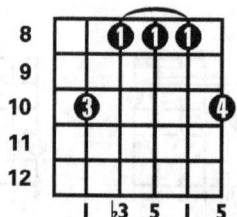

B♭7
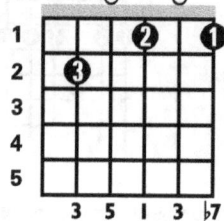
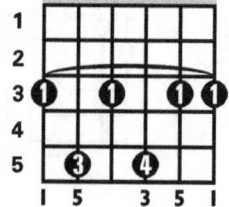
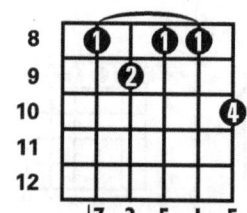

B♭m7
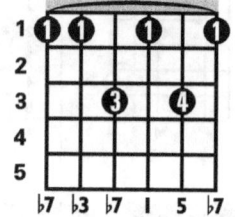
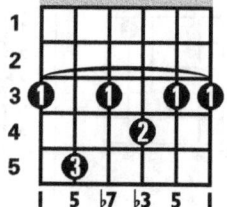
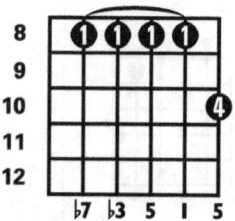

B♭5
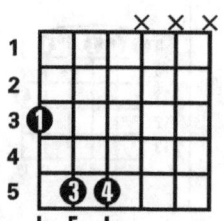
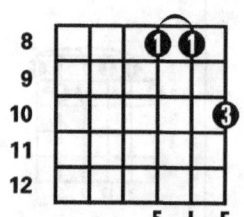

B♭6
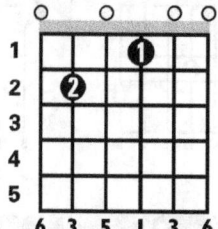
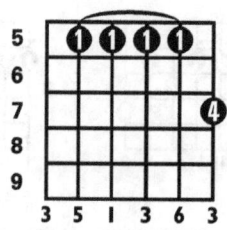
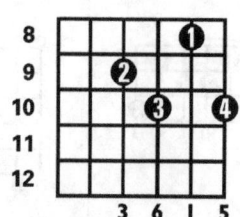

B♭m6
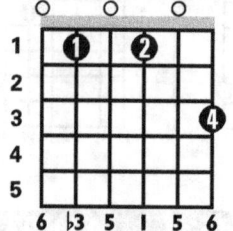
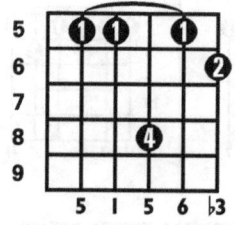
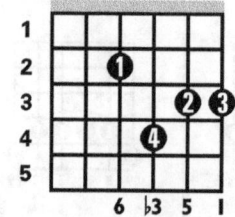

B♭maj7
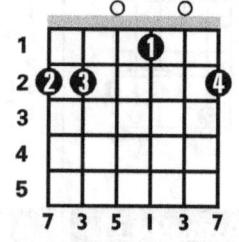
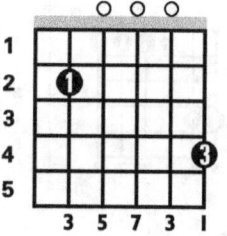
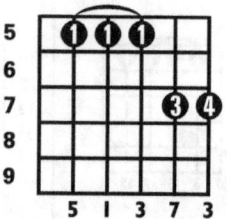

A#/B♭ Chords

B♭°
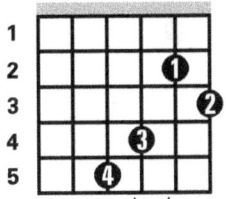
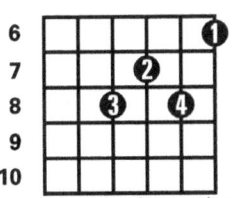
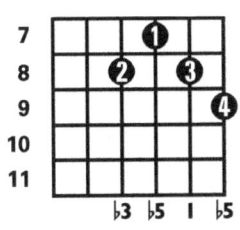

B♭°7
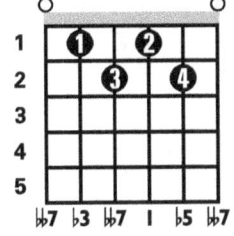
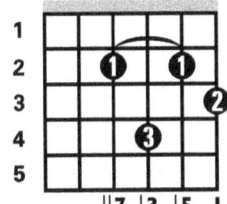
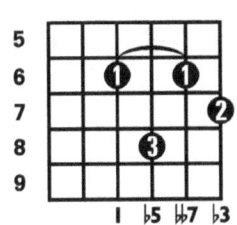

B♭-5
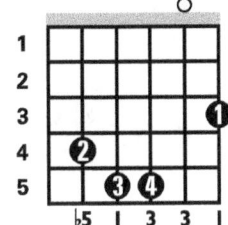
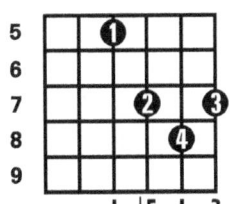
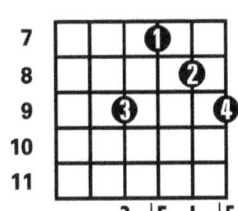

B♭+
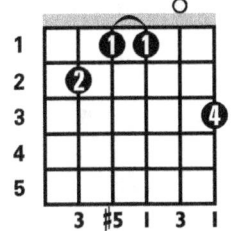
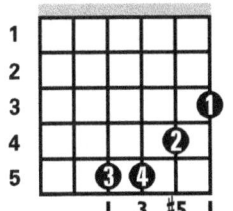
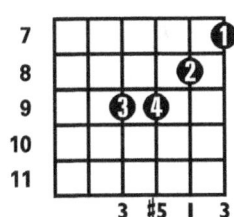

B♭sus2
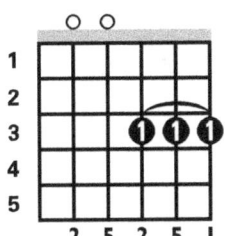
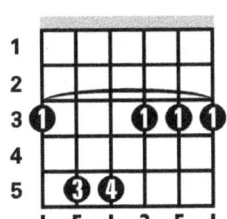
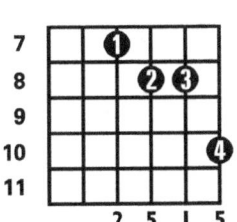

B♭sus4
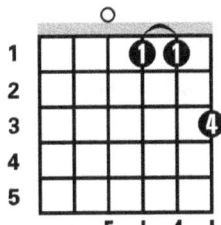
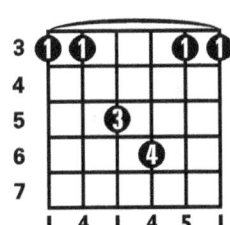
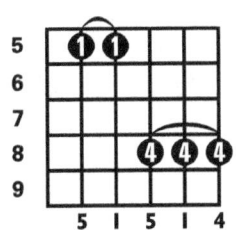

B♭7sus4
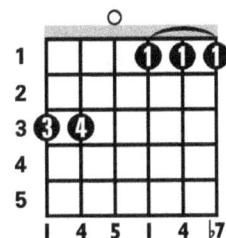
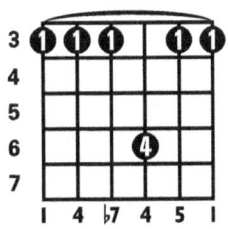
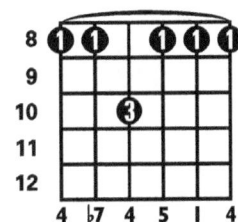

B♭m7-5
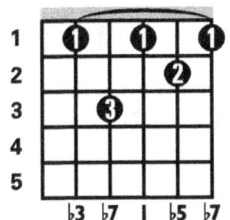
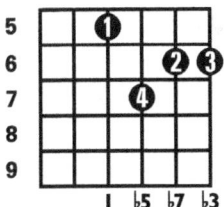
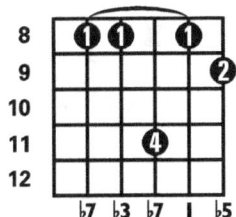

A# / B♭ Chords

B♭add9
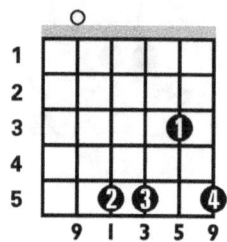

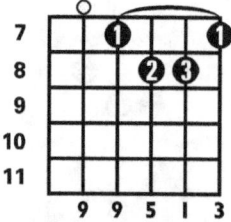

B♭madd9
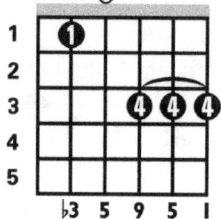
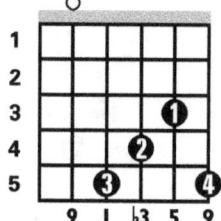
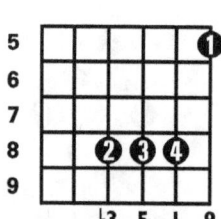

B♭6add9
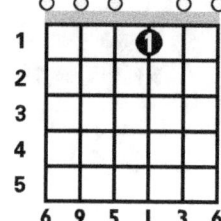
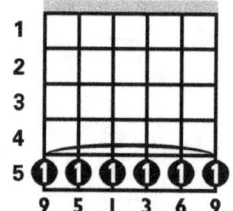
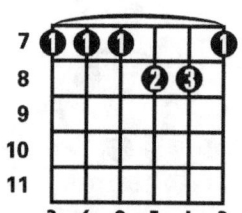

B♭m6add9
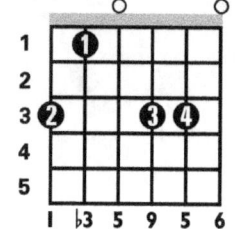
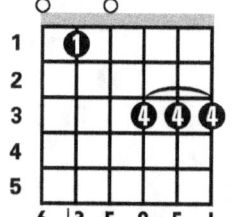
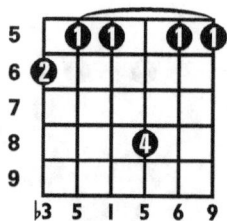

B♭7-5
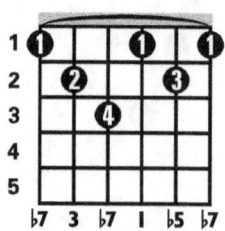
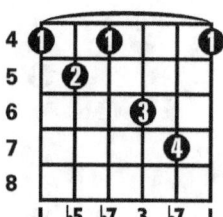
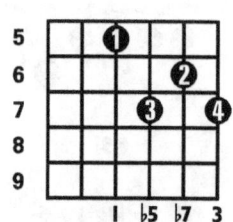

B♭7+5
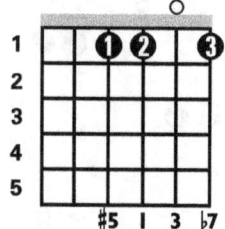
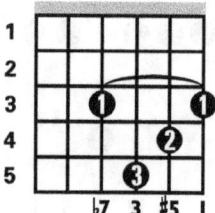
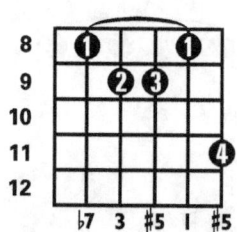

B♭7-9
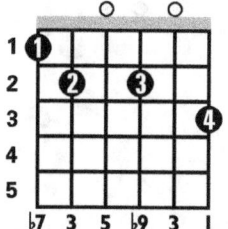
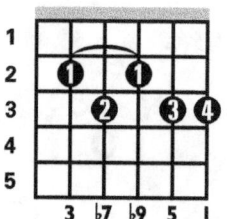
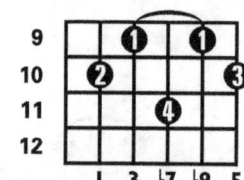

B♭7+9
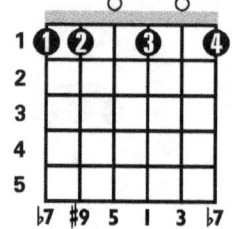
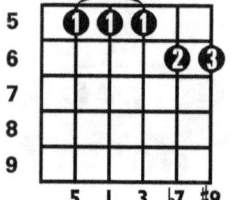
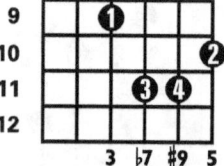

A#/ B♭ Chords

B♭m(maj7)
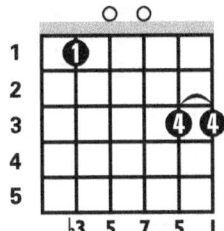
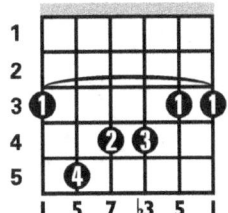
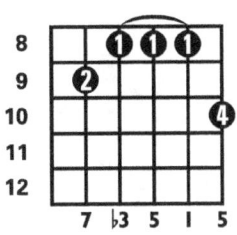

B♭maj7-5
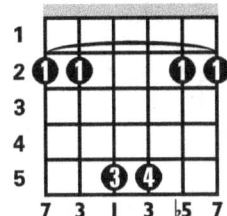
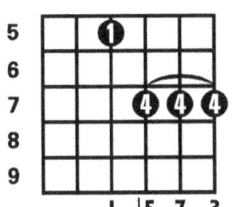
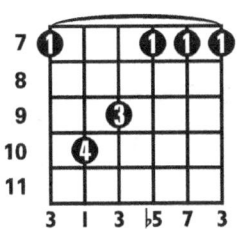

B♭maj7+5
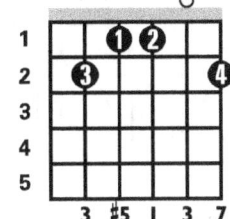
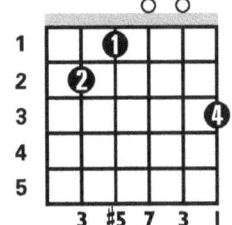
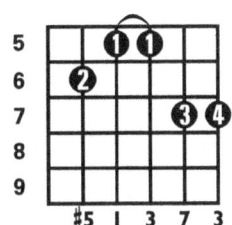

B♭9
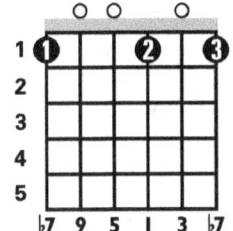
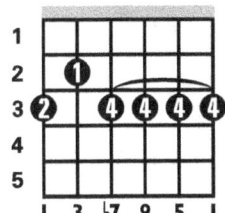

B♭m9
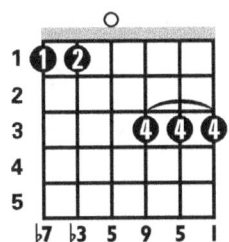
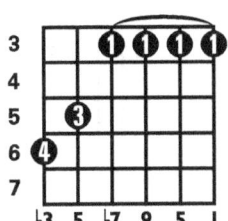
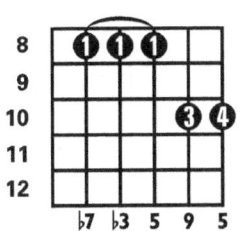

B♭maj9
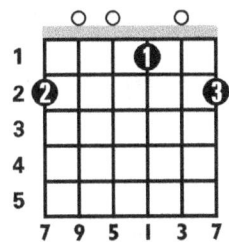
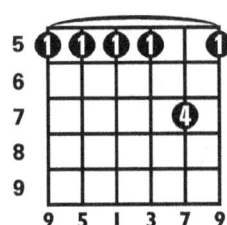
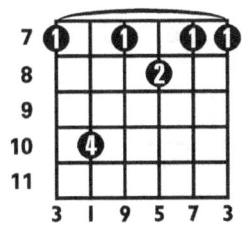

B♭11
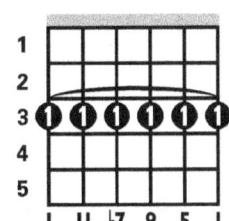

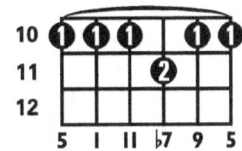

B♭13
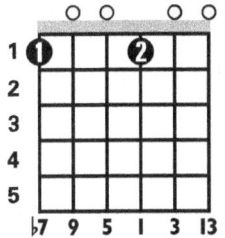
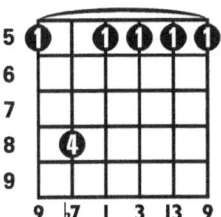
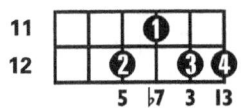

A# / B♭ Chords (Advanced)

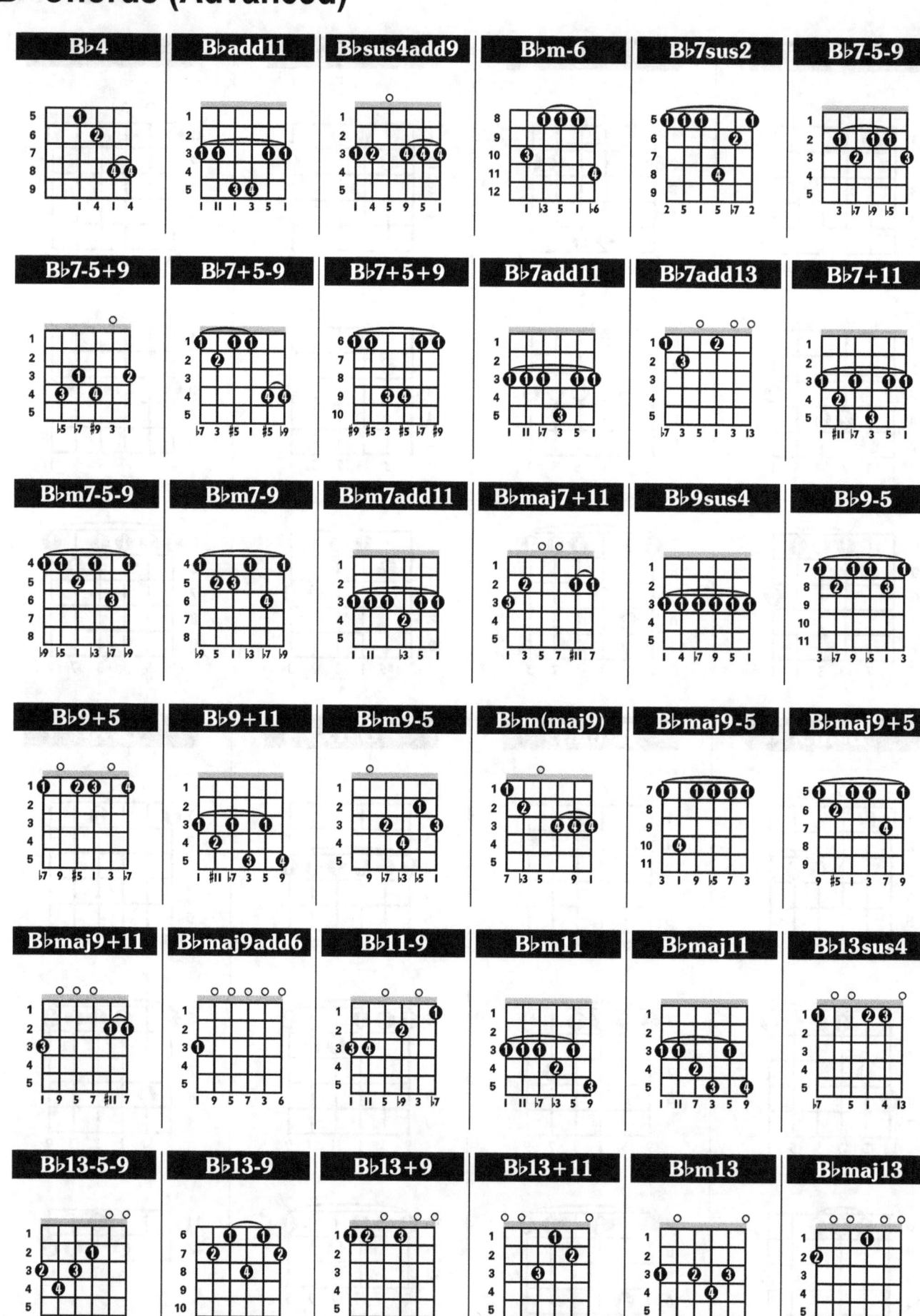

B Chords

B
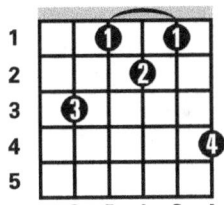

Bm
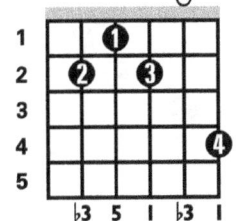

B7
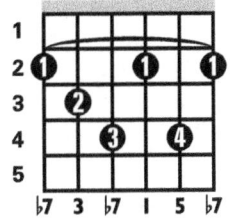

Bm7
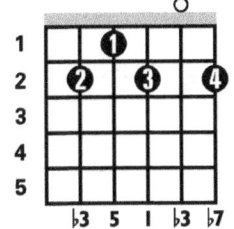

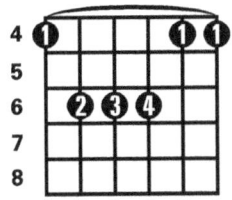
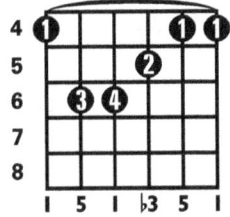
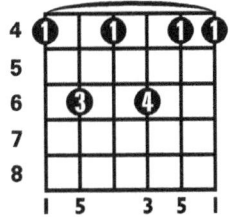
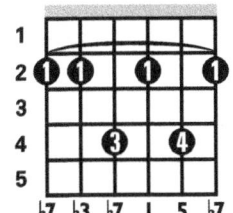

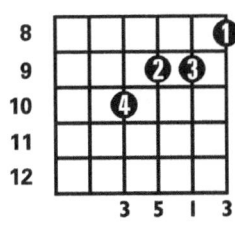
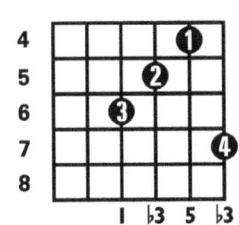
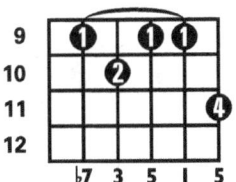
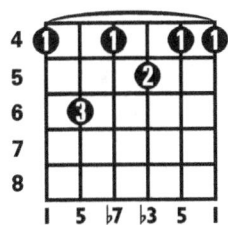

B5
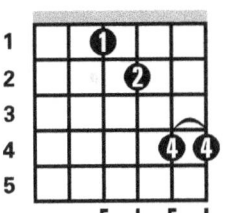

B6

Bm6
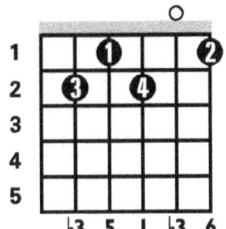

Bmaj7
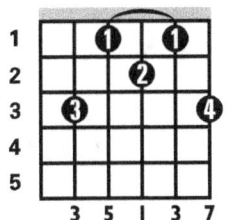

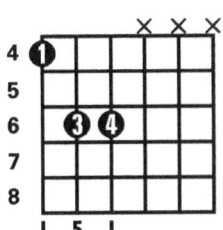
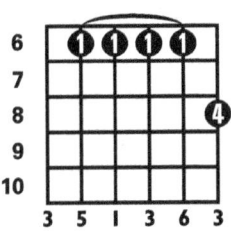
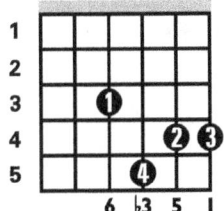
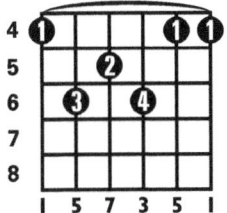

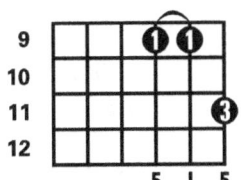
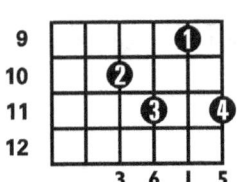
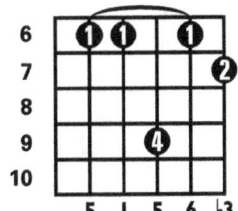
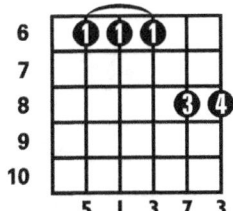

B Chords

B°	B°7	B-5	B+
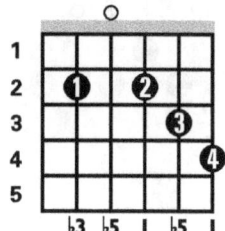	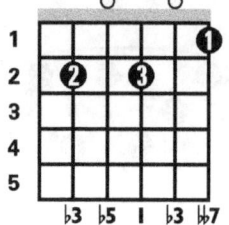	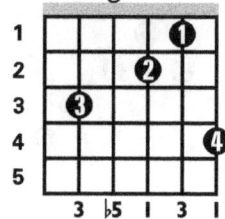	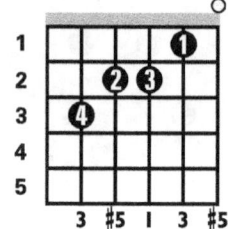
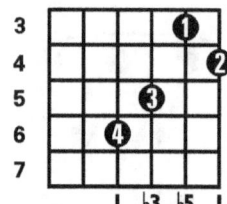	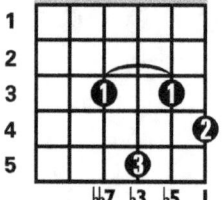	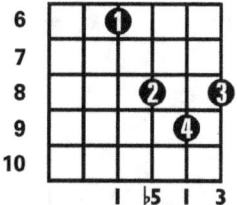	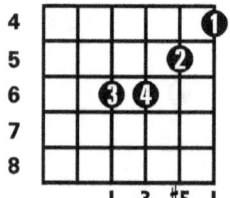
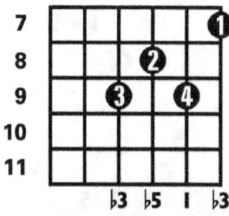	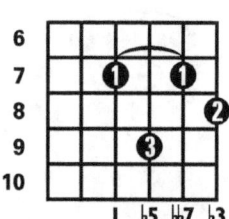	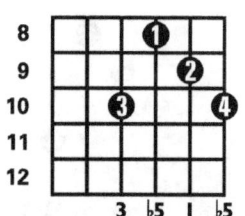	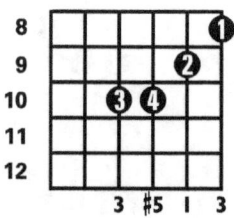

Bsus2	Bsus4	B7sus4	Bm7-5
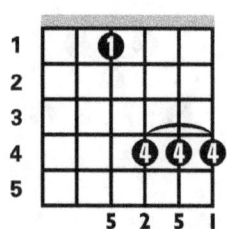	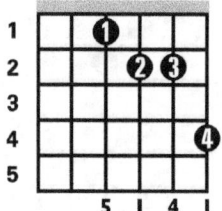	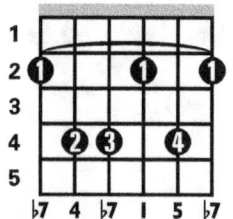	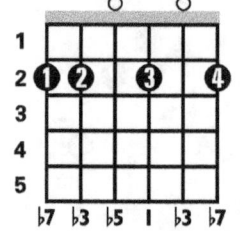
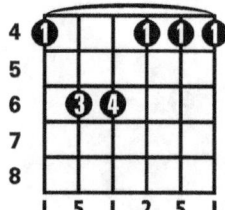	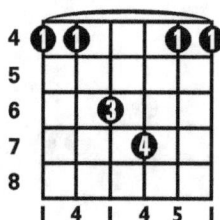	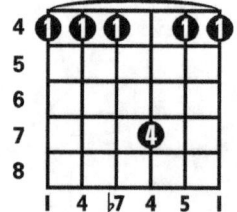	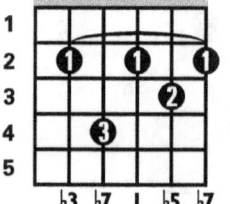
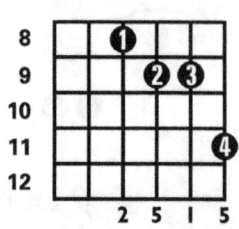	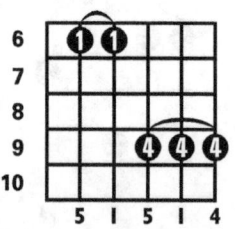	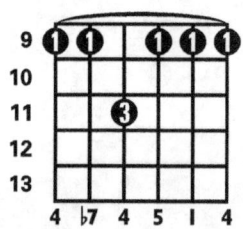	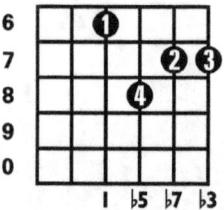

B Chords

Badd9
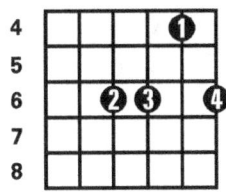
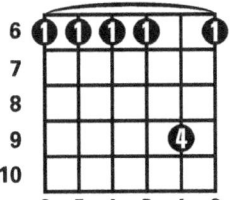
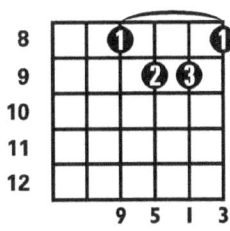

Bmadd9
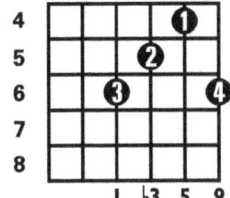
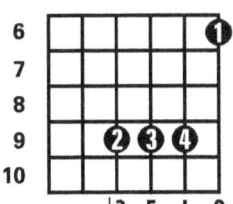
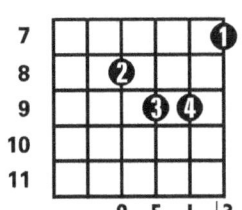

B6add9
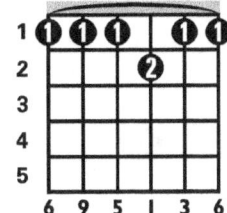
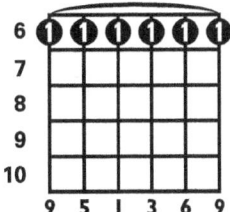
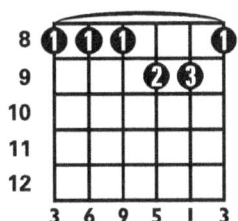

Bm6add9
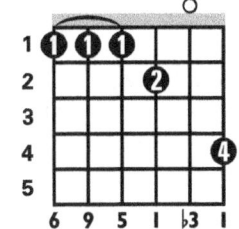
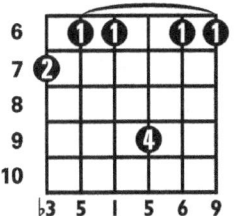
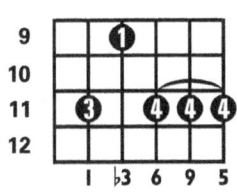

B7-5
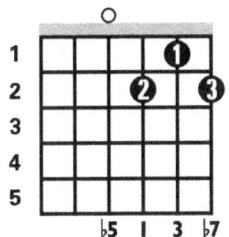
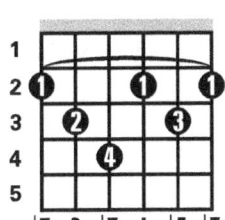
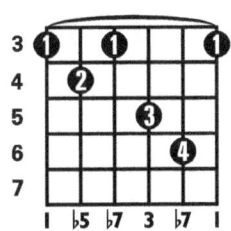

B7+5
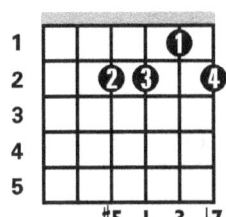
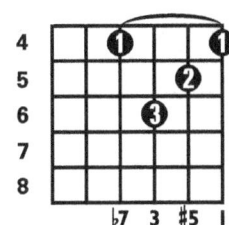
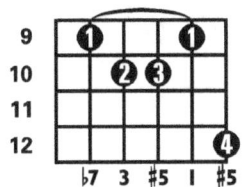

B7-9
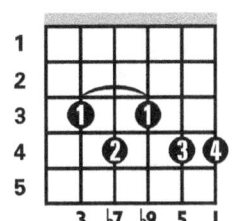
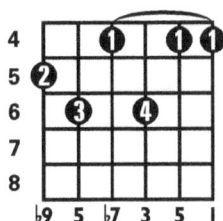
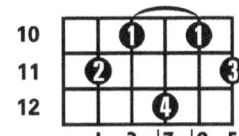

B7+9
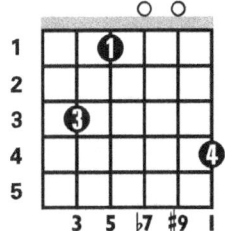
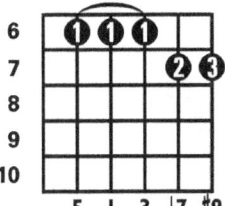
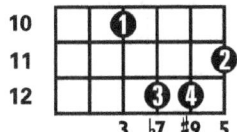

B Chords

Bm(maj7)
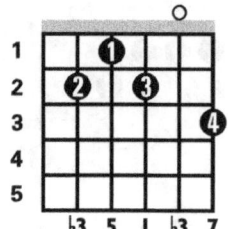
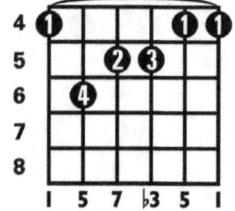
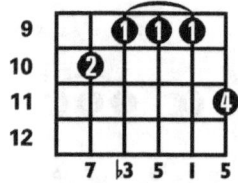

Bmaj7-5
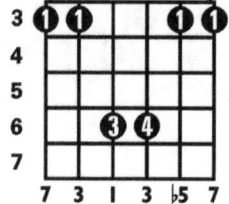
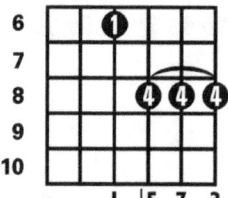
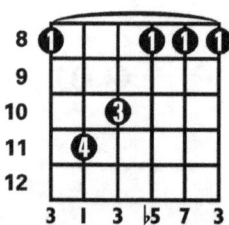

Bmaj7+5
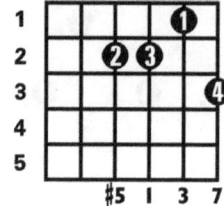
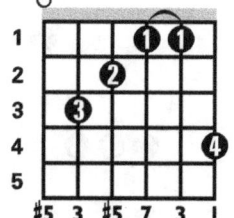
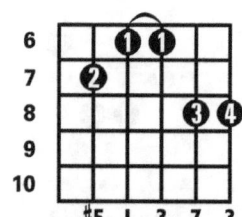

B9
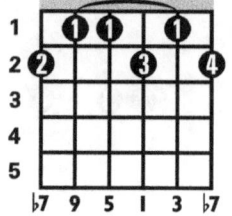
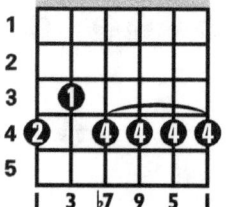

Bm9
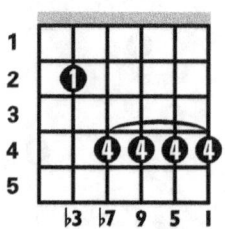
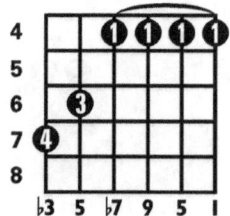
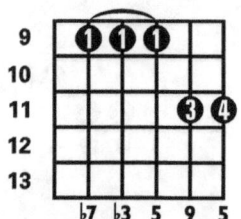

Bmaj9
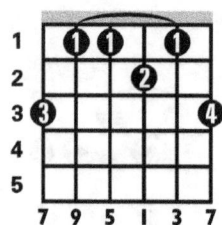
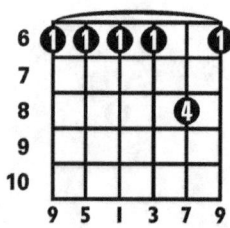
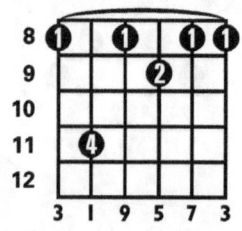

B11
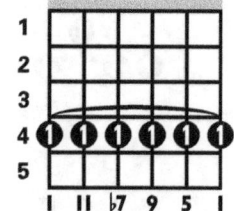
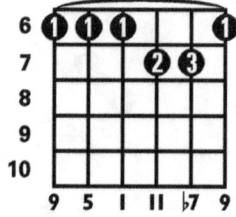
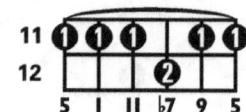

B13
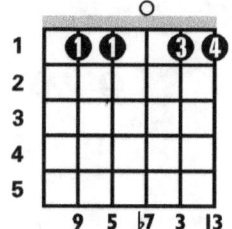
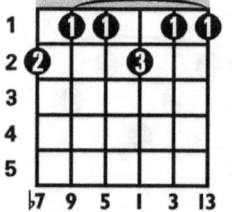
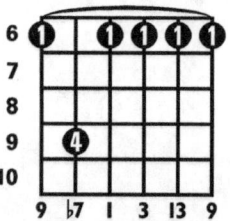

B Chords (Advanced)

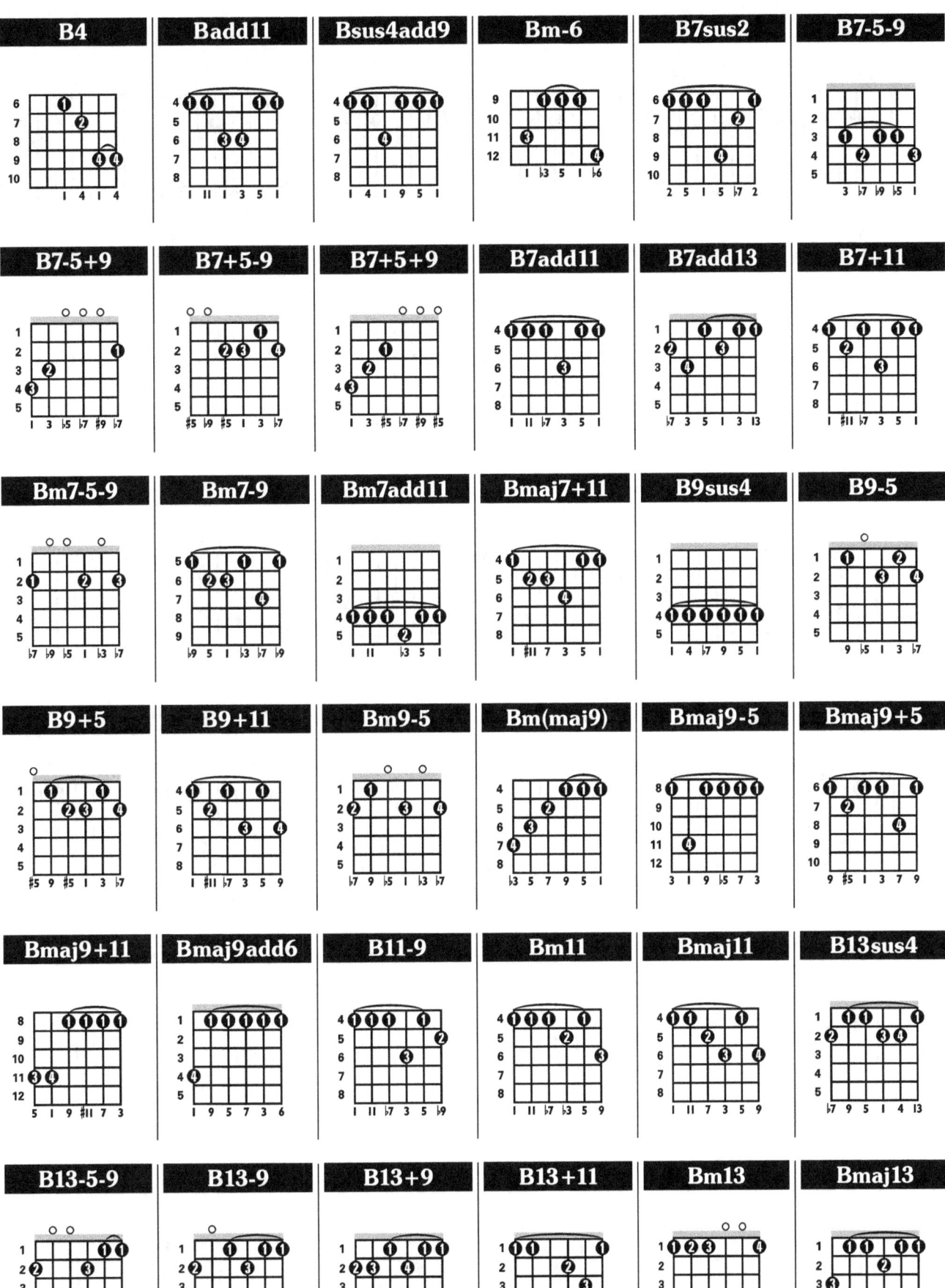

Major Slash Chords

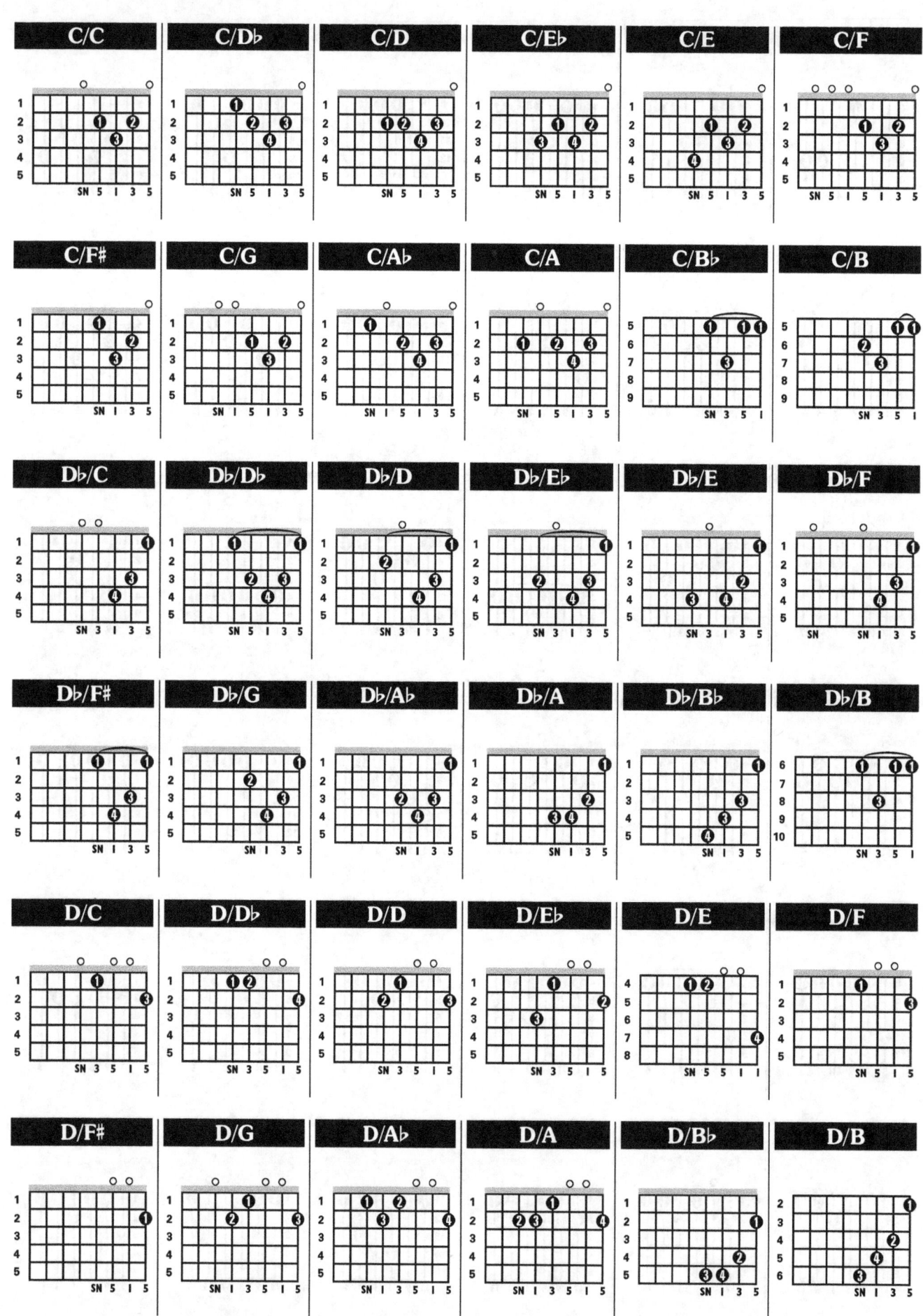

Major Slash Chords

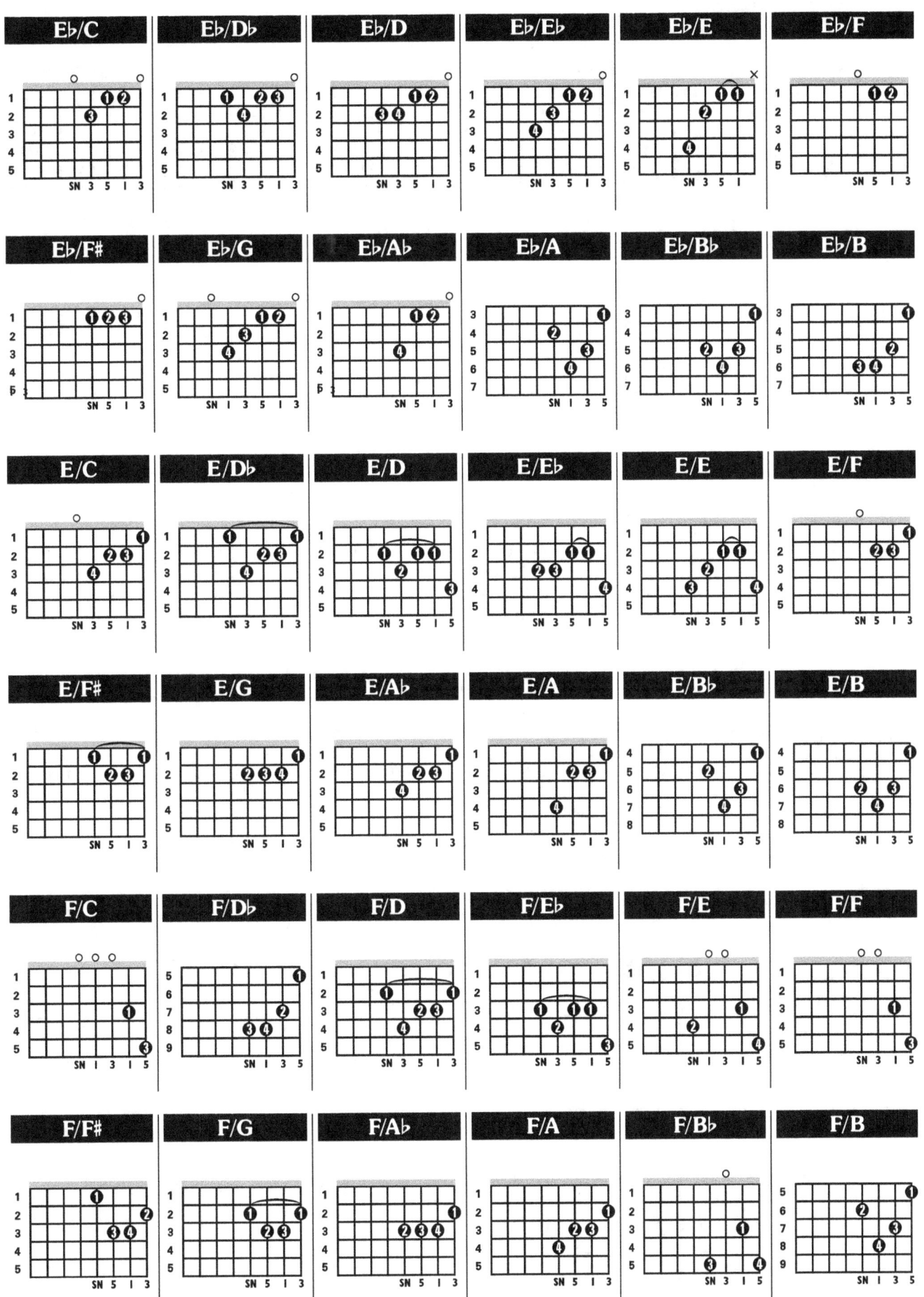

Major Slash Chords

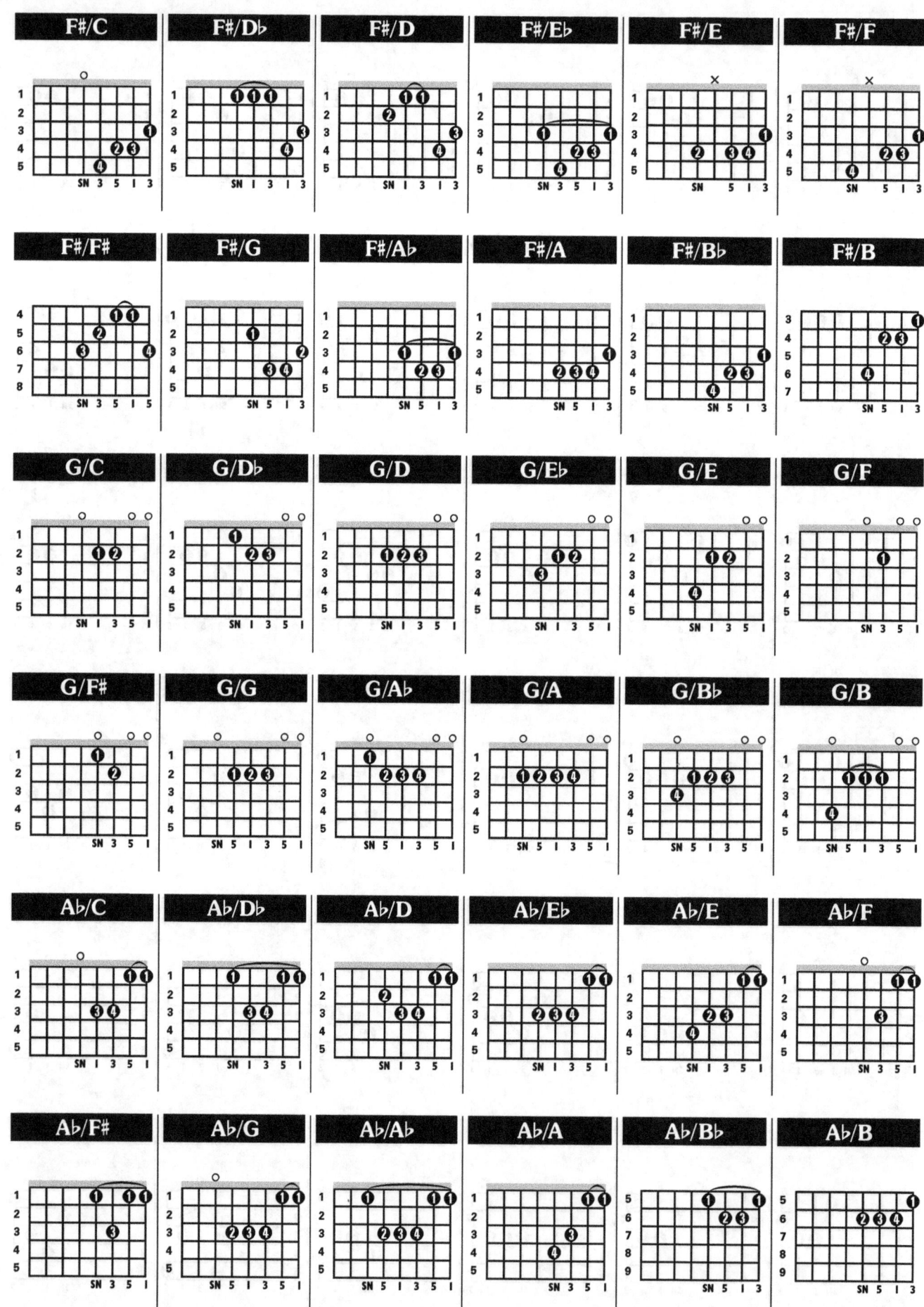

Major Slash Chords

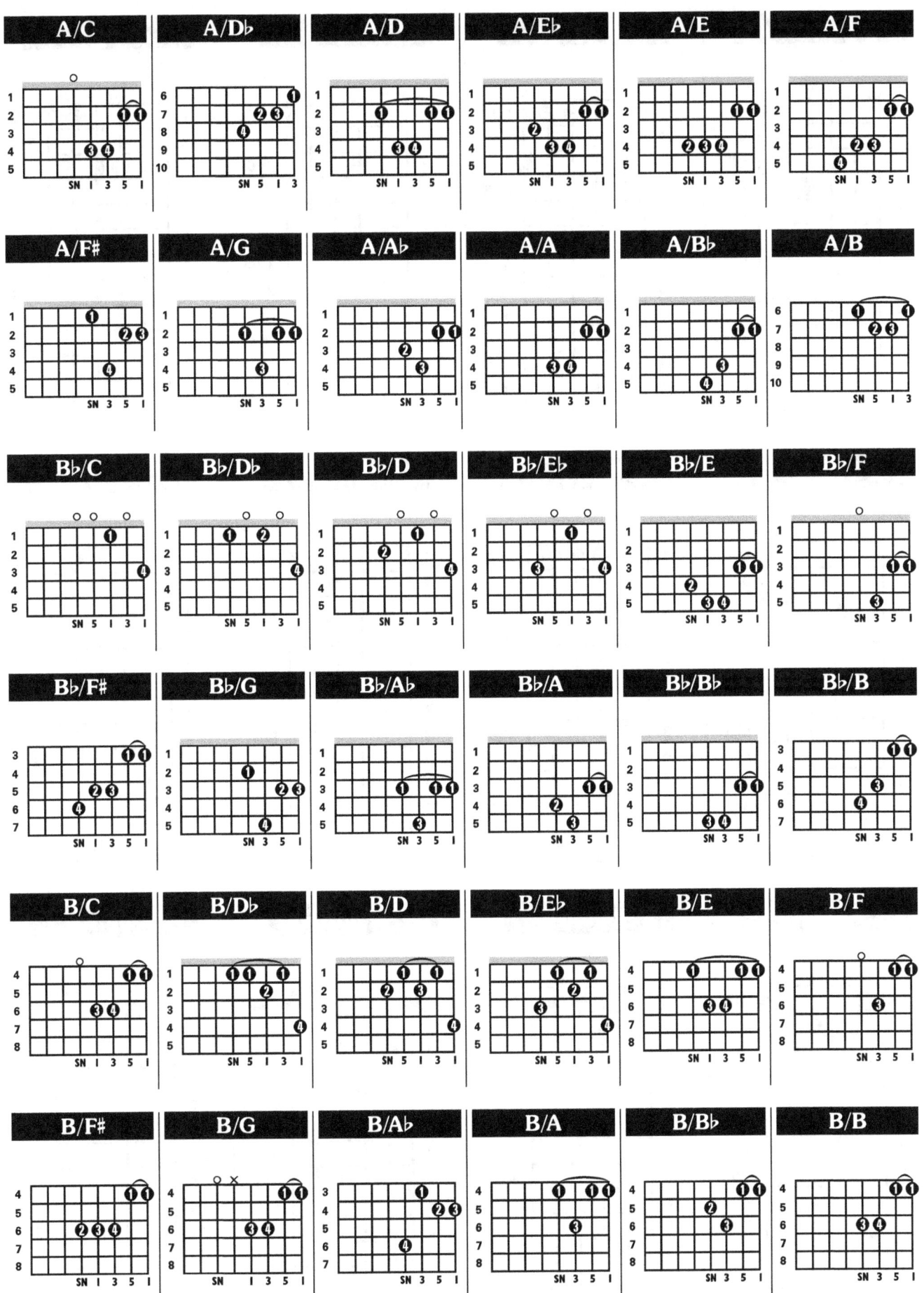

A Selection of Moveable Chord Shapes

Major
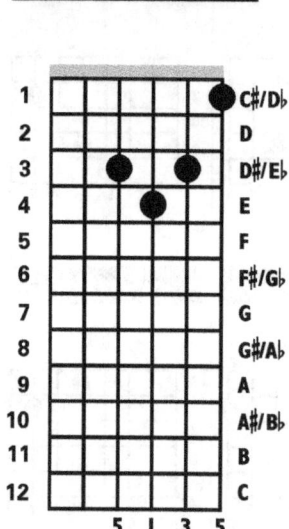

Major
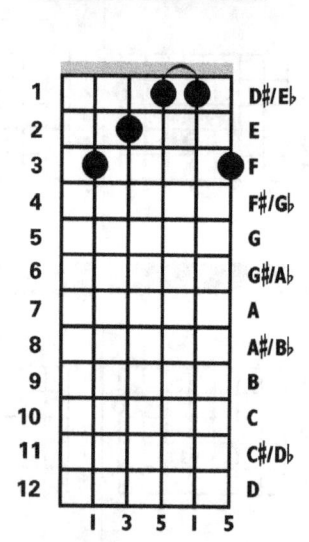

Major
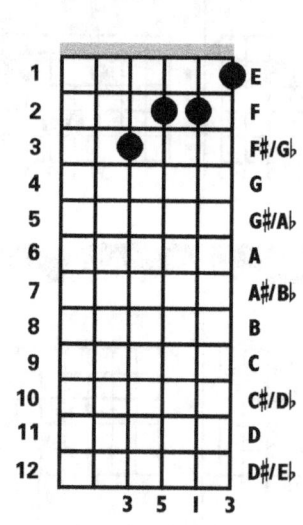

Major
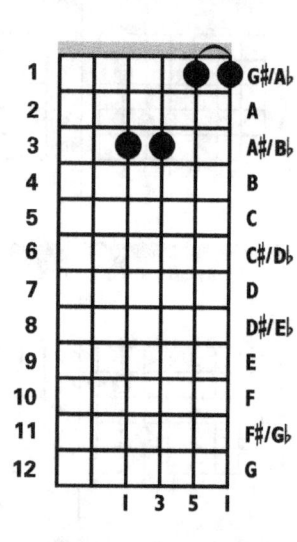

Minor
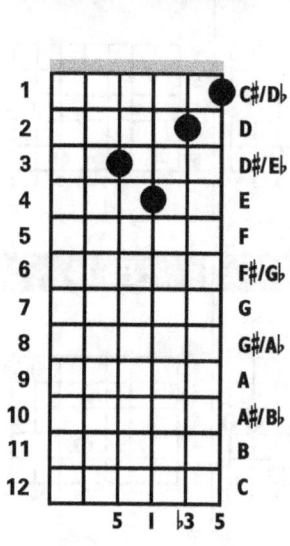

Minor
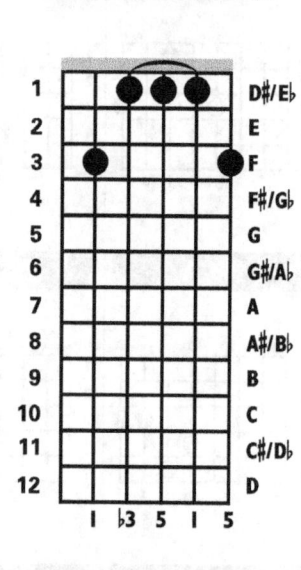

Minor
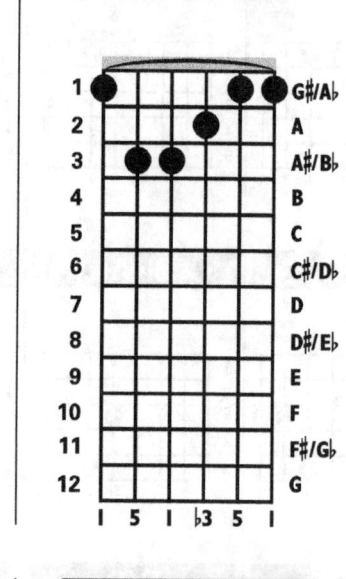

Minor
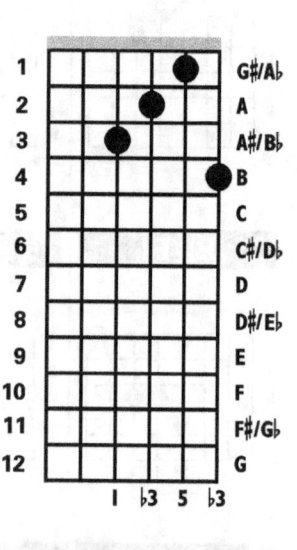

Seventh
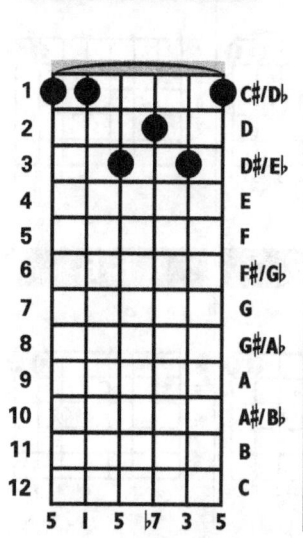

Seventh
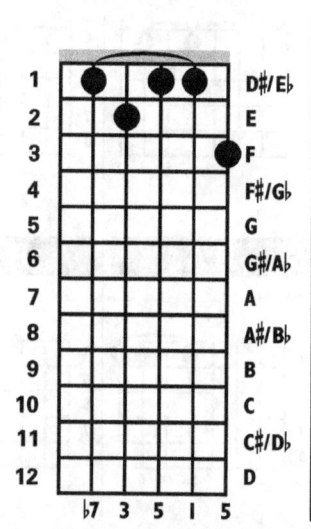

Seventh
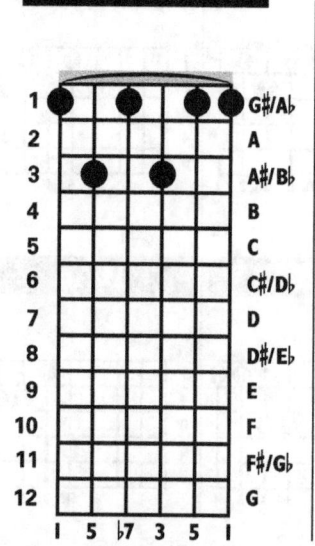

Seventh
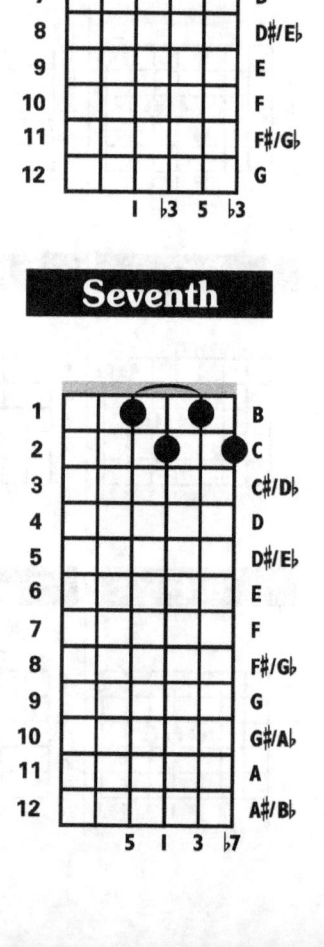

A Selection of Moveable Chord Shapes

Minor Seventh
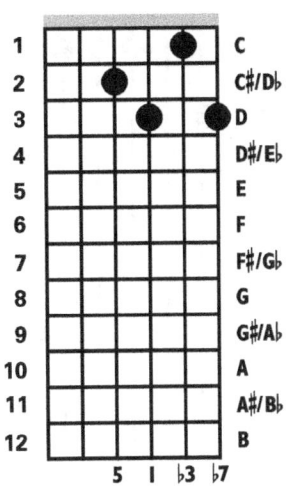

Minor Seventh
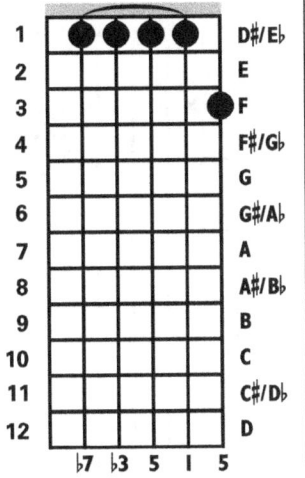

Minor Seventh
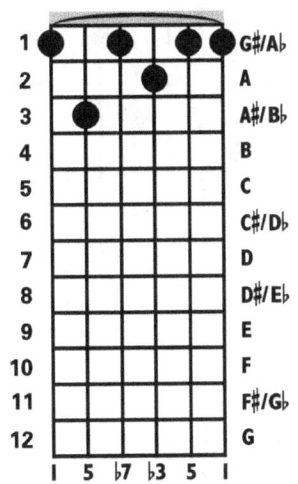

Minor Seventh
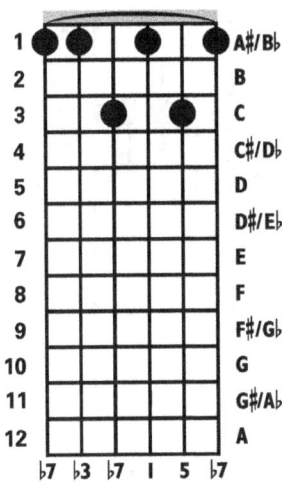

Sixth
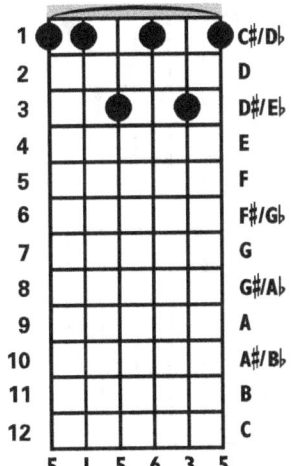

Sixth
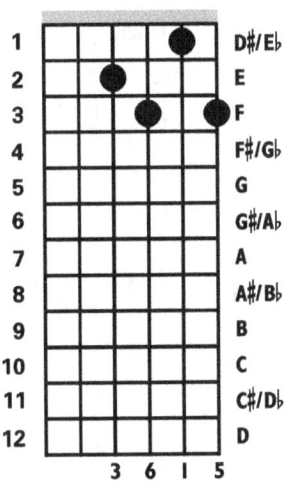

Sixth
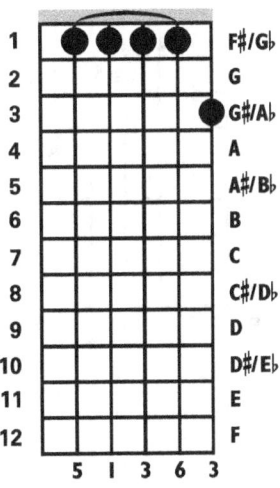

Sixth
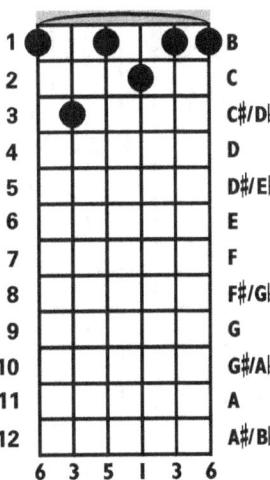

Minor Sixth
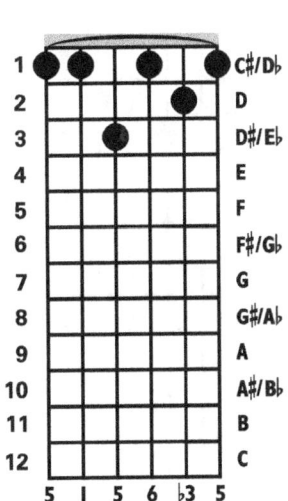

Minor Sixth
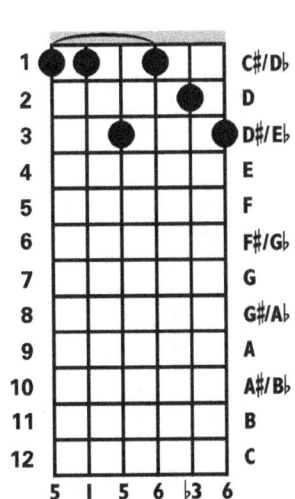

Minor Sixth
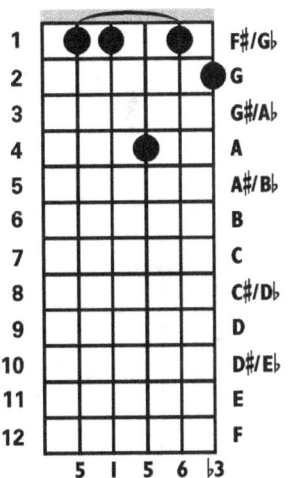

Minor Sixth
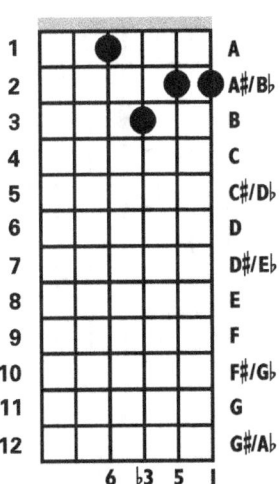

A Selection of Moveable Chord Shapes

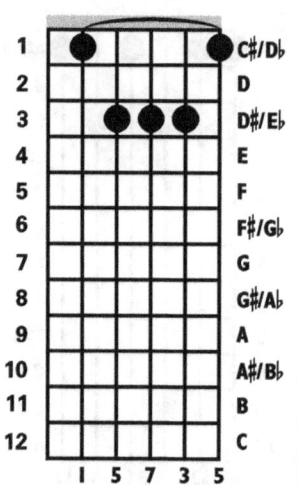
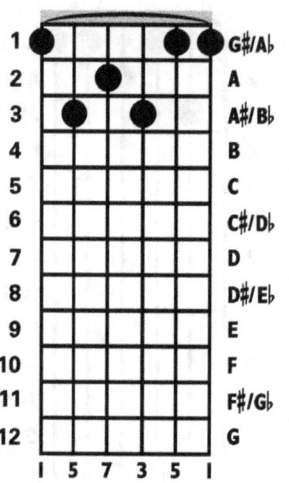
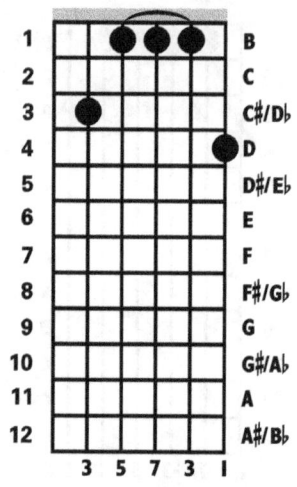
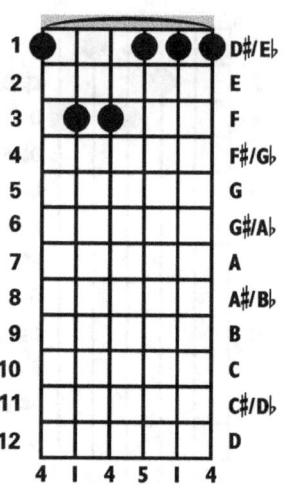
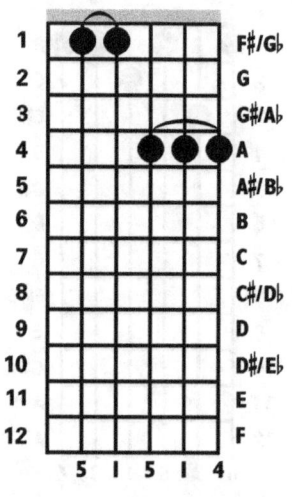
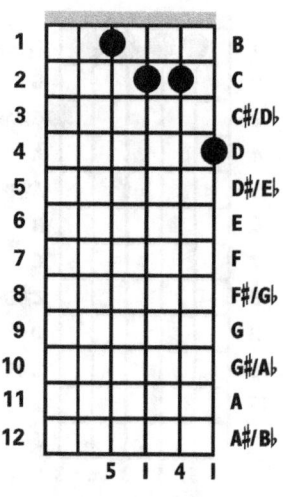
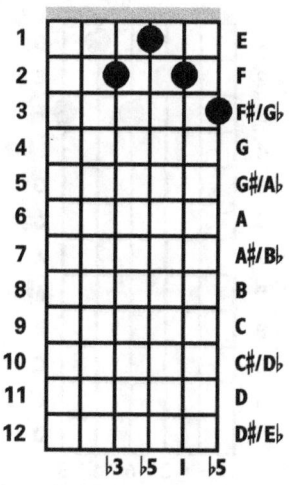
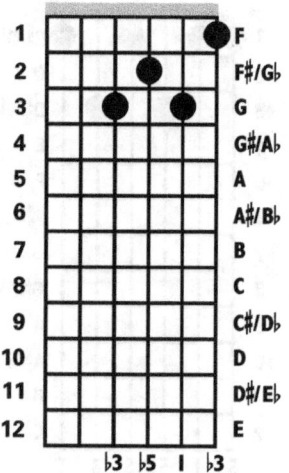
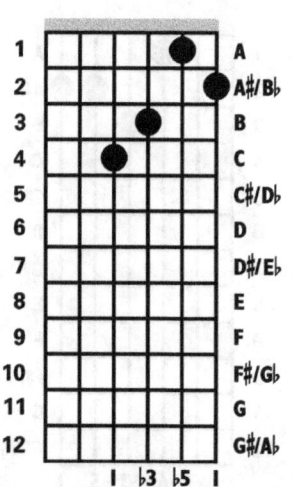
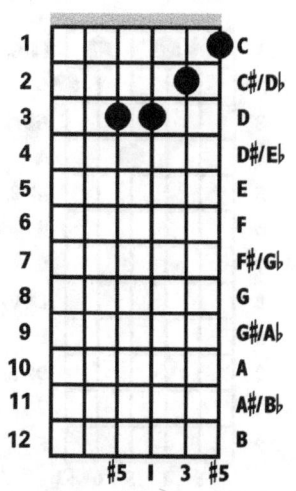
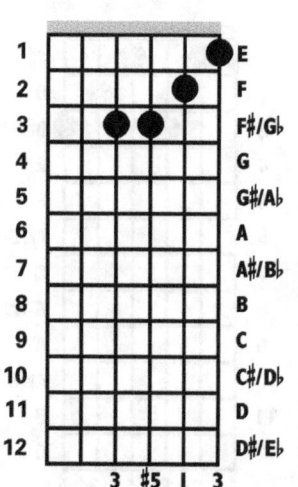
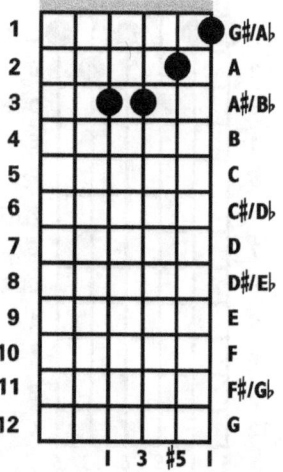

A Selection of Moveable Chord Shapes

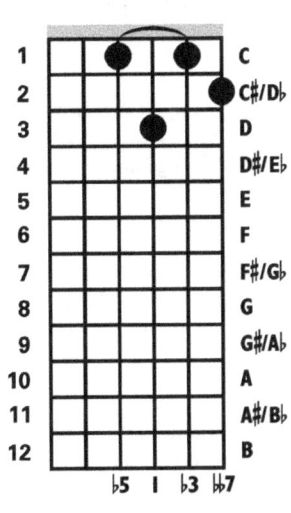
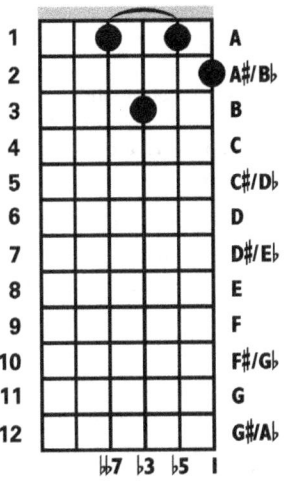
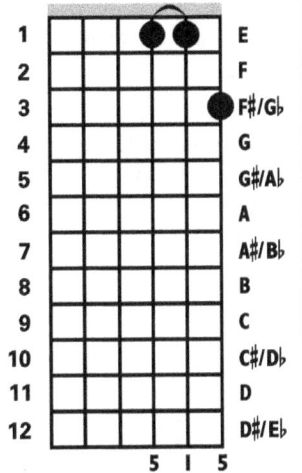
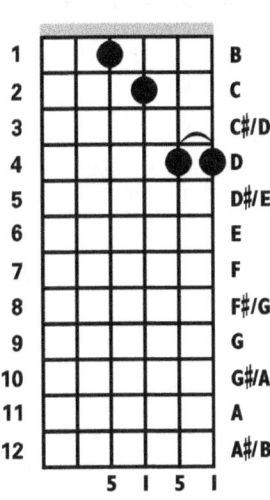
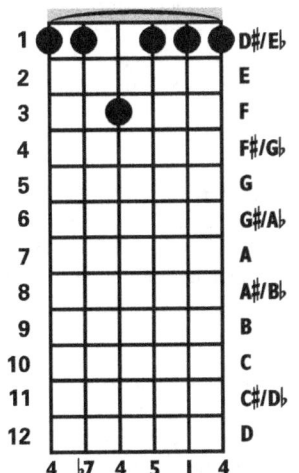
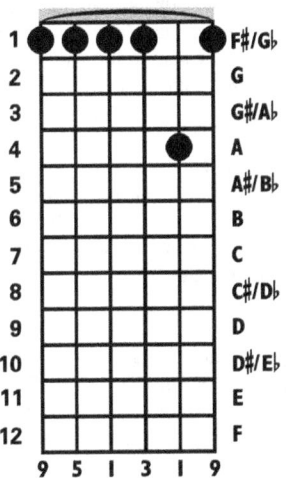
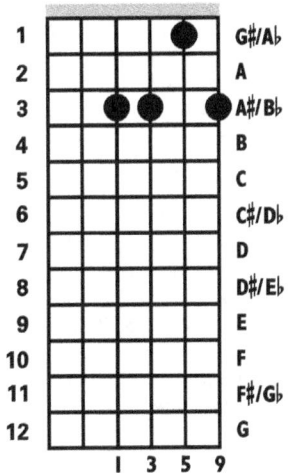
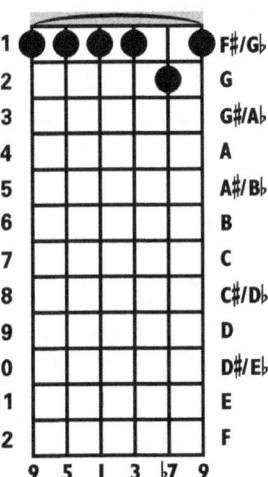
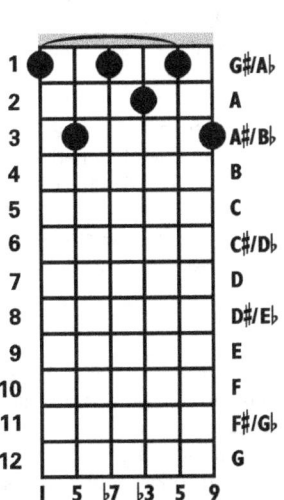
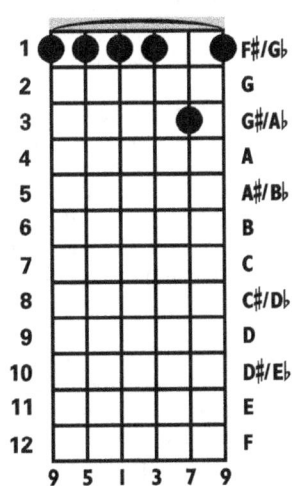
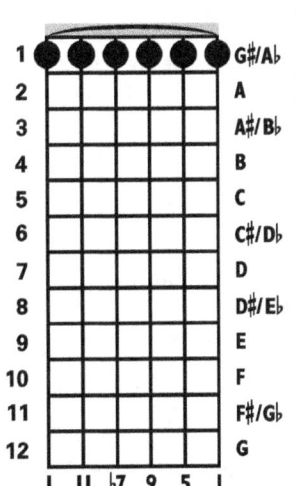
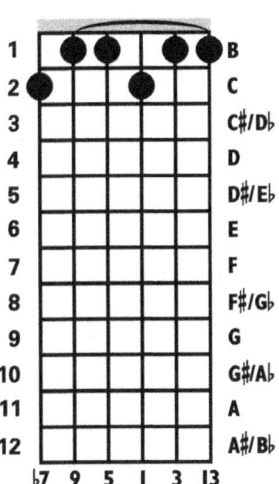

THE LUTE FAMILY FACTFILE

Angélique
The angélique made its first appearance during the baroque era and bears a resemblance to its cousin, the theorbo, with its double peg box and long extended neck. Very much like a harp, it featured diatonic tuning spread over 15 to 17 strings. Normally, the instrument featured 8 to 10 bass strings.

Archlute
The archlute was designed to fall somewhere between the very long necked theorbo family of bass lutes and the shorter Renaissance lute. The tuning configuration, like its Renaissance cousin featured perfect fourths and a third (GCFADG - similar to a guitar capoed on the 3rd fret) on the first 6 courses. The diapasons continued on from the 7th to the 14th course in the following order - FEDCB♭AGF.

Bandora
An instrument dating from around 1560 designed by English luthier John Rose, featuring metal strings and a body shape resembling the orpharion. The stringing arrangement featured 6 or 7 paired unison courses, rather than octaves, again, much like that of the orpharion and was generally included in a musical consort involving the lute, cittern, violin, viola da gamba and flute.

Baroque Lute
While retaining many of the physical characteristics of the Renaissance instrument, the Baroque lute added a more complex neck arrangement to accommodate the additional diapasons. The German design added a swan neck with some of the bass strings still remaining frettable, whilst others were free-strung away from the neck. The French version, on the other hand, retained the traditional right angled pegbox with the addition of an extended *rider* section for the bass strings. The tuning of the Baroque lute is set to a D minor chord (AA dd ff aa d'd' f'f') and featured between 11 and 13 courses of strings.

Chitarrone
A long necked lute with double pegboxes, being virtually identical to the theorbo. Its ancestry, though, can be traced back to the *chitarra italiana*, a lute style instrument with 4 or 5 single or double strings. What makes it recognisable from other long necked instruments was the introduction of three soundhole rosettes, rather than the usual one seen on most lutes. When used within an orchestra context, the chitarrone was used to beat time for the other musicians by the player swinging the neck back and fourth. For tuning conventions see *Theorbo*.

Colascione or Calascione
A seventeenth century Italian lute with a small body and long neck, strung with 3 or 4 bass strings. It was ostensibly used in the *Commedia dell 'Arte* - a form of improvised character-based theatre that was very popular in 16th century Italy.

Liuto Attiorbato
Another of the theorbo-styled lutes, but featuring a different pegbox configuration. In the liuto attiorbato, the first pegbox is totally straight, unlike a typical theorbo or chitarrone. The second or upper pegbox also differs by bending in an unusual way from back to front. Liutos were mainly owned by the upper classes or the wealthy and tended to be built with a high degree of decorative adornment to show off the owner's social and financial status.

Lute Guitar, Lutar, Guitar Lute or Wandervogellaute
A German invention which was designed to look like a lute, with its teardrop-shaped body and additional soundboard mounted frets. It arrived in the mid-nineteenth century and remained popular well into the 1920's. Most were strung like a guitar with the standard 6 strings, whilst variants borrowed the extended theorbo-ised swan neck to include additional plucked bass strings. The repetoire was more likely to feature traditional folk songs than baroque stylings. Today, the instruments are regularly snapped up by interested parties on popular internet auction sites. Normally tuned like a regular guitar (EADGBE) or like a transposed Renaissance lute (EADF#BE).

Mandor
A small tenor instrument of the lute family which utilised 4, 5 or 6 single gut strings tuned in fourths or fifths. A very similar instrument called the Scottish mandora also existed. This had paired strings tuned to d-g-d'-g'-d".

Mandora *or* Gallichon
A bass lute from 18th century Germany and Bohemia. It featured 6-8 double courses of strings set over a long fingerboard, more akin to a guitar, than a lute (it's very likely that the lute guitar owes much of its design to the mandora).

Medieval Lute
Physically, the medieval lute featured a much rounder body than the teardrop-shaped instruments that appeared later on. Although it included the standard single string on the first course (the *chanterelle*) and paired doubles on the remaining courses, octave strings were yet to appear.

Orpharion
A curious instrument with an instantly recognisable wavy body shape, that owed more to a guitar or cittern than a lute. This hybrid featured 6 or 9 double courses of metal strings, rather the usual gut and was tuned like a Renaissance lute. To add to the orpharion's unique architecture, it also features slanted frets and a strange d-shaped neck, where the player would rest palm of his hand. Because of the shared tuning, lute and orpharion music was interchangeable.

Oud *or* Ud
A fretless short-necked lute probably originating in the Middle East. The oud features strongly in Arabic, North African, Greek, Byzantine, Turkish and Jewish music. It's also thought to be related to the guitar. The oud has many different tunings according to the regional music it is be used for.

Renaissance Lute
Where the Renaissance lute differed from its earlier medieval ancestor becomes immediately apparent when you compare the two. The rounded body is transformed into the much more recognisable teardrop shape and the number of string courses increased to as many as 10. The tuning of the first six courses remained basically the same, but with the addition of octavised diapasons (or bass strings) in the lower ranges. Where these differ from the long necked lutes such as the theorbo and chitarrone is that all the strings from the 1st to the 10th courses are frettable, although in most situations the outer courses would be plucked open rather than fretted. The tuning on the lower courses was also alterable, according to the piece of music being played. In this book, the 2 outer courses are tuned to D and F, but this arrangement is flexible.

The Renaissance lute also came in a variety of sizes and pitches to accommodate the vocal range of different singers. Each lute had a note designation (i.e. the *g* lute as seen in this book) to distinguish it from other sizes and pitches of instruments. The most popular being the tenor (f, g *or* a), the treble (c *or* d) and the bass (C *or* D). The repetoire of the Renaissance lute is extensive, with most of the leading works of the day still available to modern lutenists.

Theorbo
Probably the best known of the long necked lutes, the theorbo was developed at the end of the 16th century to be used in an opera context. With its additional diapasons in the lower courses, the dynamic range increased to accomodate the more complex music. The origin of the actual name is open to conjecture with Slavic and Turkish roots providing

possible insights into the meaning - *torba* meaning bag or turban. Alternatively, a Neopolitan influence might be equally valid - *tioba* (a board for grinding up herbs and essences). Neither of these sources seem to make a lot of sense within a musical setting, though.

Torban

A Ukranian theorbo-shaped instrument with additional short treble strings or *prystrunky*, strung onto the right hand side of its body. It originated in the 1700's and owes much of it's design characteristics to the angélique. The torban was also to be found in Poland and Russia at around this time. The playing style featured fingering on the fingerboard and plucking of the remaining open strings, a little like a harp-lute hybrid.

Vihuela

Tuning-wise, the vihuela was identical to the Renaissance lute (G-C-F-A-D-G), but where it differed greatly was in the design of the body and headstock. On first glance it looks very similar to a guitar, with the waisted body and flat pegbox, rather than the archetypal right angle we see on most Renaissance lutes. The strings were paired rather than octavised. The guitar-shaped design probably owes more to a wish by the indigenous Spanish to escape from the Moorish influence of the oud, than anything else. The vihuela first came into prominence in the 15th and 16th centuries and spread to near neighbours Portugal and Italy.

LUTE TUNINGS

The following list of lute tunings includes a selection of some popular standards as well as some personal favourites. Some players stick with the same two or three tunings all their lives, but others enjoy experimenting with new set-ups, but whichever you decide to do, have fun with this versatile family of instruments!

Angélique
Standard tuning	CDEFGABCDEFGABCDE
Partial diatonic tuning	ABCDEFGABCDFADF

Archlute
Standard Tuning	GCFADGFEDCB♭AGF

Bandora
Standard Tuning	GCDGCEA

Baroque Lute
10-Course (D Minor Tuning)	DEFGADFADF
11-Course (D Minor Tuning)	CDEFGADFADF
12-Course (D Minor Tuning)	BCDEFGADFADF
13-Course (D Minor Tuning)	ABCDEFGADFADF

Liuto Attiorbato
Standard tuning 1	FGABCDE
Standard tuning 2	FGCFADG

Lute Guitar
Standard Guitar Tuning	EADGBE
Transposed Renaissance Lute Tuning	EADF♯BE

Mandor & Scottish Mandora
4-Course Tuning 1	CGCG
4-Course Tuning 2	GDGD
5-Course Tuning 1	CGCGC
5-Course Tuning 2	CFCFC
Scottish Mandora	DGDGD

Mandora or Gallichon
Standard (bass) tuning 1	FGCFAD
Standard (bass) tuning 2	GADGBE

Medieval Lute
4-Course (G Tuning)	GADG
5-Course (G Tuning)	DGADG

Orpharion
The same as Renaissance lute

Oud or Ud
Arabic - Egyptian (5-course)	FADGC
Arabic - Iraqi	CDGCFF
Arabic - Syrian	CFADGC
Turkish	EABEAD

Renaissance Lute
6-Course (G Tuning)	ADGADG
6-Course (Dalza Scodatura)	GCGBEA
6-Course (Dalza Scordatura)	GDGBEA
7-Course Octave (D Tuning)	CDGCEAD
7-Course Octave (C Tuning)	A♯CFA♯DGC
7-Course Descant (B Tuning)	F♯BEAC♯F♯B
7-Course Descant (A Tuning)	GADGBEA
7-Course Alto (G Tuning)	FGCFADG
7-Course Alto (G Tuning)	DGCFADG
7-Course Alto (F Tuning)	D♯FA♯D♯GCF
7-Course Alto (F Tuning)	CFA♯D♯GCF
7-Course Tenor (E Tuning)	DEADF♯BE
7-Course Bass (D Tuning)	CDGCEAD
7-Course Bass (C Tuning)	A♯CFA♯DGC
7-Course Bass (G Tuning)	FGCFADG
8-Course Octave (D Tuning)	A♯CDGCEAD
8-Course Octave (C Tuning)	G♯A♯CFA♯DGC
8-Course Descant (B Tuning)	EF♯BEAC♯F♯B
8-Course Descant (A Tuning)	FGADGBEA
8-Course Alto (G Tuning)	DFGCFADG
8-Course Alto (G Tuning)	DD♯FGCFADG
8-Course Alto (G Tuning)	CD♯FGCFADG
8-Course Alto (F Tuning)	CC♯D♯FA♯D♯GCF
8-Course Alto (F Tuning)	A♯C♯D♯FA♯D♯GCF
8-Course Tenor (E Tuning)	CDEADF♯BE
8-Course Bass (D Tuning)	A♯CDGCEAD
8-Course Bass (C Tuning)	G♯A♯CFA♯DGC
8-Course Bass (G Tuning)	D♯FGCFADG
9-Course Alto (G Tuning)	DD♯FGCFADG
9-Course Alto (G Tuning)	CD♯FGCFADG
10-Course Alto (G Tuning)	CDE♭FGCFADG
10-Course Alto (G Tuning)	CDEFGCFADG
11-Course Alto (G Tuning)	BCDE♭FGCADG

Theorbo or Chitarrone
14-Course (A Tuning)	GABCDEFGADGBEA
15-Course (A Tuning)	FGABCDEFGADGBEA
19-Course (A Tuning)	BCDEFGABCDEFGAD GBEA
French or Lesser Theorbo	CDEFGABCDGCEAD

Vihuela
Standard	GCFADG

PITCH FOR TUNING THE LUTE
This varies according to the type of instrument, the piece of music being played and the pitch of other instruments within an ensemble situation. So-called standard pitch is A = 440Hz, but lutenists tune to a variety of pitches from 392-470 Hz. Most electronic keyboards and tuners use 440 Hz as standard.

NOTES

NOTES

NOTES

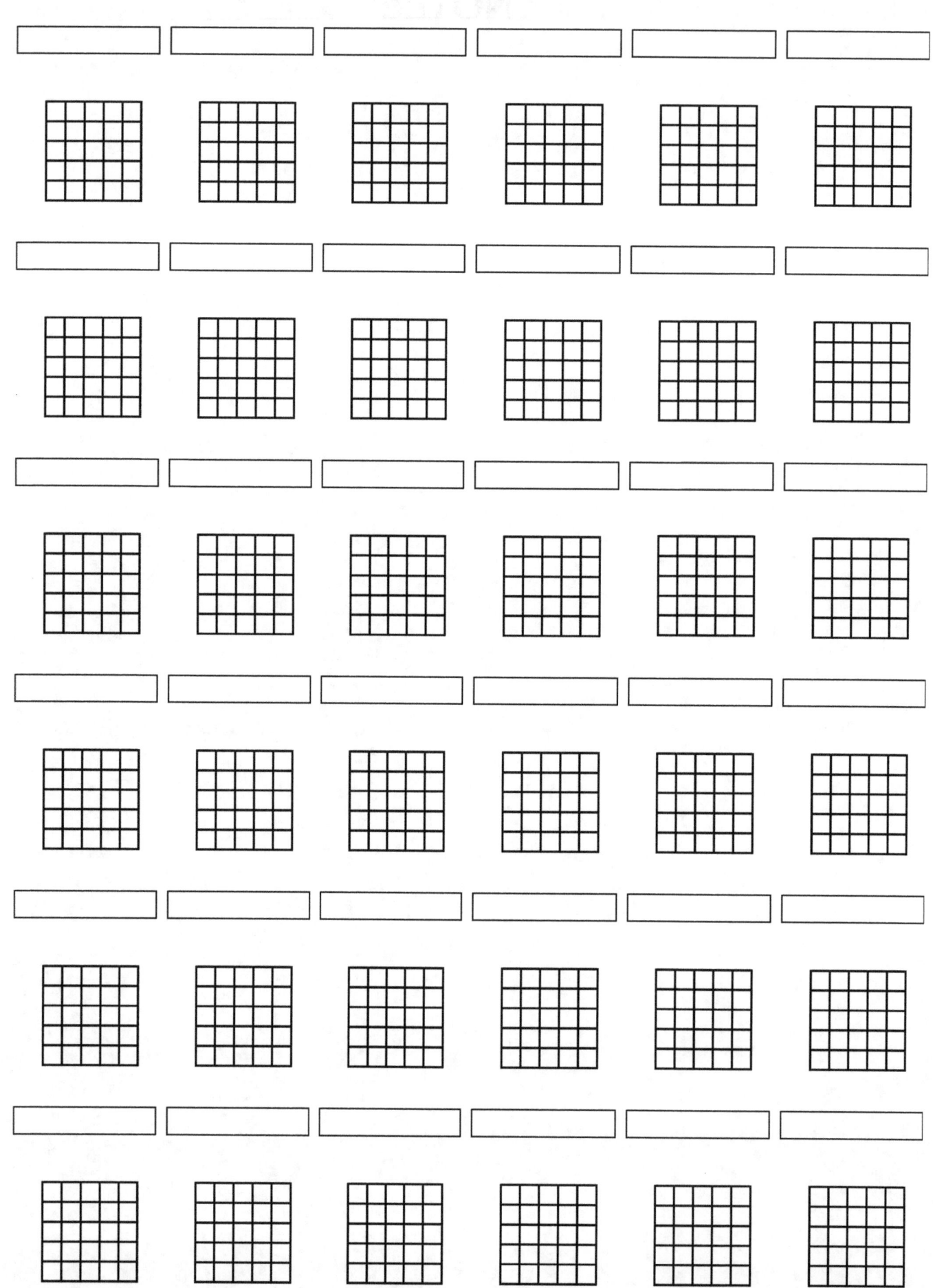

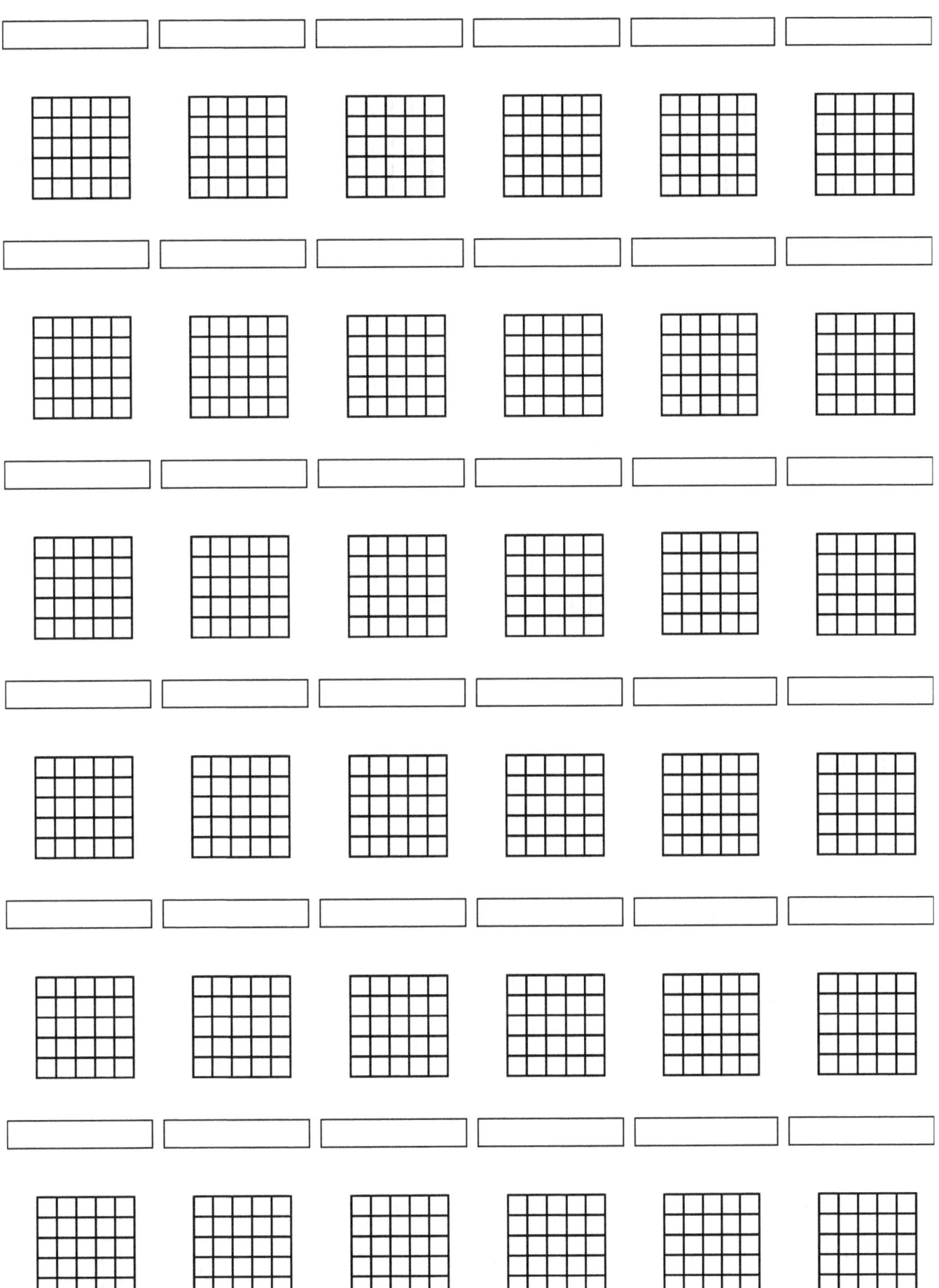

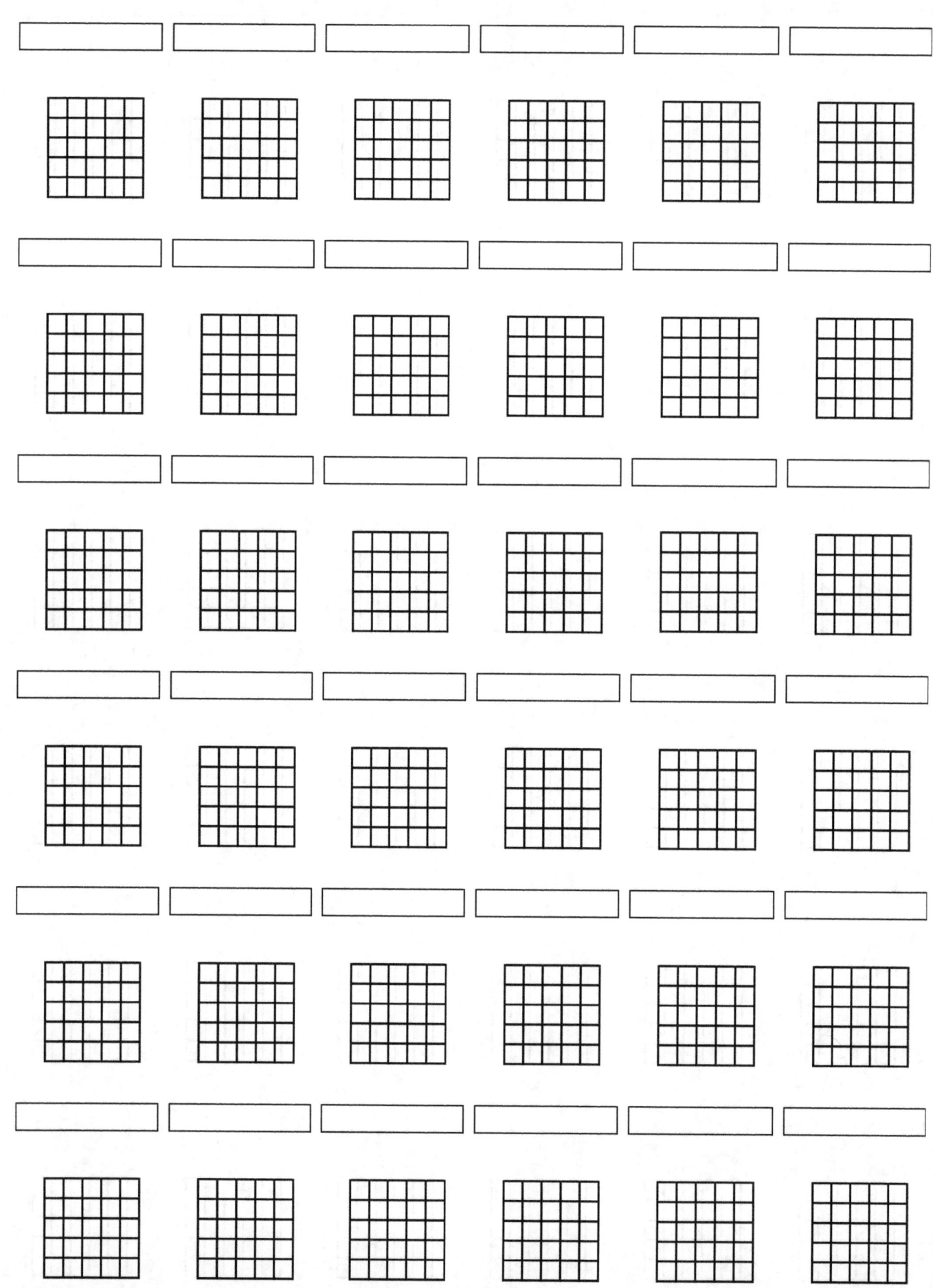

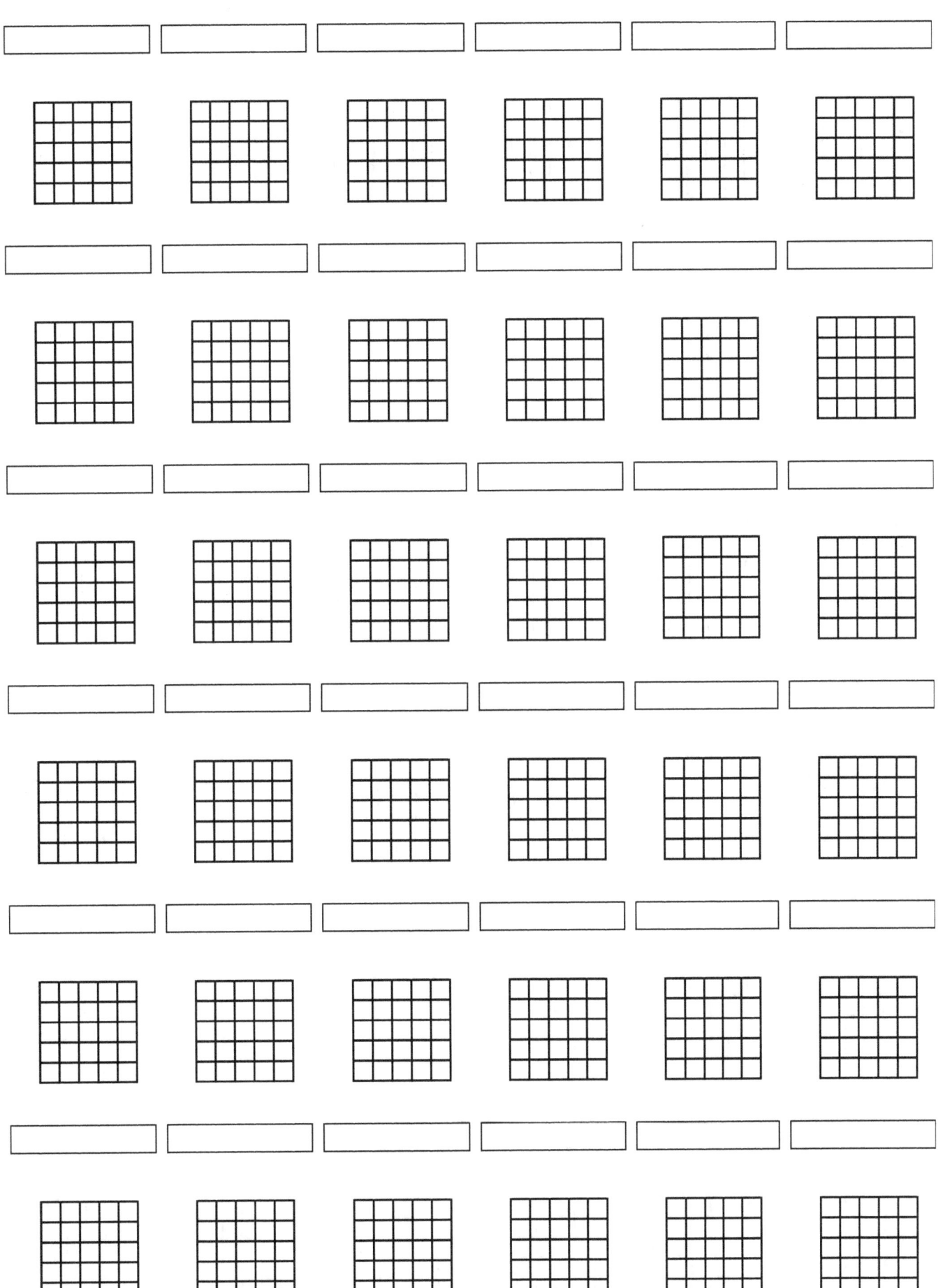

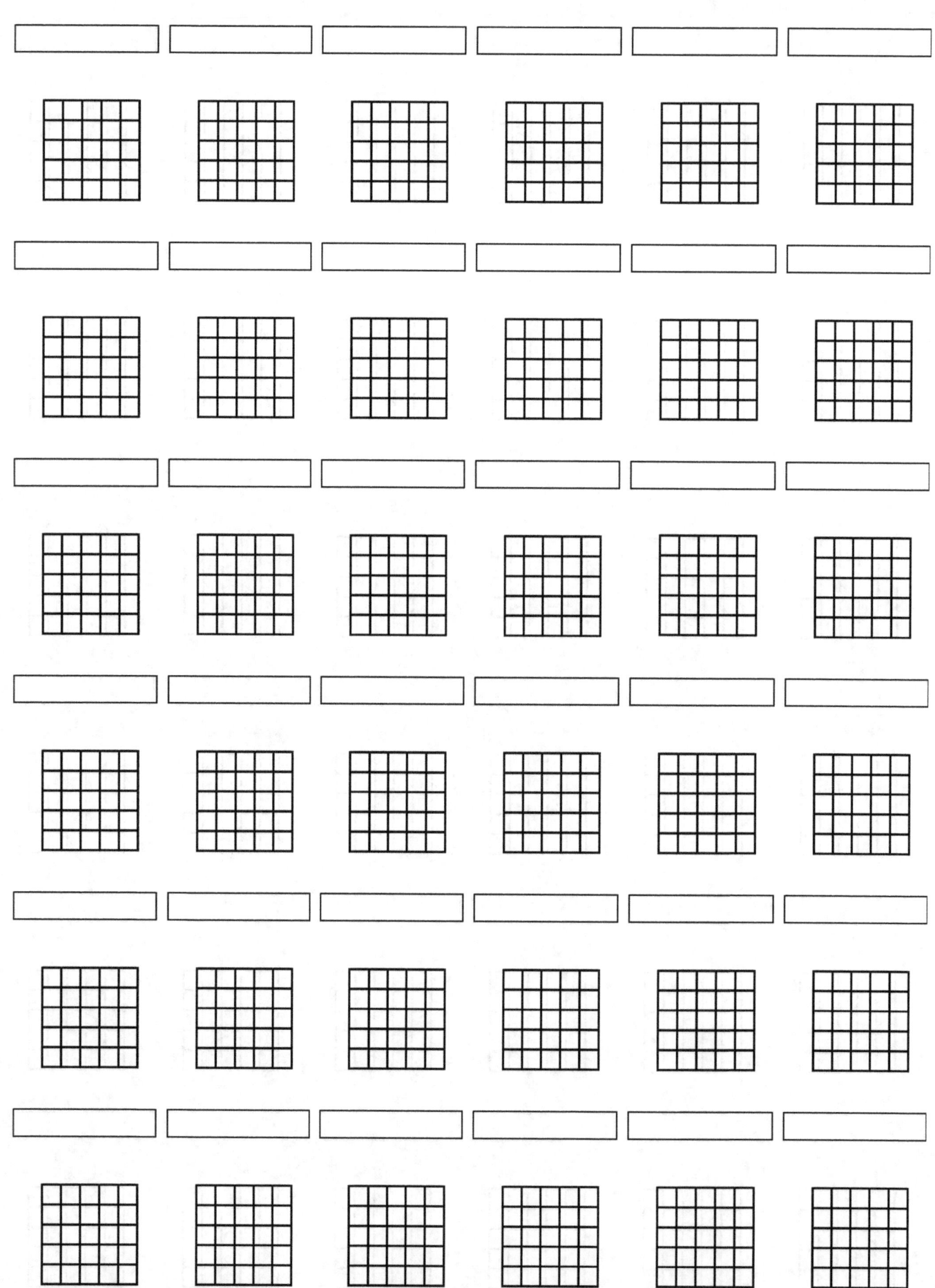

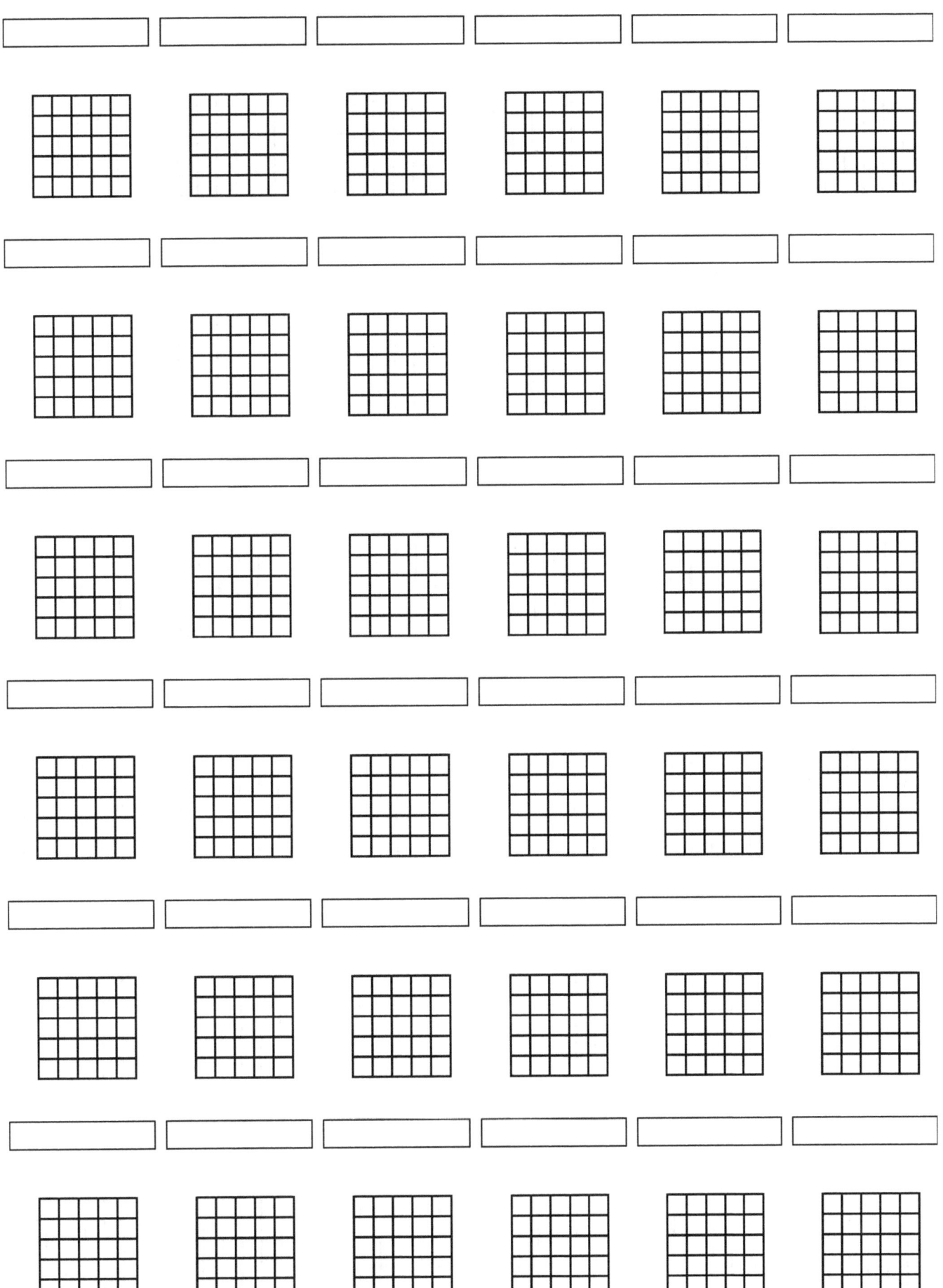

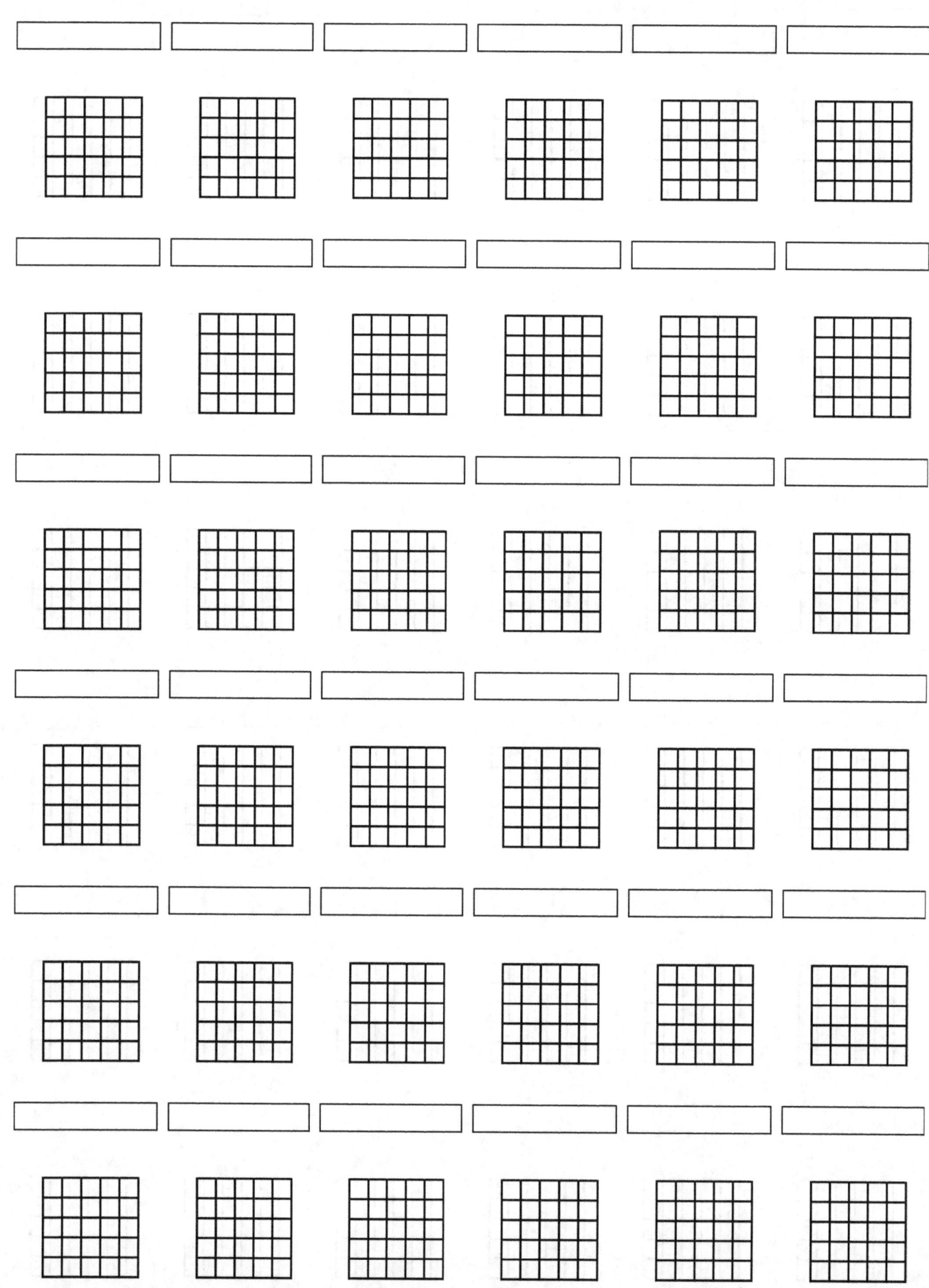

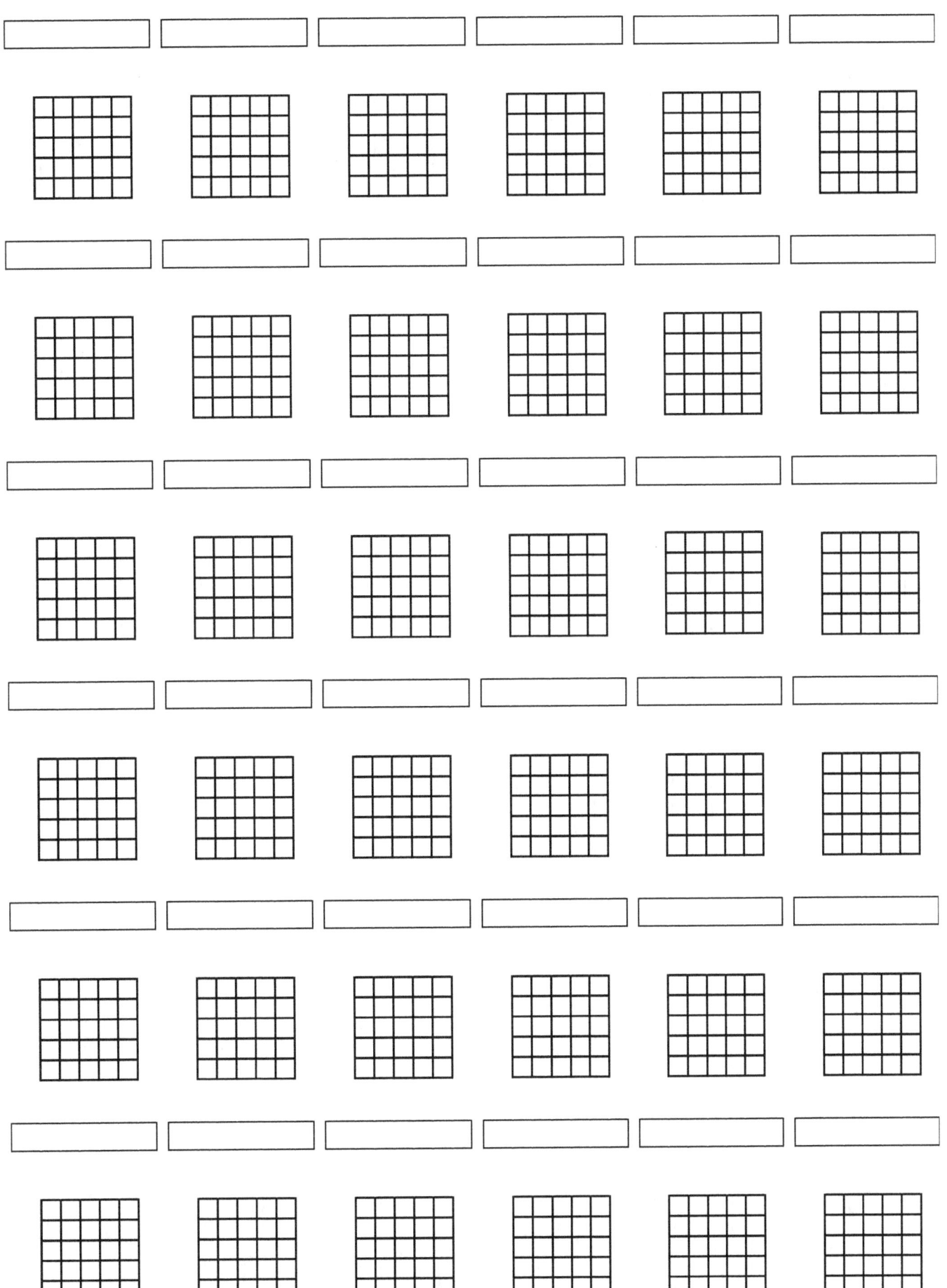

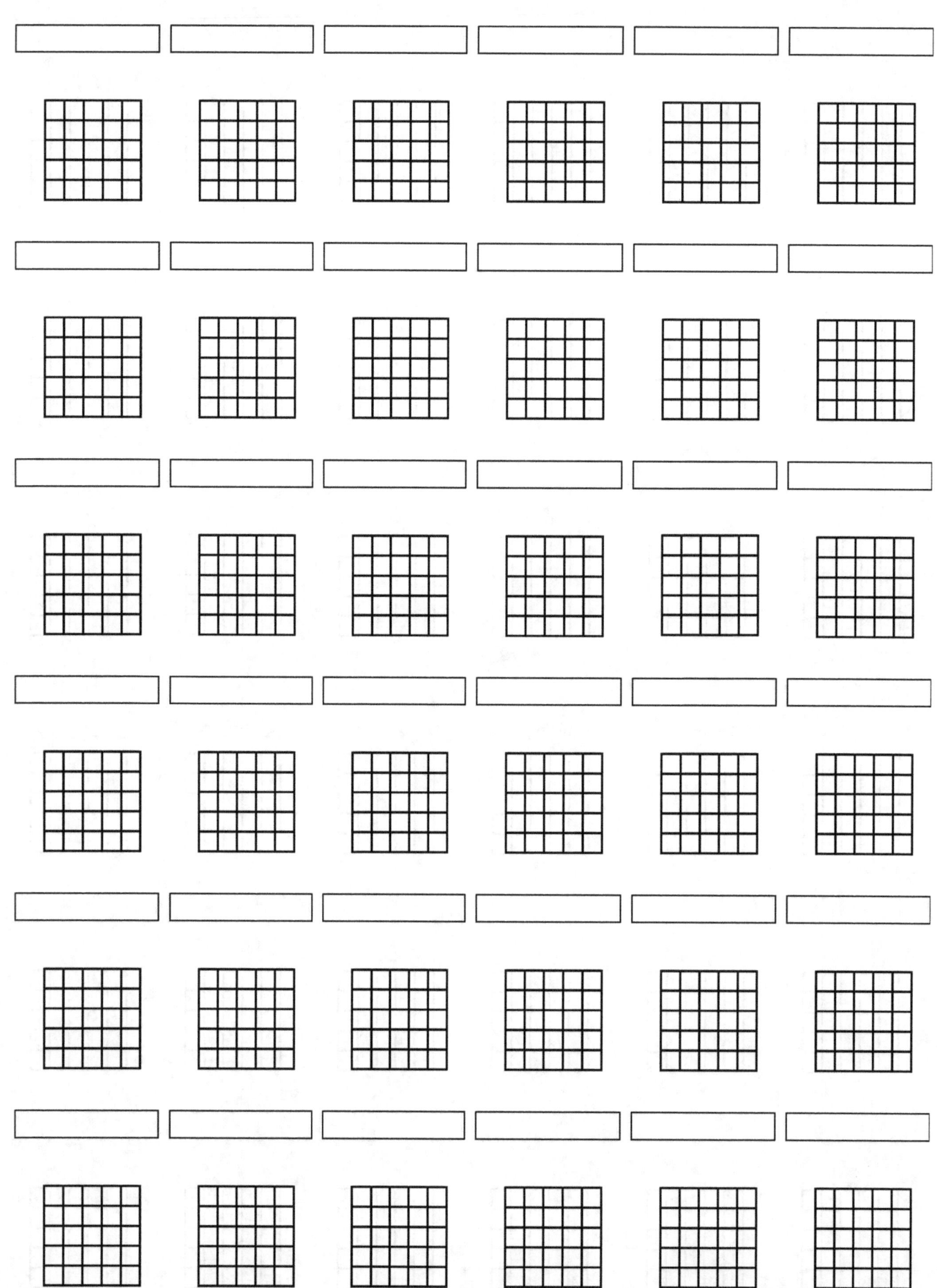

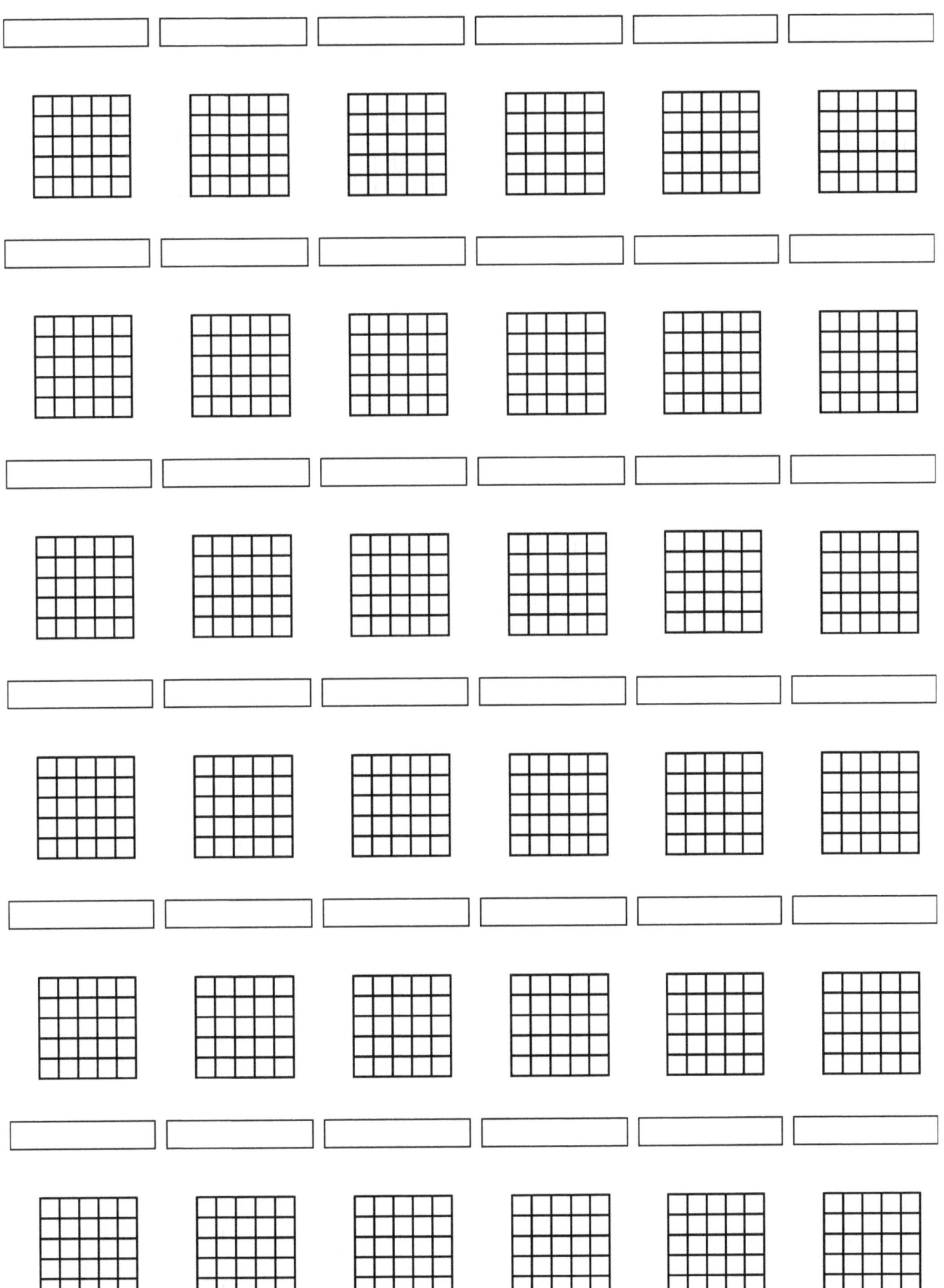

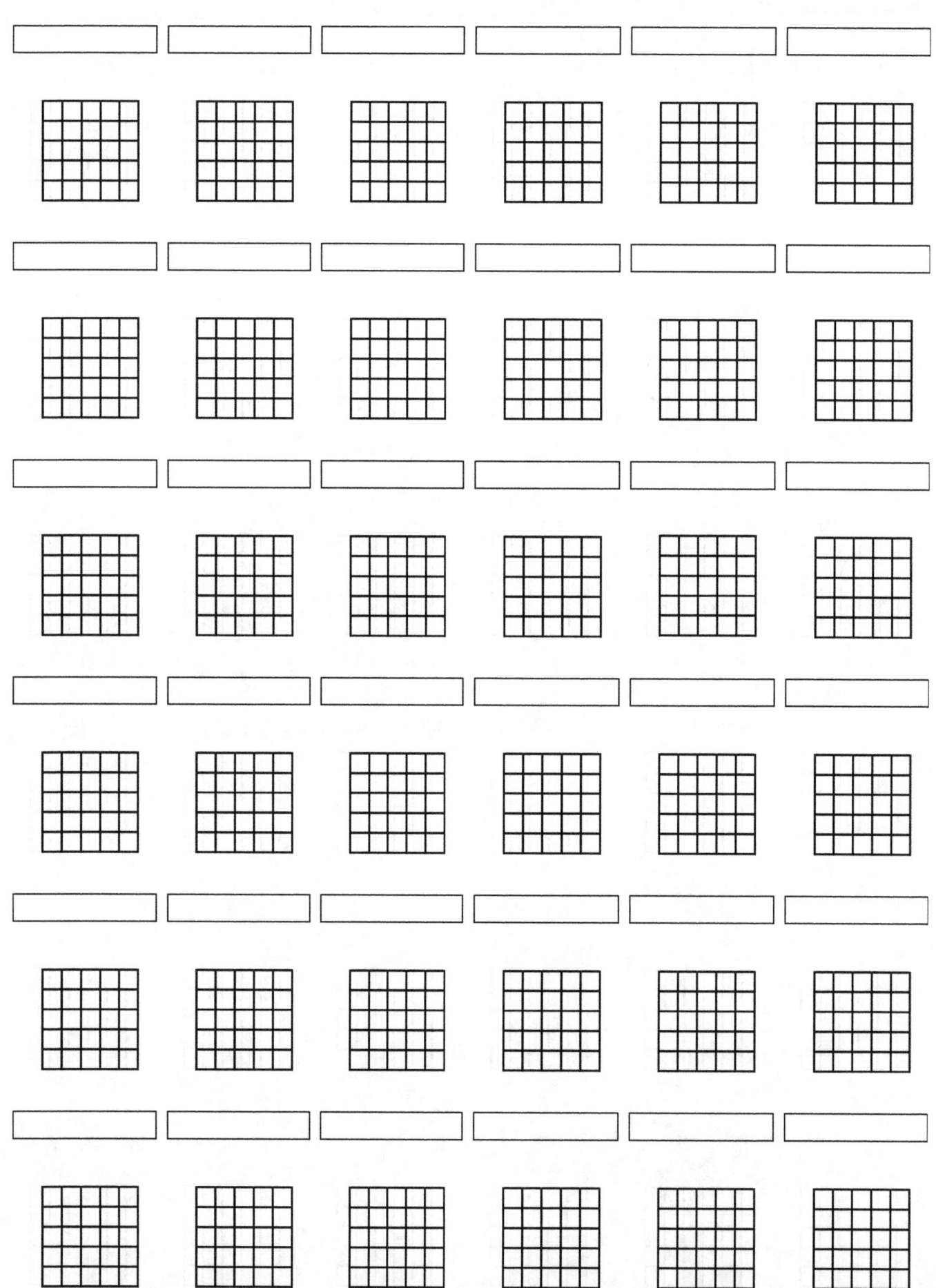

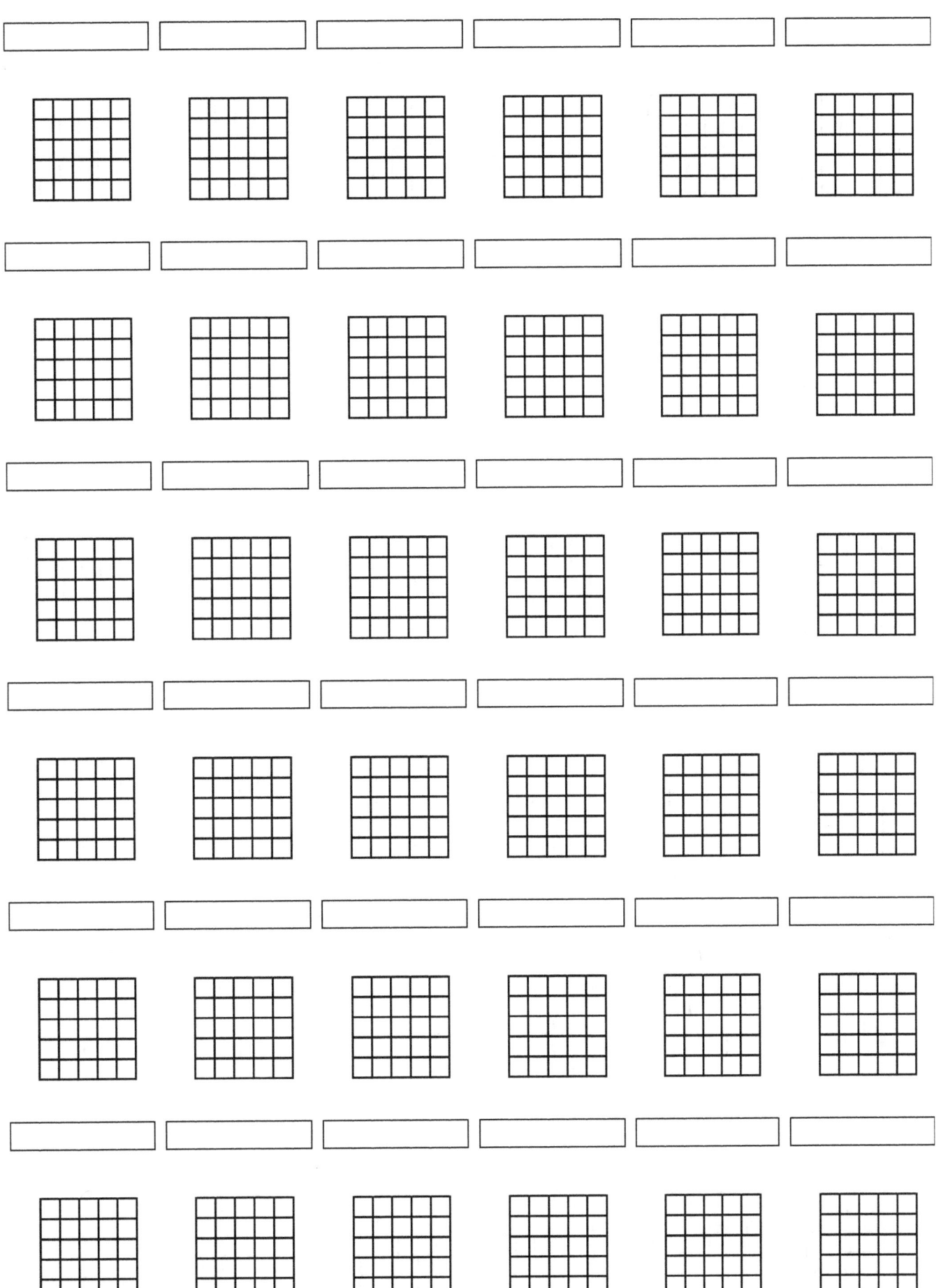

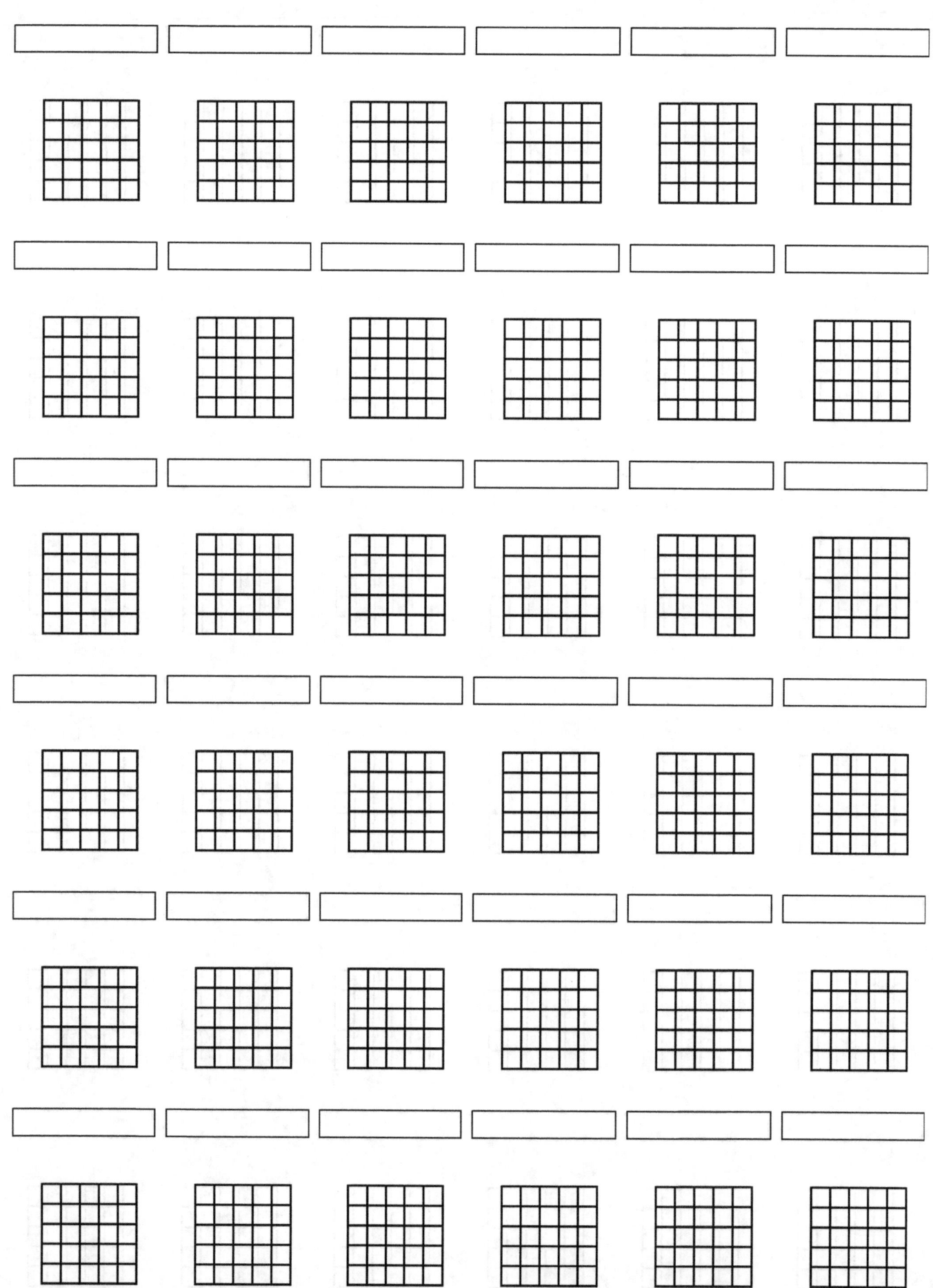

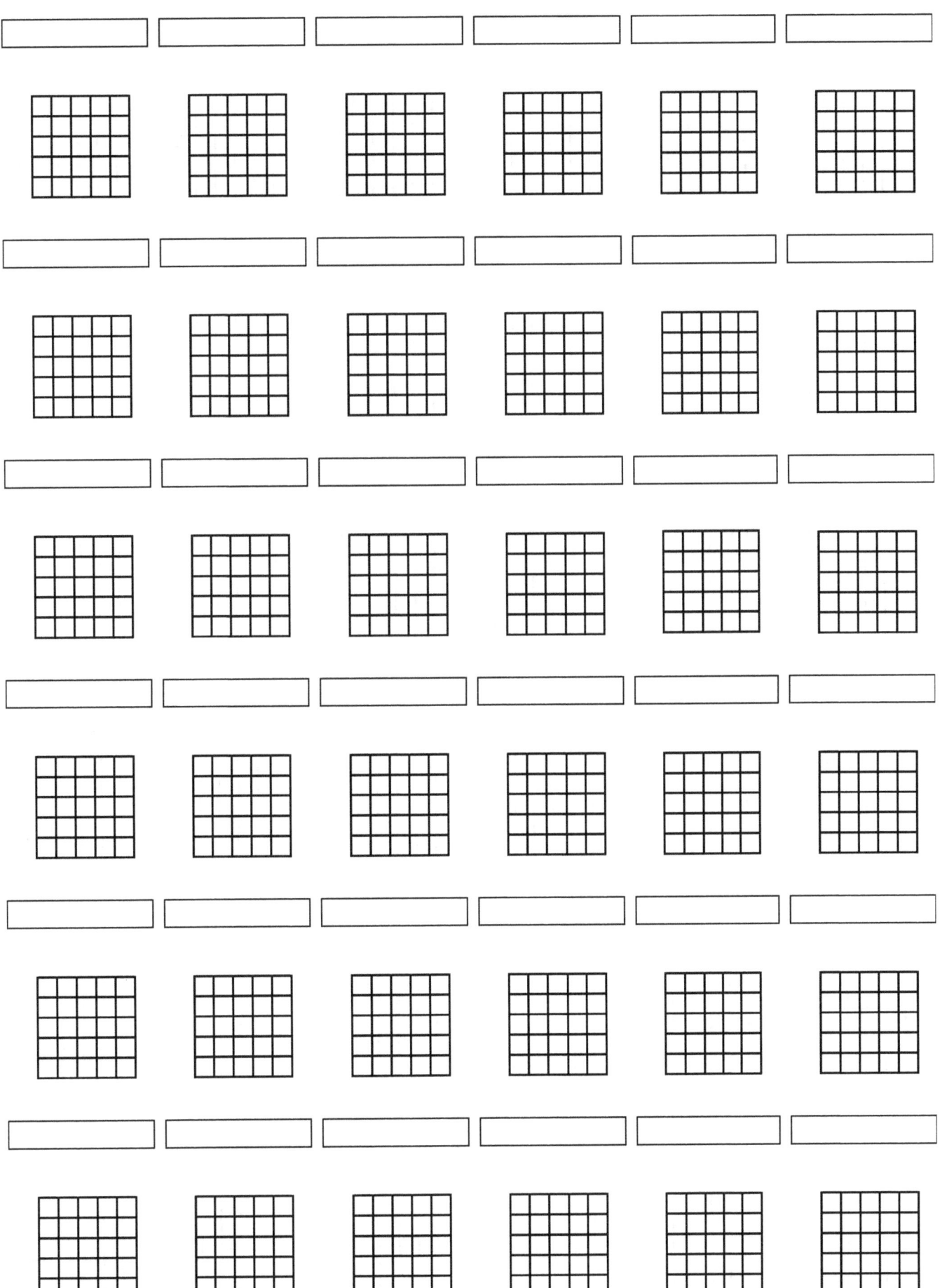

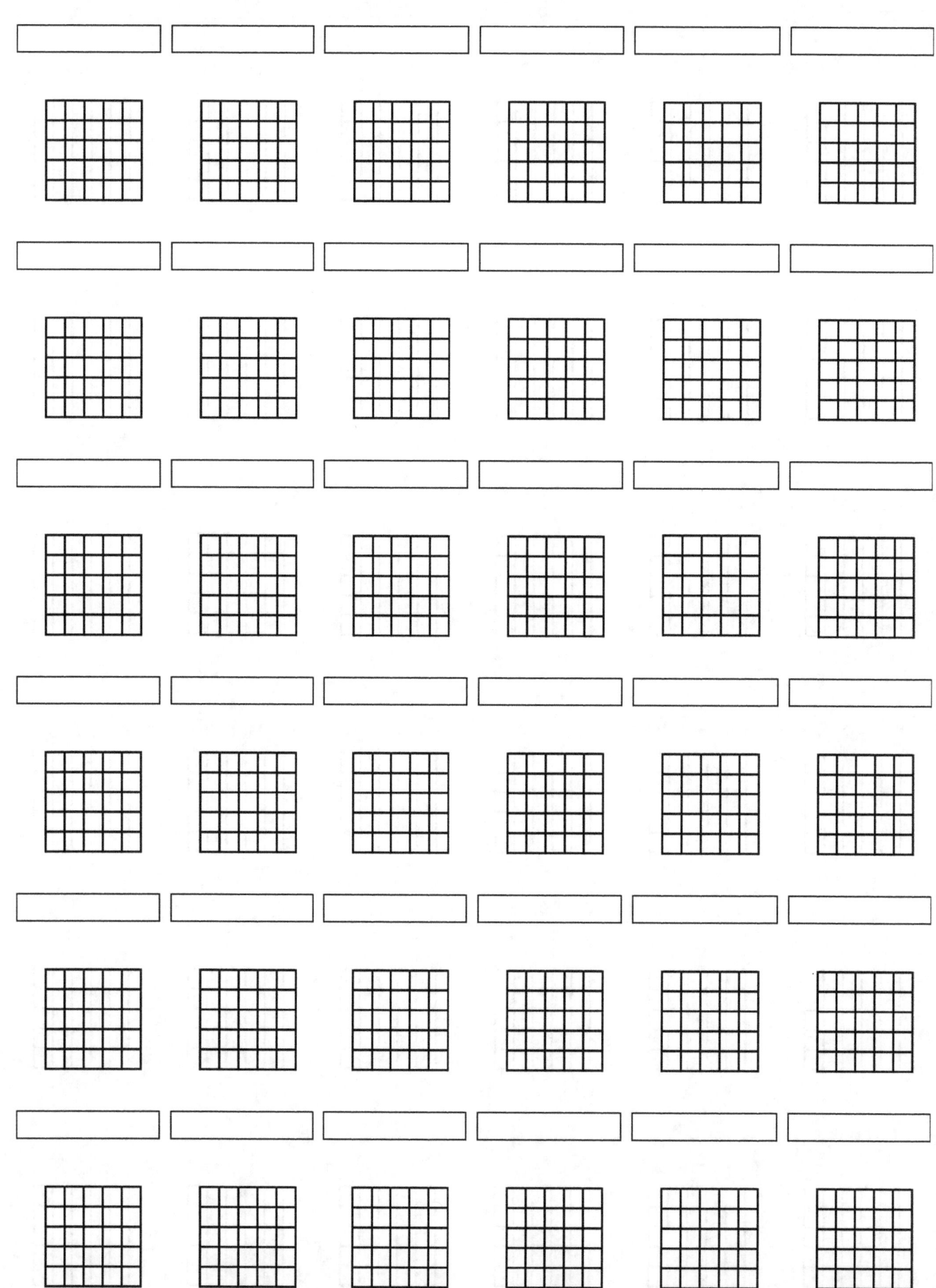

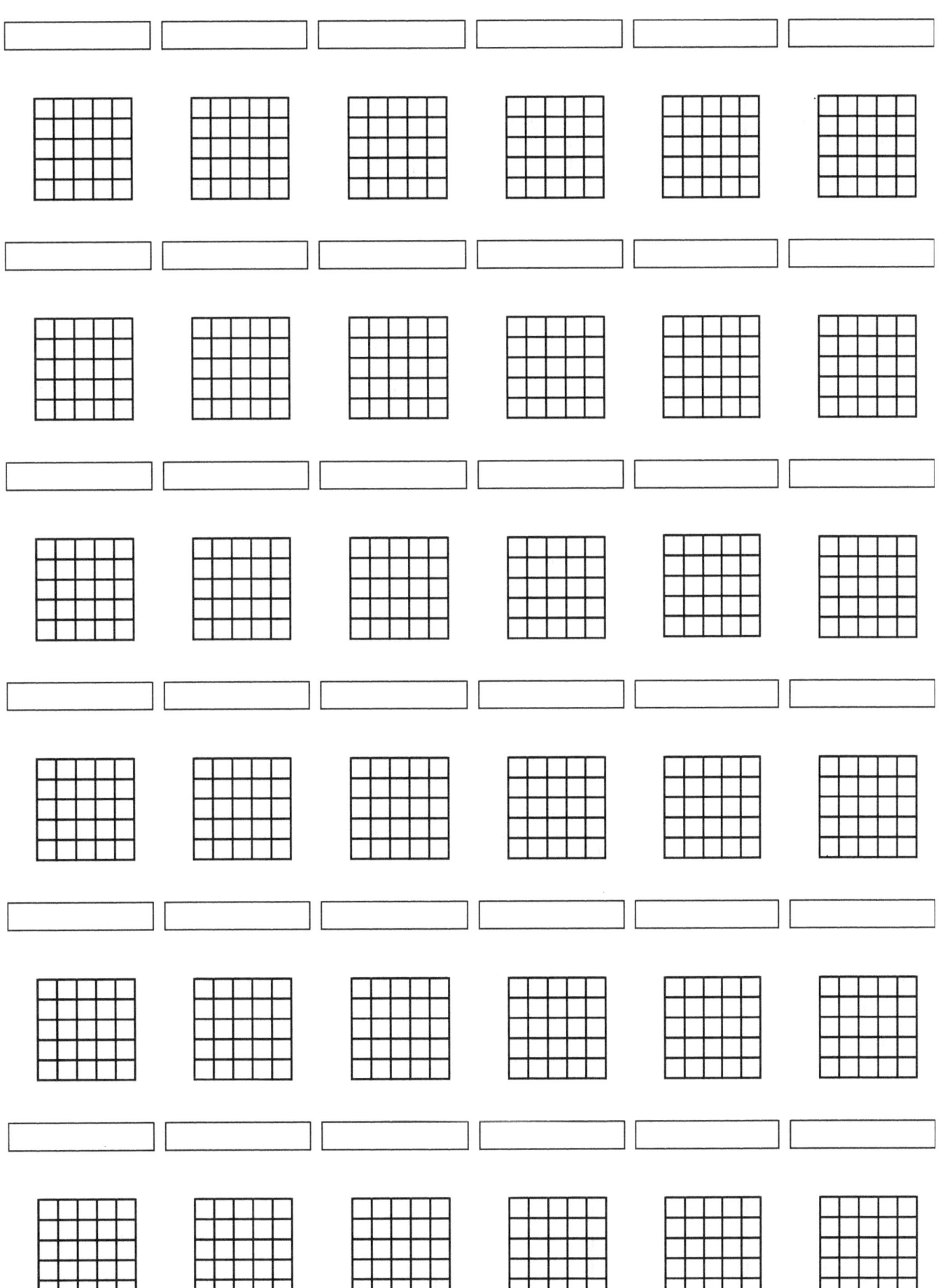

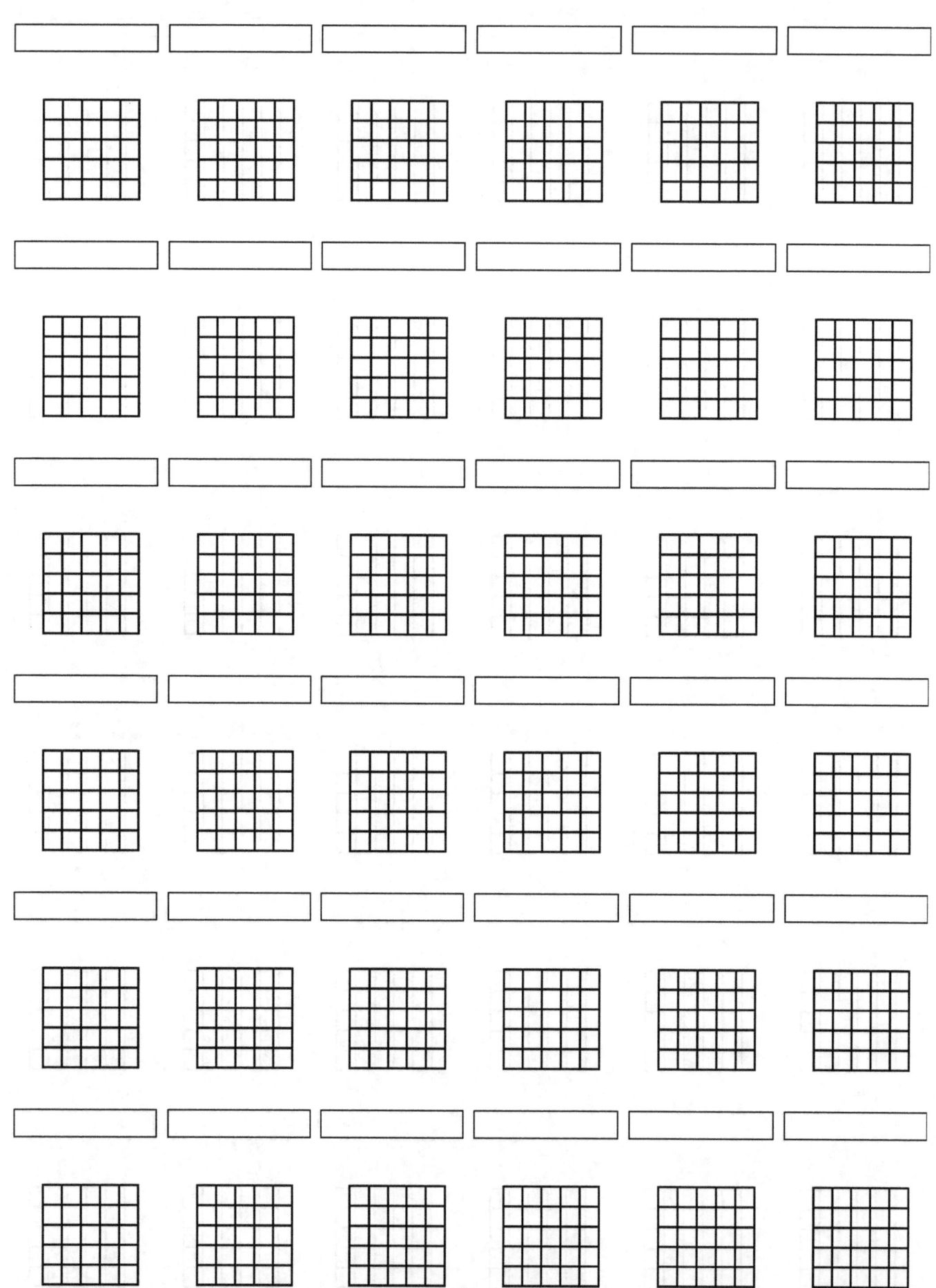

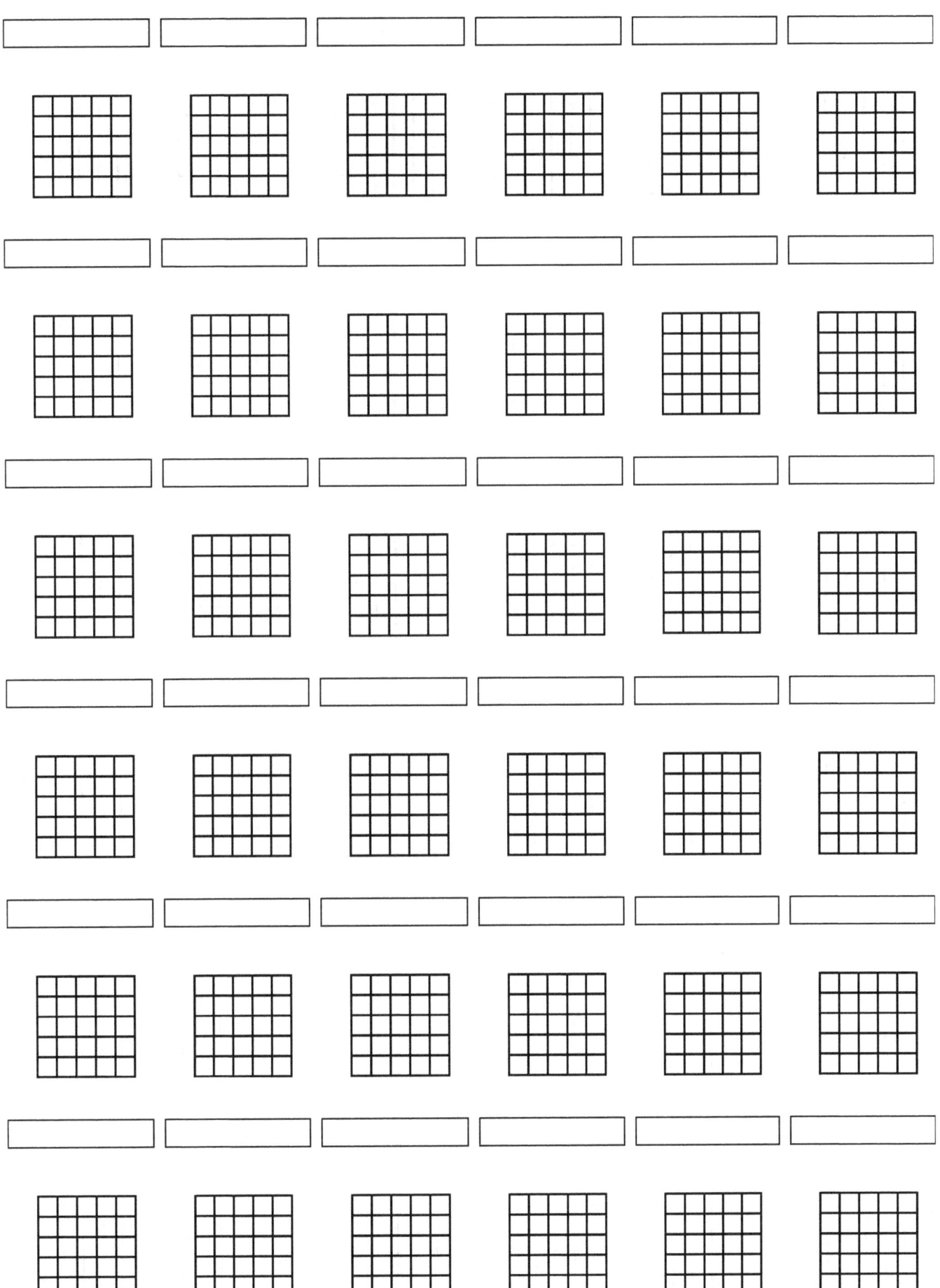

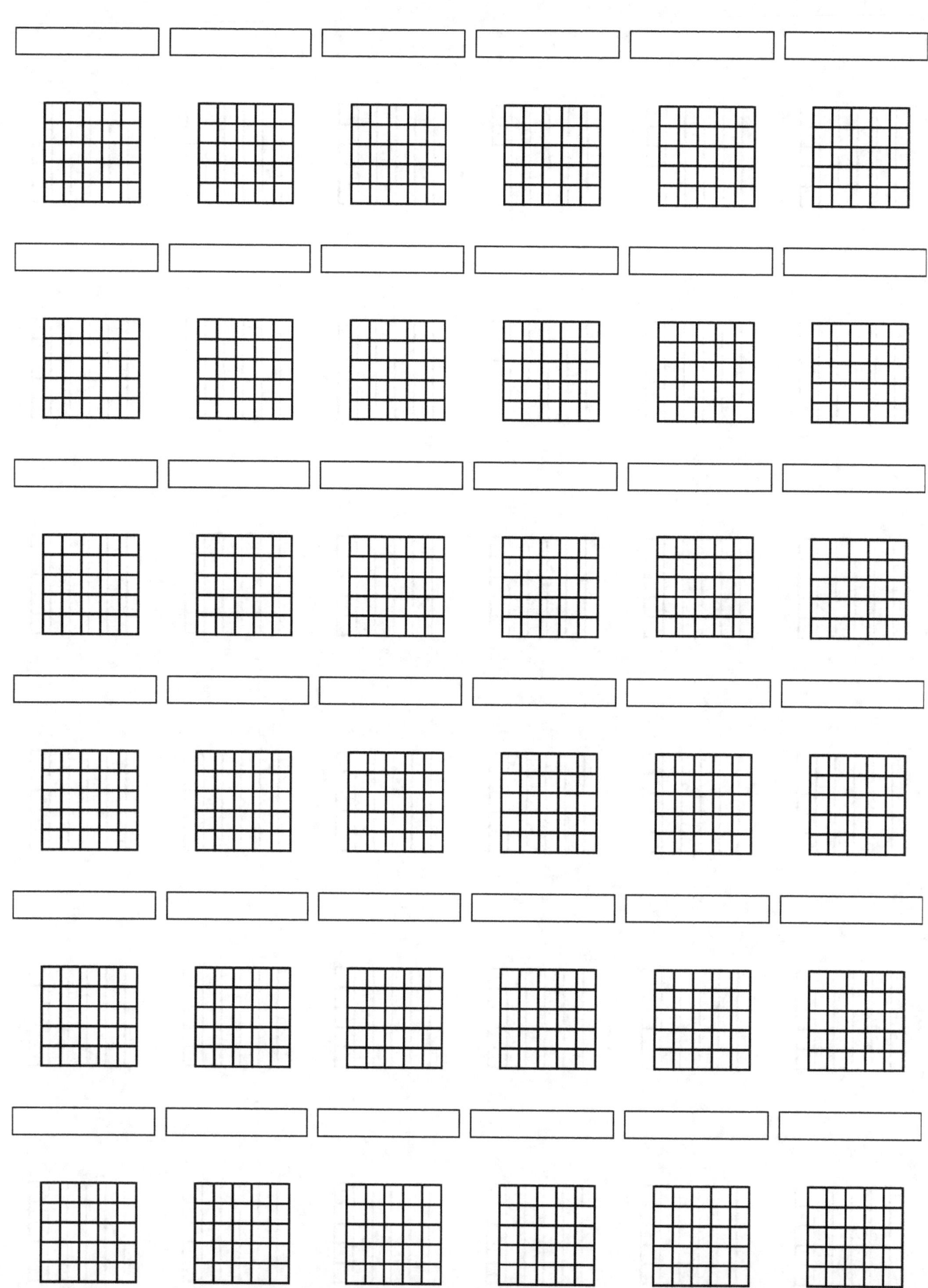

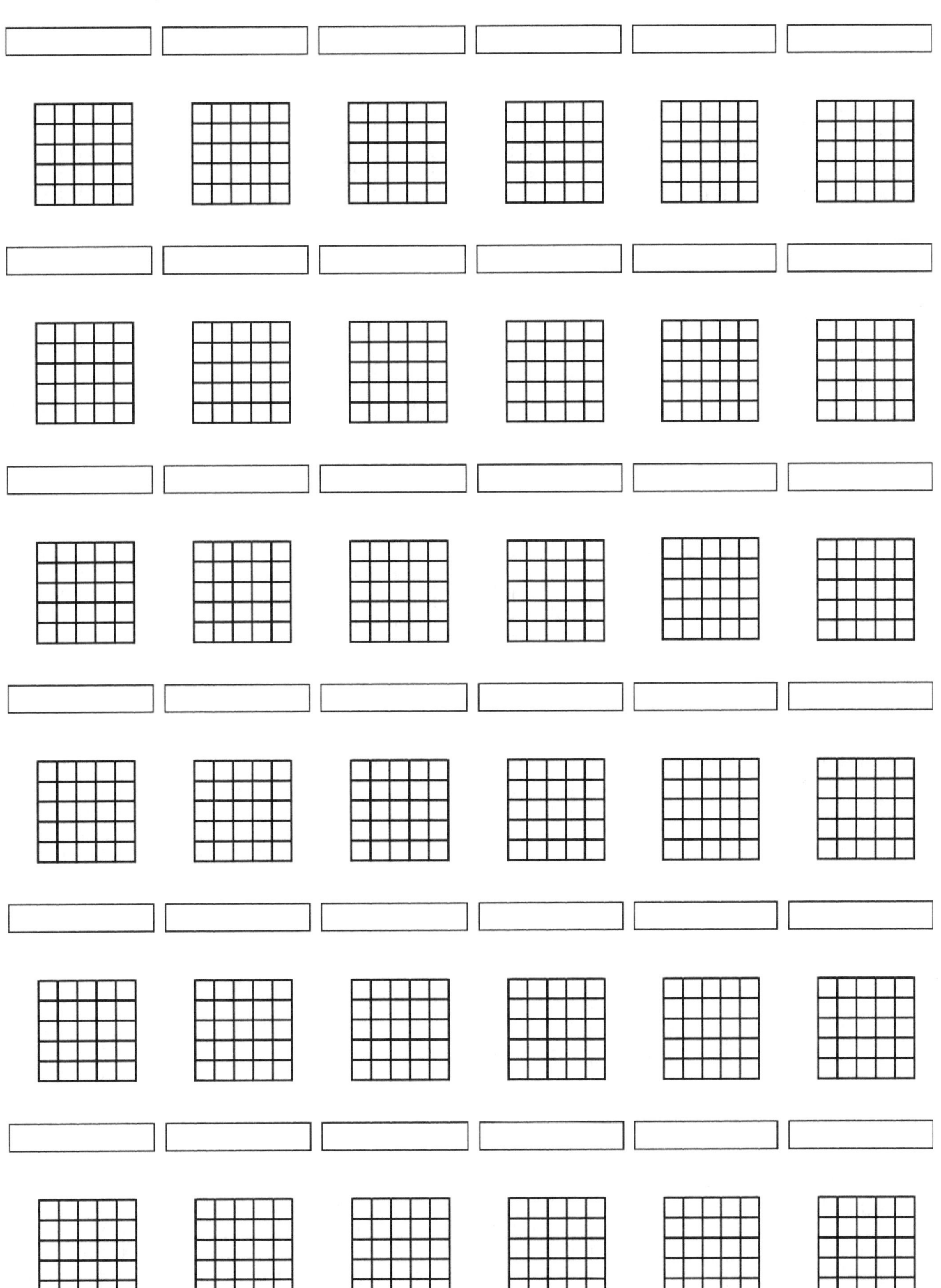

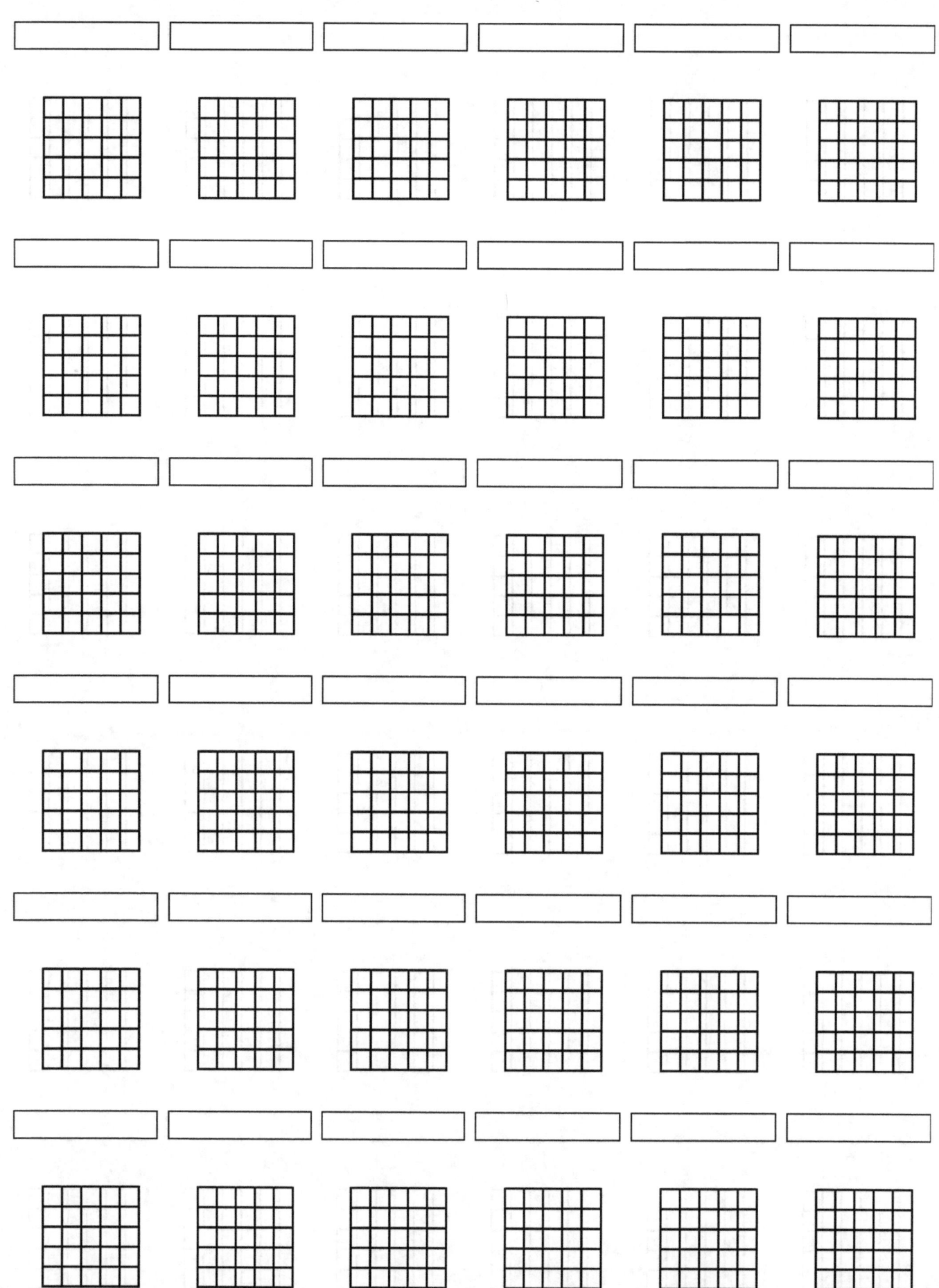

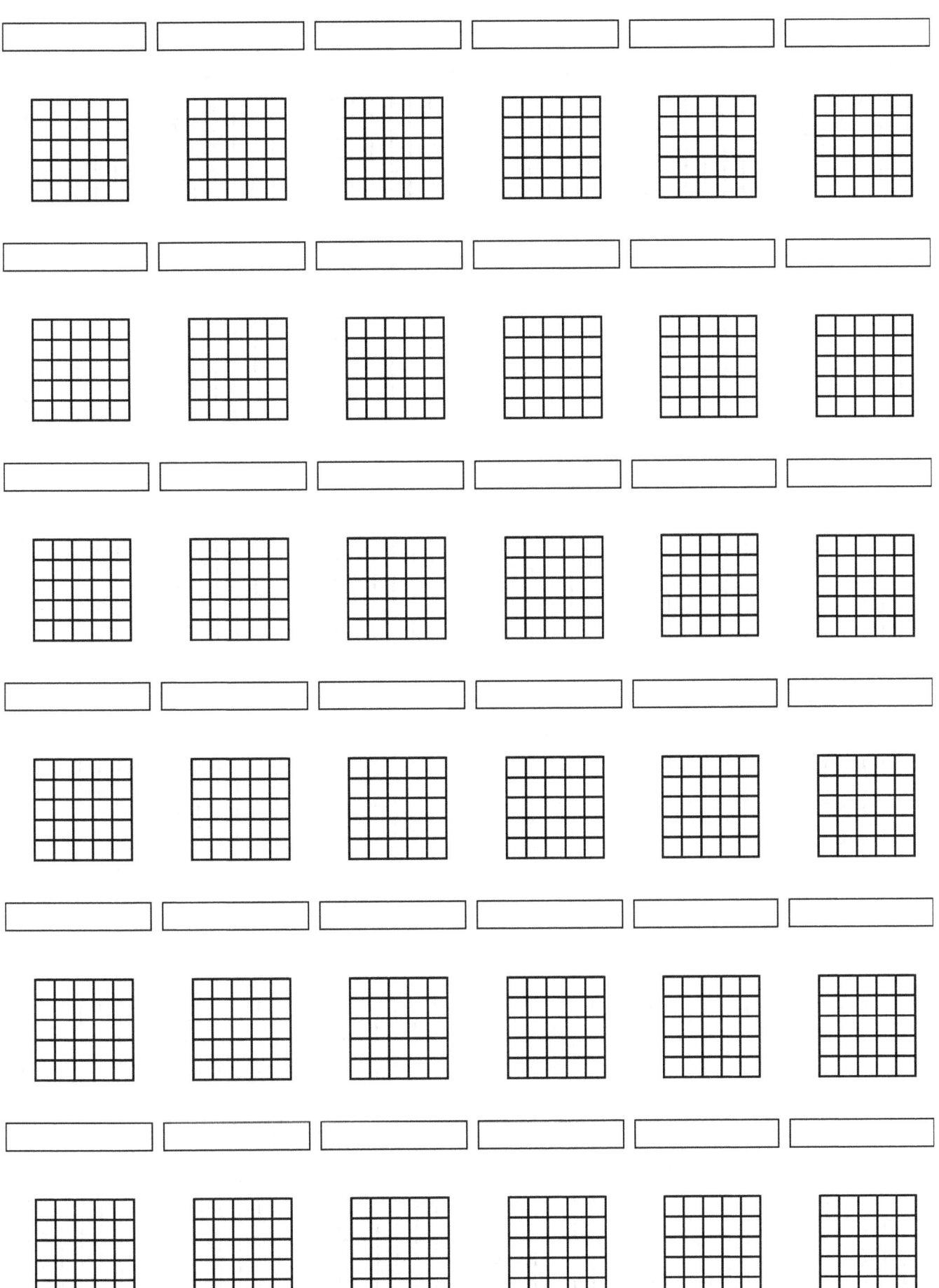

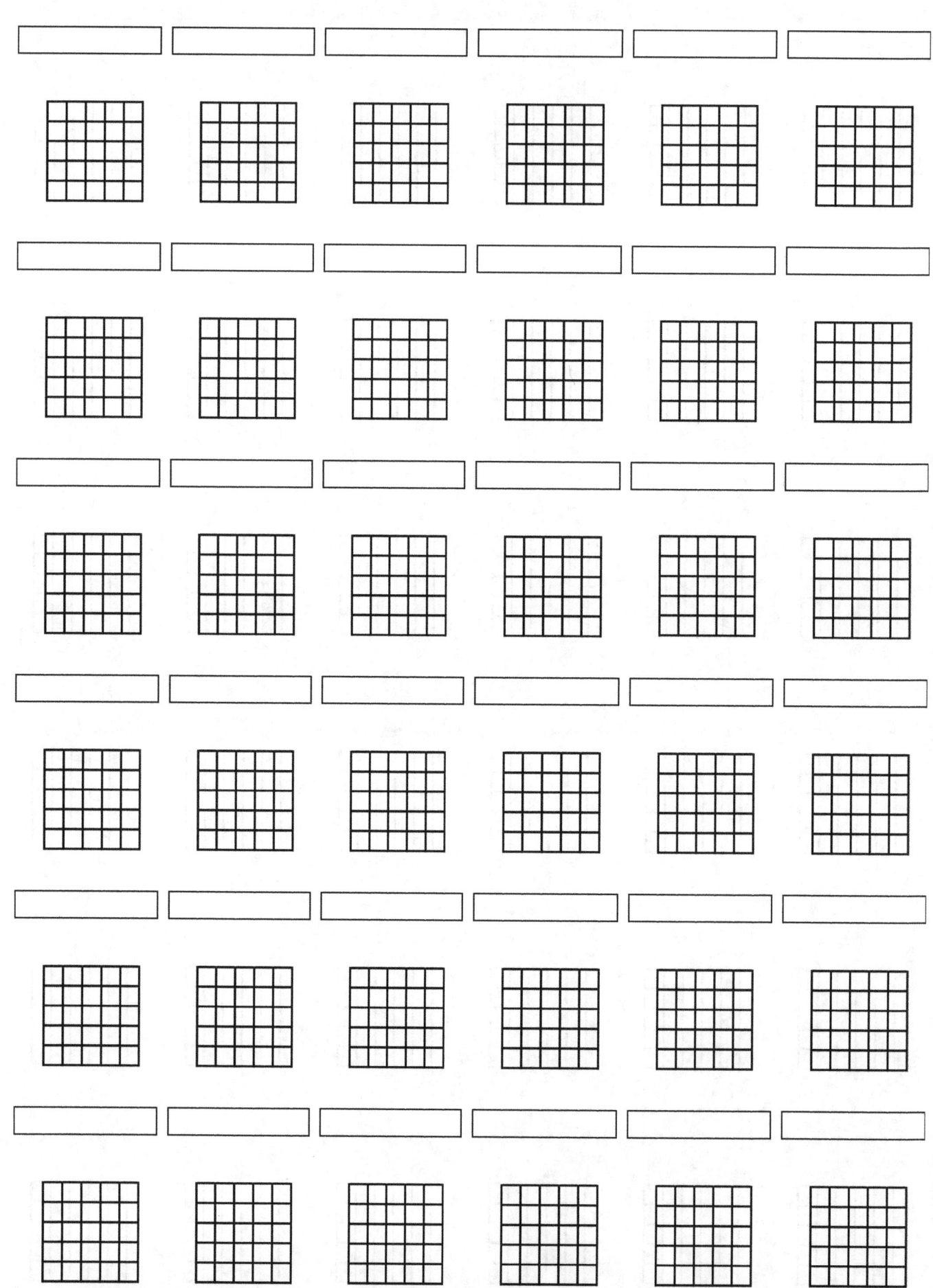